Siege and Survival

Siege and Survival

HISTORY OF THE

MENOMINEE INDIANS,

1634–1856

▼▼▼

David R. M. Beck

UNIVERSITY OF NEBRASKA PRESS

LINCOLN & LONDON

Portions of chapter 1 have been
previously published as
"Return to *Namä'o Uskíwämît:*
The Importance of
Sturgeon in Menominee Indian History,"
Wisconsin Magazine of History 79, no. 1
(1995): 32–48. © Wisconsin
Historical Society.

Publication of this book was
assisted by a grant from
The Andrew W. Mellon Foundation.

Library of Congress
Cataloging-in-Publication Data
Beck, David, 1956–
Siege and survival: history of the Menominee
Indians, 1634–1856 / David R. M. Beck.
p. cm.
Includes bibliographical references and index.
ISBN 0-8032-1330-1 (cloth : alk. paper)
1. Menominee Indians—History.   2. Menominee
Indians—Government relations.   I. Title.
E99.M44 B43 2002
977.4004'973—dc21
2002003088

I dedicate this
work to those no longer
among us whose vision and
work bring hopes for a
brighter future.

Contents

Illustrations

Maps

Tables

In the appendix

Acknowledgments

Numerous people helped me with their generosity, hospitality, criticism, advice, input, and encouragement. I would like to especially thank Rebecca Alegria, Steve Askenette, John Aubrey, Bob and Ellie Beatty, Katy Beck, George and Lucy Bennett, Shirley Burton, Bruce Calder, Chris Caldwell, Cawtackasic (Honorable Louis Hawpetoss), Art and Lucille Chapman, Michael Chapman, Mae Chevalier, Bette Crouse, Mary Danowski, Ada Deer, Verna DeLeon, Bob Dignan, Carol Dodge, Robert V. Dumont Jr., R. David Edmunds, Scott Forsyth, Neil Froemming, Roy Froemming, Fran Gamwell, David J. Grignon (Nahwahquaw), Gloria Hamilton, Alice and Jerry Hammett, LaDonna Harris, Peggy Hoge, Grace Sims Holt, Brian C. Hosmer, George Howlett Jr., Terry Johnson, Basil Johnston, Rita Keshena, Louis B. Kuppenheimer, Rosalyn LaPier, Nancy O. Lurie, Harvey Markowitz, David Reed Miller, Glen Miller, Marion Miller, Mavis Neconish, Roger L. Nichols, Jay Oleson, Susan Otto, Otto Pikaza, David C. Ranney, A. LaVonne Brown Ruoff, Leo Schelbert, Honorable Sarah Skubitz, Faith Smith, Robert J. Smith, Terry Straus, Eli Suzukovich, Gary and Mary Jo Swanson, Sol Tax, Mark Thiel, Scot and Cathy Thomas, Anne Valdez, Bernard Vigue, Angeline Wall, Cheryl Warrington, Karen Washinawatok, Hilary "Sparky" Waukau, and the students I have had the pleasure of working with at Native American Educational Services (NAES) College. Joerg Metzner deserves special recognition for the maps he created for this book.

Organizations that provided important help were Americans for Indian Opportunity, the Denver Art Museum, the Field Museum of Natural History, Marquette University Archives, Menominee Tribal Archives, the Milwaukee Public Museum, National Anthropological Archives at the Smithsonian Institution, National Archives and Records Service in Washington DC and Chicago, the Newberry Library, Northwestern University Government Publications, and the State Historical Society of Wisconsin.

I would also especially like to thank the Menominee Conservation Commission, the Menominee Historic Preservation Department, the Menominee Public Relations Office, the Menominee Treaty Rights and Mining Impacts Office, the Menominee Tribal Archives, the Menominee tribal chairman's office, Menominee Tribal Enterprises, the Menominee tribal legislature, and NAES College for their help with this project.

Introduction

In the early seventeenth century the European invasion of North America began to impact directly the Indian nations of the Upper Great Lakes area. Thus began a centuries-long siege on Indian societies and cultures that destroyed tribal economies, decimated or diminished their populations, subverted their governments, and forced many to migrate from their homelands. Some tribes disappeared entirely; others survived the onslaught and created a base from which they could eventually regain some of the political and economic control that had eroded over the years.

The Menominee Indians of Wisconsin, the state's original residents, began the period of Euro-American invasion as a fully sovereign nation, cautiously welcoming and often resisting wave after wave of newcomers from the east. These newcomers included the French, displaced or forcibly resettled Indian tribes, the British, and the Americans; they came as government officials, soldiers, traders, and seekers of land and resources, as well as loggers, missionaries, and settlers.[1]

The Menominee have had to deal not only with invading people but with the institutions they brought with them, including European, federal, tribal, state, and local governments; religious institutions of Indian and non-Indian origin; and corporations in search of fur, timber, and real estate.[2] The newcomers often had conflicting desires and ambitions, reflecting at times personal and at other times institutional motivations. Yet they all tried to impose themselves upon the Menominee in various ways. Through their own institutions and individual actions, the Menominee sought consistently to maintain political and economic sovereignty and cultural identity.

Despite the vagaries of war and alliance, and despite the massive upheavals caused by the fur trade and those who brought it, the Menominee nation retained complete independence in its own land for nearly two centuries, until its country was claimed in 1815 by the United States in the aftermath of war. Then came the most serious period of crisis in the nation's history, a span of forty years in which its political independence was crippled, its economy destroyed as nearly the entire tribal land base was swept away, and its people placed under the intense pressures not only of privation and disruption but of powerful outsiders attempting to force severe changes in the very foundations of their culture. Although few could have predicted it at the time, the tribe, despite the pressures, was able to maintain a viable homeland in a small part of its original territory. Nearly a century and a half later, at the beginning of the twenty-first century, this homeland would provide a base from which the Menominee could not only survive but regenerate, culturally and politically, bringing hope that the Menominee nation could be made whole again.

This study follows that process from the time of earliest recorded contact until the Menominee secured their current land base in 1856—the year in which they signed their last treaty with the U.S. government and began in earnest to create reservation-based communities. It reassesses the history of Menominee-white contact by positing the Menominee as a people not only with the power and internal motivations to shape their world but who use that power to do so. It reexamines the wealth of primary sources with the aid of present-day oral sources, as well as those recorded by ethnologists in the past.[3]

The primary question guiding this work throughout has been how the Menominee survived the increasing encroachment by Europeans and Americans. The account that follows is guided by a simple thesis: since the 1630s, and probably before, the Menominee have been under siege from a variety of sources, nearly all caused directly or indirectly by white expansion. This siege built slowly to a crescendo that almost proved overwhelming after the arrival of the Americans. The tribe's economic base and thus its political independence have constantly been threatened. At every stage of this interactive process, Menominee individuals and leaders worked to shape the tribe's future as they envisioned it. In doing so, they forged what historian Richard White has termed a "middle ground" between themselves and the encroaching societies, adapting their political, economic, and social structures as necessary, yet retaining an essentially Menominee cultural context.[4]

Although the study covers the same timespan for both Menominee and white history in Wisconsin, these histories have developed within slightly different frameworks. Most commonly, even in books purportedly written to include an American Indian perspective, Old Northwest history is partitioned into three time periods: the French, the British, and the American eras, with the latter sometimes being further divided into territorial and statehood phases. Menominee history, in the context of the questions raised in this study, more properly falls into three different periods: a preinvasion phase, in which the tribe was remote from the centers of European power; a trading frontier phase, at the end of the European and the beginning of the American years; and finally a period of direct white encroachment into their lands, resources, and culture (see chart).

This study presents the story of the dynamic interaction between a succession of invading groups and one indigenous Native American nation. All participants need to be studied on their own terms. The French, British, Indians, and Americans, including tribal leaders, U.S. officials, traders, entrepreneurs, and settlers, all pursued their own goals and interests. Within the Menominee world goals also varied among groups and from one historic situation to another. In the words of historian Colin G. Calloway, the interactions between these groups created "new worlds for all" of them. "The making or remaking of early America was not a

Figure 1. Periods in Menominee history: A visual timeline

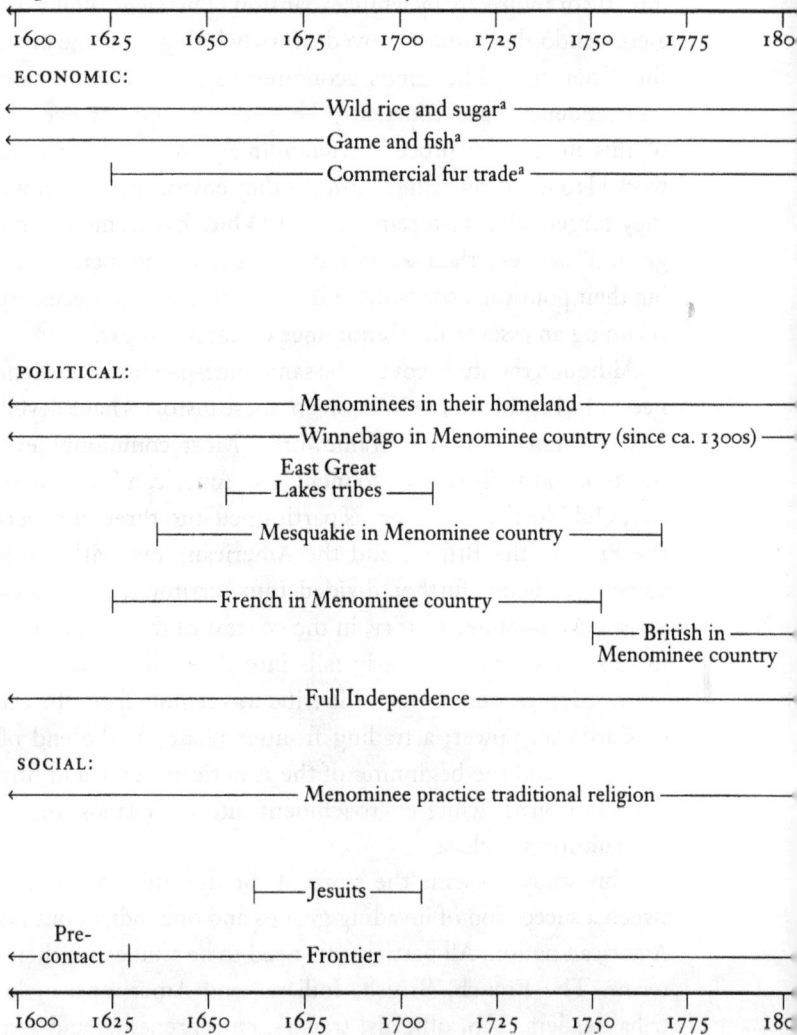

```
 1600   1625    1650    1675    1700    1725    1750    1775    180
```

ECONOMIC:

←——————————————————————— Wild rice and sugar[a] ——————————————→

←——————————————————————— Game and fish[a] ——————————————————→

|————————————————————— Commercial fur trade[a] ——————————————→

POLITICAL:

←——————————————————— Menominees in their homeland ————————————→

←——————————————————— Winnebago in Menominee country (since ca. 1300s) ——→

East Great
|——— Lakes tribes ——|

|——————————— Mesquakie in Menominee country ———————————|

|——————————— French in Menominee country ———————|

|——— British in ——→
Menominee country

←——————————————————— Full Independence ————————————————→

SOCIAL:

←——————————————————— Menominee practice traditional religion ——————→

|——— Jesuits ———|

Pre-
←—— contact ——|——————————————— Frontier ————————————————→

```
 1600   1625    1650    1675    1700    1725    1750    1775    18c
```

a The Menominee did not stop using these at the dates indicated, but they became relatively unimportant to the tribal economy at those times.

|825   1850   1875   1900   1925   1950   1975   2000 →

Termination

├Land Cession┤─────────── Dependence ──────────┤──┤───→

Restoration

Logging[b]

├── 1 ──────┼──── 2 ─────┼── 3 ─┤── 4 ──┤─5─┤─ 6 ──→

├───→

Gaming

──→

├── Oneidas, Stockbridge, Munsees in Menominee country ───────→

───────────┤

──────── Americans in Menominee country ────────────→

├─Weaker─┤──────── Wardship ────────┤────┤─Increased→
ut independent   Termination Sovereignty

├──── Dream Dance ────┤

├── Peyote/Native American Church ──→

├──────────── Catholic ────────────→

├───── Scholars in Menominee country ─────→

├─────────── Surrounded ───────────→

|825   1850   1875   1900   1925   1950   1975   2000

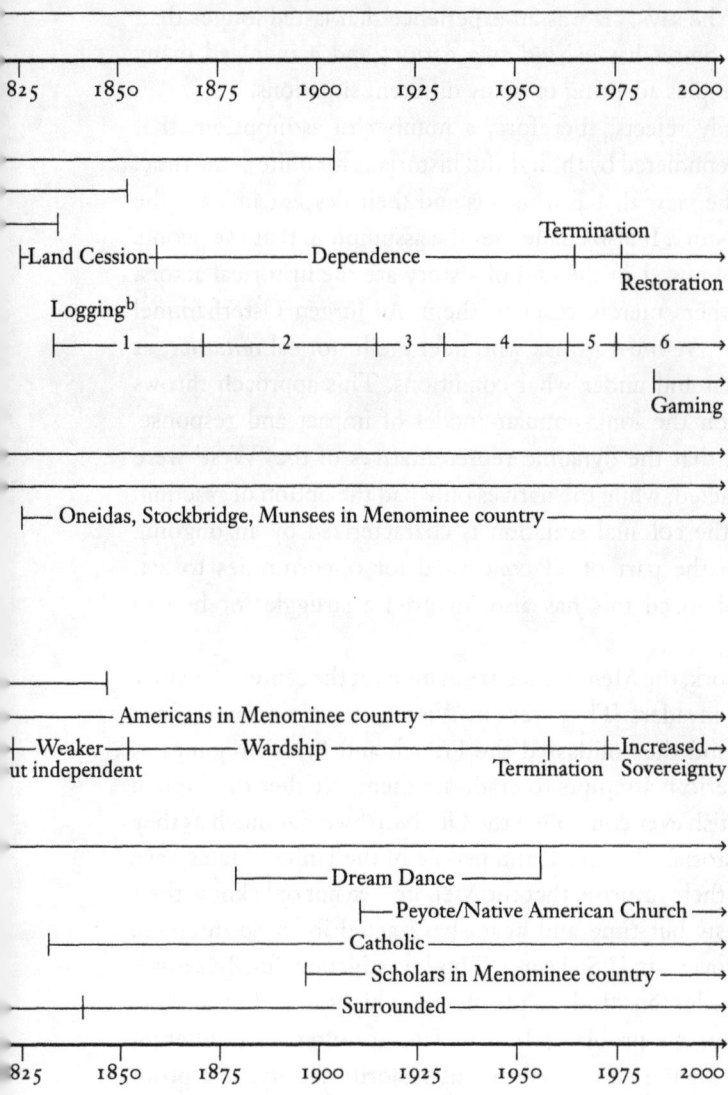

) The six periods in Menominee logging are (1) 1830s–1871: whites log Menominee timber, legally and illegally; (2) 1871–1908: Menominees and whites
log Menominee timber, legally and illegally; (3) 1905–27: gross federal mismanagement of Menominee timber, despite 1908 LaFollette Act; (4) 1927–61:
selective cutting under various jurisdictions and leaders; (5) 1961–73: termination, outside management tries "modernization"; and (6) 1973–present: restoration, tribally run Menominee Tribal Enterprises, Inc., effectively oversees resource.

'moment,'" he says, "It was an experience that lasted longer than the United States has existed as a nation, and it involved many different peoples adapting to many different situations."[5]

This study rejects, therefore, a number of assumptions that have been repudiated by thoughtful historians for quite some time. It refutes the view that Europeans and their descendants are the center of history. It also challenges the assumption that the people who control power in the end of a story are the historical actors, while all others merely react to them. As Jürgen Österhammel points out, "We must . . . ask who held the historical *initiative*, as well as when and under what conditions. This approach throws into question the long-popular model of impact and response, which held that the dynamic representatives of the 'West' were those who acted, while the natives only had the option of *re*acting. In reality, the colonial situation is characterized by an ongoing struggle on the part of all concerned for opportunities to act. For the colonized this has also involved a struggle for human dignity."[6]

In this work, the Menominee are as much at the center of history as are their invaders. They were in Wisconsin for centuries, if not millennia, and they outlasted the French and British regimes as well as American attempts to eradicate them. Neither the French nor the British ever controlled the Old Northwest as much as they or their historians believed; and people of the United States have learned, to their surprise, that the Menominee not only know their own interests but time and again have acted in those interests, often controverting U.S. desires. This investigation, finally, refuses to acknowledge an "Indian problem." This was and is a white construction; the problems Indians face are often very different from those attributed to them by the majority society. The problems have been defined in the wrong terms by the wrong people. Attempts by white society to solve Indian problems, therefore, have generally failed, often only exacerbating existing troubles. Thus, the federal government's efforts to remove the Menominee from Wisconsin in the mid–nineteenth century failed. These pursuits of

American needs and desires ran counter to Menominee needs in the context of Menominee conditions.

This history shows how the Menominee constructed their future during the era of European and American imperial expansion, essentially from the early seventeenth through the mid–nineteenth centuries: first, as their country remained independent within the imperial hinterlands of France and Britain, then as it became part of the British and American frontiers, and finally as it became surrounded by Americans. Europeans and Americans both attempted to take political and economic control of the Menominee people and their resources and, in the process, tried to reshape tribal culture in a Western image. Such control was pursued by public officials and private citizens, as well as by mixed-blood people caught between cultures and races, sometimes with the help of Menominees.[7] It was generally resisted by Menominee leaders and individuals and, to some extent, by some mixed-blood and non-Menominee (including non-Indian) friends of the tribe from outside of the community.

During this time the Menominee nation was able to retain not only self-definition but also control over a portion of its land base, resources, and governance. Thus the tribe's adaptation to the changes it encountered is a sign of success rather than decline. This study demonstrates the survival strategies adopted by a small indigenous nation in the face of various waves and forms of incursion from Euro-Americans and other Indian entities, which put it in a state of siege. As such, this study is neither white nor Indian history but rather an investigation of a complex and dynamic enmeshment.

Siege and Survival

I

The Menominee World
before Invasion

The Menominee have lived in Wisconsin longer than anyone
else.[1] Their own name for themselves, Kayaes Matchitiwuk, which
translates as "original men" or "original people," indicates this.[2]
Both the tribe's own oral traditions and archaeological evidence
suggest that they never migrated from anywhere else. According to Menominee history, the Bear clan first organized at the
mouth of the Menominee River and the Thunder or Golden Eagle
clan emerged at Lake Winnebago.[3] Some tribal members say the
Menominee originated at the Keshena Falls on the Wolf River.
Thus numerous, sometimes conflicting beliefs about the origin
of the clan system exist. According to the official history of the
Menominee tribe, the Bear, the Thunderer or Golden Eagle, the
Moose, the Crane, and the Wolf became the five principal clans.
Approximately two dozen other clans were also adopted in time.
Each of these was organized under one of the five main clans, which
in turn were responsible for specific functions within Menominee
society. The Bear served as "speakers and keepers of the law"; the
Thunder clan, or Thunderers, were in charge of "freedom and jus-
tice"; the Moose maintained "community or individual security";
the Crane oversaw "architecture, construction and art"; and the
Wolf regulated "hunting and gathering." These clans formed the
basis of Menominee social structure.[4]

The archaeological record shows that Indians moved into Wisconsin with the creation of the modern landscape, as the glaciers
receded about twelve thousand years ago. Scholars largely agree

that these earliest known Indians were Menominee.[5] Menominee history posits that the Menominee were placed in their homeland by the creator and that since they were the first ones there the creator taught them how to live in that land. Since the creator knew that other Indians would be moving into that country, the Menominee were given the responsibility of showing them how to live there, especially in terms of surviving the harsh northern winters.[6]

Indeed, other groups of people lived nearby or soon moved into Menominee country and for the most part maintained good relations with the Menominee historically. Some of these groups are still locally represented in modern Indian nations. From the north and spreading to the west came Ojibwe bands of Anishinabeeg, who lived in what is now Ontario and Michigan's Upper Peninsula. The Ho Chunks probably arrived from the south centuries before the appearance of French explorer Jean Nicolet. The Menominee formed their strongest political alliances with the Ho Chunks and Ojibwes in the years preceding European contact. Other groups that lived in Wisconsin include the Santee Dakotas, whom the Ojibwes eventually drove to the west, the Mesquakies, and groups whose traces cannot be found in modern peoples.[7]

Most significant and intriguing of this last category is a group known to us by the mounds it left behind. Located primarily along the Mississippi River basin, with a significant number as far north as the southern half of Wisconsin, some of these mounds also have been found on or near the present Menominee reservation. Built primarily between 700 and 1200 A.D., these mounds are known as effigy mounds because many are shaped like animals. Both archaeological and oral historical evidence posit that these mound builders may be ancestors of the Ho Chunk and Iowa tribes before these two groups split, leaving the Ho Chunks in the vicinity of Lake Winnebago. Some evidence also suggests that mound builders in the north are ancestors of the Dakotas. However, the relationships and identity of mound builders in the precontact period are "currently a matter of intense debate in

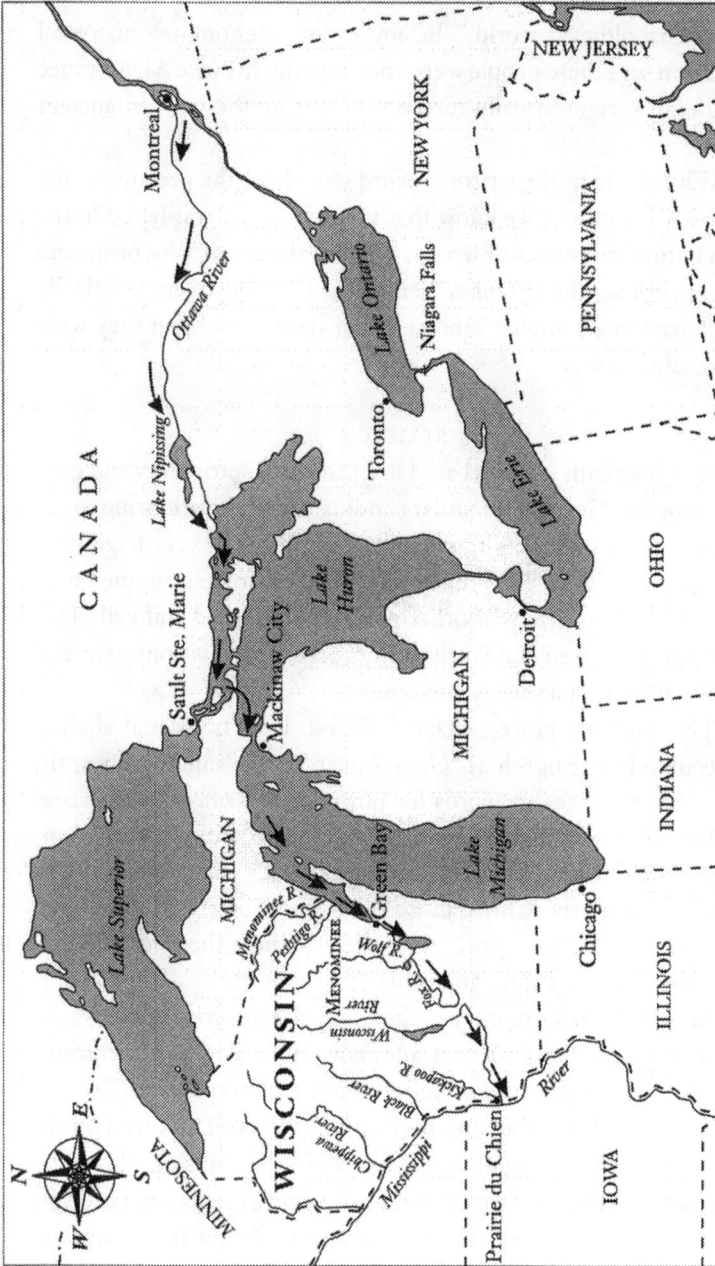

Map 1. The Upper Great Lakes tribes in 1634

the archaeological world." In any event, Menominee historical tradition says these people were enemies who invaded Menominee land and were eventually forced out of it by the tribe in ancient times.[8]

While little in the written record elucidates the precontact life of the Menominee, we know that their economy was based in the rich natural resources of what is now northeastern Wisconsin and Michigan's southern Upper Peninsula, that they were politically organized in a complex band and clan system, and that they were intensely spiritual.

RELIGION

Menominee daily life was based in a profound spirituality and governed by the Menominee understanding of their relationship to the world. The tribe traces this understanding to the very beginning of the world. The Menominee recognized a single supreme being who oversaw a variety of other powers, both good and evil. This dualistic view predated Christianity's arrival to this continent and differs from it in a variety of ways.[9]

The supreme power, Māēc Awāētok, later translated slightly inaccurately in English as "Great Spirit," is the sun. Significantly, three interchangeable words for power (*tatāhkesīwen, meskōwesen,* and *ahpēhtesēwen*) translate roughly to mean "that which has energy or life," "that which has strength," and "that which is valuable."[10] While the Christian god's power is based on dominion, Menominee spiritual power was based on these three foundations of energy/life, strength, and value.

According to Menominee cosmology the sun created the world, including good powers that reside above and evil powers that reside below. The earth is the dividing line for these powers. The sun then created Māqnabus and his brother, the Wolf, to dwell on the earth. The underground spirits slew the Wolf, causing Māqnabus to react with grief and rage. He embarked on a retaliatory rampage, slaying several of the underground spirits. Adept in the ways of the trickster, for example, he made himself appear as a doctor to gain entrance to their homes. The evil spirits, seeking an end to Māqnabus's actions, asked Māēc Awāētok for help.

Māēc Awāētok forged an agreement between the parties in which Māqnabus would cease his murderous spree in exchange for some of the powers of the belowground spirits. These powers included the healing powers of medicines that grew up out of the ground and would lengthen people's lives. Māqnabus was to share his new knowledge with the people, who were the Bear and Thunder clans of the Menominee.

Māqnabus was instructed by the powers in the ways he was to honor them when asking for their help. In turn, he was to act as an intermediary between Menominee people seeking help from the powers and the powers themselves. Māqnabus was to instruct individuals in the use of tobacco and medicine bundles, which were to be kept in a sacred way and offered to the spirits at the time of seeking.[11] This formed the basis for the traditional religion and also for the daily activities of tribal members.

Each individual used power derived from the spiritual powers to carry out his or her daily activities. People began to do this upon passing from childhood to adulthood, and the educational system for children focused in part on preparation for this. Menominee boys and girls at their coming of age gained access to these powers by undertaking a great fast that lasted several days or longer. Throughout childhood they prepared for this fast by taking smaller (one- to two-day) fasts and by receiving instruction from elders regarding the ways in which the world worked and how Menominee adults functioned in that world.

During the great fast the seeker hoped to receive a vision. The vision identified the powers that would relate to that person throughout life and defined also how the person would honor the powers. The great fast was practiced regularly until sometime early in the twentieth century. The powers also communicated with individuals through dreams.[12]

In addition to the daily maintenance of their religious activity, which helped keep the world in proper balance, the Menominee invoked spiritual aid in religious ceremonies centering around seasonal needs or specific events, performing them before and after harvesting rice, hunting, and going to battle enemies. It would have been unthinkable for them to attempt any sort of activity based on human prowess alone.[13]

In Menominee spirituality, or to put it another way, in Menominee daily existence, the world was defined as a whole in which all parts were imbued with a spiritual base. One recent historian has said, "Both animate and inanimate objects in their world possessed spirits that had to be propitiated and manipulated through proper ritual procedures. Each animal had a spirit that had to be treated with proper respect. . . . Even tools, like weapons and pots, possessed spirits that demanded proper attention in order to perform in useful ways."[14]

More properly, however, animacy was conceived differently in the Menominee world-view than in the atomistic Western view that pervades American society today and even than in the spiritually based Western society of the seventeenth century. Menominee language structure reflects this understanding: objects that modern Americans consider inanimate are given animate form by the language. This implies a relationship not only between humans and other living beings but between humans and other parts of both the natural and man-made environments, in which, because of this spiritual base, things are accorded respect as sacred. The basis of Menominee prayer and spiritual activity was the sacredness of the objects of everyday life; the purpose of the prayer and spiritual activity was to permit the individual or community to use those objects for their intended purposes. When objects were used in those ways the economic and political base of the nation (or band or individual) was secure, food could be collected in adequate abundance, enemies could be forced to retreat, and leaders could direct their people in proper directions, which would secure the well-being of the nation.[15]

RESOURCES

The natural resources that were the foundation of the Menominee world formed a key base of the tribe's identity in economic, social, political, and spiritual terms, although these sociological divisions did not occur in Menominee terminology or thought. Menominee tradition says that when the Bear invited the Thunderer to become his brother, the Bear brought wild rice and the Thunderer brought corn and fire to the new family. This family consisted of distinct band units comprising from several dozen to over one hundred members who made their summer homes along several rivers flowing into Green Bay: the Menominee, the Oconto, the Peshtigo, and the Big Suamico.[16] Menominee land also overlapped into an area of mixed forest that supported large game.[17] However, because the Green Bay area's soil and climate were insufficient to support widespread large game populations or extensive agriculture, the Menominee relied largely on water-based resources, especially rice and fish.[18]

The Menominee tribe's modern name derives from the Algonquian word *manōmin*, which means "wild rice," and the Menominee are known to their Algonquian neighbors as Wild Rice People. The Menominee too recognize wild rice as an important feature of their identity, and it shaped their understanding of the seasons and the landscape around them. When Albert Ernst Jenks wrote a monograph on the importance of wild rice to Upper Great Lakes tribes he observed that the Menominee called the month of September "Pohia-kun ka-zho." This translates as "wild rice threshing moon."[19] When the Menominee translator John Satterlee collected oral history, the Menominee words he recorded in relation to rivers named settlements, rapids, falls, and rice beds.[20] Geographic locations on rivers, the main thoroughfares for Menominees, thus described places where people lived, dangerous areas, and the sources of the all-important rice. The French, in even the earliest written references to the tribe, called them the Folles Avoines, the French term for wild rice, literally meaning "false or wild oats."[21] Jenks found that, according to Menominee sacred beliefs, the tribe never had to sow the rice; wherever they went, it followed in their wake.[22] This is no doubt true, because during the process of gathering the rice from rice beds, when the rice is beaten off the stalks into canoes with sticks, much of the seed falls into the water, planting more for the next year. When harvested, the rice self-multiplies.[23]

Wild rice, "the modern Menomini claim, [was] given by the spirit powers to be forever their special privilege," according to Felix Keesing.[24] Jenks made similar observations in his fieldwork conducted in 1899: "[T]he Menomini came into possession of wild rice at the very inception of their tribal organization. Mä'näbush . . . created the bear . . . [and] determined to make an Indian of the bear. . . . He called the Indian 'Shekatcheke'nau.' . . . Then taking the Indian to the river he showed it to him and gave it into his hands, with all its fish, its great beds of wild rice, and many sugar trees along its banks. He said, 'I give these things to you, and you shall always have them — the river, the fish, the wild rice, and the sugar trees.'"

When Weskineu the Thunderer came from Lake Winnebago to the Menominee River, the Bear clan turned everything, including the river and the wild rice, over to the Thunderer. But the Thunderer always brought rain and storms, so the rice harvest was ruined. Weskineu then returned the rice to Sekatsokemau. "So after that when rice harvest came Shekatcheke'nau called all his people together, and they made a feast, and smoked, and asked the Great Spirit to give them fair weather during the harvest. Since then there has always been a fine, stormless harvest season."[25]

Wild rice, a seed rather than a grain, is both highly nutritious and tasty. It can be dried, stored, and used through the winter. Growing in wetlands, it attracts an abundance of waterfowl, which flock to it especially in autumn, and it can feed large groups of people during harvesttime. The Menominee probably harvested rice just before it fully ripened, "to avoid heavy grain loss to birds."[26] Northern Wisconsin, which the glaciers left dotted with lakes, flowing with rivers, and smothered in wetlands, provides much ideal environment for wild rice.

The game the rice attracted helped the people build up strength for the winter, and the rice also helped see them through until the maple sugar and sturgeon in springtime could rebuild their strength. Jenks, whose study remains the most significant work on the topic, provided test results showing that wild rice was more nutritious than any other naturally available food in the area and that only sturgeon and dried beef surpassed it as "richer in flesh producing substance." He adds that the Menominee are "unique" in that "Unlike other Indians who, for short periods, have been named because of their intimate relations with the grain, the Menomini have always been known, so far as Indian tradition and authentic history are concerned, as the 'Wild-rice Indians' par excellence." He describes Menominee country as being in the heart of the United States' "wild-rice district" and remarks, perhaps with some exaggeration, that "no other section of the North American continent was so characteristically an Indian paradise, so far as a spontaneous vegetal food is concerned, as was this territory in Wisconsin and Minnesota. . . . [T]he most princely vegetal gift which North America gave her people without toil was wild rice."[27]

The first French missionary to establish a mission in Menominee country, Father Gabriel Dreuillettes, distinguished the Menominee from other tribes in the area by their location in the best wild rice lands. "They reap, without sowing it, a kind of rye which grows wild in their meadows, and is considered superior to Indian corn," he wrote in the late 1650s in a report titled "The Names of Many Recently-Discovered Nations," which appeared in *The Jesuit Relations*.

Father Claude Dablon, who reported on French Jesuit Catholicism in Menominee country in 1670 and 1671, wrote in describing local tribes, "A[nother] Nation, known as 'the Wild-Oats people,' because this grain grows in their country, dwells on the banks of a river of considerable beauty, which empties into this same Bay

[Green Bay], 15 or 20 leagues from its head." Dablon referred to the Menominee in Algonquian terms as Oumaloumines—"the wild-oats Nation."[28]

When Father Marquette made his famous first voyage through Menominee country, in his travels up the Fox River between Green Bay and Lake Winnebago, he observed the abundance of wild rice: "The way is so cut up by marshes and little lakes that it is easy to go astray, especially as the river is so covered with wild oats that one can hardly discover the channel."[29] Father Marquette was possibly the first European to describe the process of gathering wild rice as the Menominee practiced it:

The [Menominee] Gather and prepare it for food as Follows. In The month of September, which is the suitable time for The harvest, they go in canoes through these fields of wild oats; they shake its Ears into the Canoe, on both sides, as they pass through. The grain falls out easily, if it be ripe, and they obtain their supply In a short time. But, in order to clean it from the straw, and to remove it from a husk in which it is Enclosed, they dry it in the smoke, upon a wooden grating, under which they maintain a slow fire for some Days. When The oats are thoroughly dry, they put them in a Skin made into a bag, thrust It into a hole dug in the ground for This purpose, and tread it with their feet—so long and so vigorously that The grain separates from the straw, and is very easily winnowed. After this, they pound it to reduce it to flour,—or even, without pounding it, they Boil it in water, and season it with fat. Cooked in This fashion, The wild oats have almost as delicate a taste as rice has when no better seasoning is added.[30]

Women played the key role in the harvesting process. According to ethnologist Walter James Hoffman, "the women, and frequently the men as well," paddled the boats to the rice fields and beat the rice into the boats. Women made the special bags to hold the rice before it was lowered into the holes, stamped the rice, and processed it as well.[31]

The rivers coursing through Menominee country, as well as Green Bay, Lake Michigan proper, and the many inland lakes, also provided seasonal abundance of fish for the tribe in the prereservation years. The Menominee speared fish in spawning season—some in the fall, such as whitefish, cisco, and lake trout, which could be dried for winter use; others in the spring, which provided needed nutrition after the harsh winter.[32] Especially important to the Menominee, and a significant part of the tribe's social, political, and spiritual life, were the sturgeon, or *namāēw* in Menominee terms, large fish that swam upstream in the spring, some from Lake Michigan, some from Lake Winnebago, and others that lived in the rivers year-round. Alanson Skinner observed that "Sturgeon played so important a part in early Menominee economy that they receive frequent mention in mythology."[33] The sturgeon play significant roles in several recorded versions of the tribe's origin story, from being the first food the Bear caught and ate to being the first spiritual offering to the powers that provided them with food.[34]

In 1913 Skinner described the tribe's origins as related to him by a tribal elder. When the two Bears first became a man and a woman at the mouth of the Menominee River, the man immediately built a wigwam. His next act was to build a canoe "in order that he might go out on the waters and catch sturgeon, which were very abundant at the foot of a nearby cataract, where they had been created for the use of man. [He] was very successful in taking sturgeon." His wife then prepared the abundant catch of sturgeon. "First she split them from the head down and drew them; then she hung them over a frame to dry. When they were sufficiently cured she cut them into flakes and made the first sacrifice and feast to all the powers."[35] The sturgeon were thus from the beginning a part of Menominee spiritual life.

In one version of the story, the first Menominee who came into the world brought a kettle with them. They carried the kettle to the river, which they found to be "full of sturgeon," and the tribe's leader used the kettle to feed sturgeon to his people. Because he was thus able to provide for his people, the other clans brought him their own foods and joined the Bear.[36] The leader not only provided for his people, a critical role, but also displayed the generosity that has long remained part of Menominee cultural institutions.

In one case, two of the tribe's bands fought over the all-important sturgeon. One band lived upstream, and the other lived at the mouth of the Menominee River. When the lower band built a dam blockading the river, preventing the sturgeon from ascending, the two bands traded insults and eventually attacked each other. According to a U.S. army officer who recorded this story, this was the only civil dissension of any importance in precontact tribal history. Significantly, the disruption of the supply of sturgeon in the spawning season caused the conflict. Had the band upstream not been able to catch sturgeon during the short-lived spawning season, many would have starved.[37] The downstream band reportedly escaped by canoe down the eastern shores of Lake Michigan and joined a Potawatomi band, leaving their Menominee brethren forever.[38]

The sturgeon supplied not only food but a variety of other uses as well. The jawbone could be shaped into a scraper; other bones were used for utensils; the backbone was processed into a glue; and oils and the skin provided a variety of medicinal uses, including for minor injuries and maladies such as earaches, headaches, and eye aches.[39]

A variety of large and small game, including deer, bear, raccoon, moose, caribou, elk, squirrel, rabbit, muskrat, and beaver, lived in Menominee forests and wetlands. Bison lived nearby, but larger hunting expeditions were required to bring this meat back to the villages.[40] Since the larger game was less populous than the fish or small game, the tribe's separate bands returned to their favored winter camp areas between Lake Michigan and the Mississippi River or spread along the shores of the waterways in winter to hunt for the larger animals. The forests also provided berries in the fall and sap from maple trees in the spring. To this day, many favorite Menominee recipes include maple sugar, berries, wild rice, and fish or game.

After a difficult winter the fish and maple sap provided much needed nutrition. Without the spring sturgeon the Menominee would have starved, and often the maple provided a buffer from starvation in the critical period before the sturgeon spawn began.[41] But the natural abundance of resources through much of the year, along with the farming that some of the southern bands practiced, provided a good, if harsh, living. For generations Menominees followed this pattern of subsistence, each of several bands, governed by a complex system of democracy, in its own territory, joining together only at times of rice harvest and religious ceremony.

LAW

The Menominee were able to maintain their relationship to the land, the spiritual world, and each other because their society had established sophisticated codes of conduct or tribal customary laws that ensured a stable, functional environment. Menominee political and legal systems were highly structured and dealt with both conflict and relationships at a variety of levels: within clans, between clans, between villages, as a whole nation, with allied or friendly tribes, and with enemy tribes. Laws, though not written, were well known to every member of the community starting at a young age. They were taught and reinforced through the education system, through stories, through ceremony, through remembered history, and through constant practice.

These tribal customary laws defined behavior in all areas. Societal norms and expectations provided for or empowered these codes of conduct, which were based on hundreds, even thousands of years of practice, and were firmly grounded in the origin stories and oral tradition of the tribe, which lends the rules both a spiritual- and secular-based significance.

Domestic law prescribed the rules for marriage, divorce, childcare, education, subsistence, cases of murder, and resource use.

Since the family, band, and clan were the primary basis of identity, and the resources were the basis of subsistence, these two areas of domestic law (family relations and resource usage) were of primary importance.

Family law was structured to ensure that every member of society was a functioning contributor to communal well-being. The act of cohabitation automatically conferred the rights and responsibilities of marriage on individuals, except in the case of adultery. Individuals could marry outside of their clans; Menominee descent was patrilineal. Men could marry more than one woman if they could support them, and they often married sisters. They occasionally took as wives other men whose roles in society were defined as female roles.[42] Divorce could be initiated by either husband or wife; in either case, the woman took on child-rearing responsibilities and the man usually continued to provide for and show affection to his children.

Family relations were strong and extended beyond what Western culture considers the immediate family. A man would be likely to marry the sister of his deceased wife; if a child's parents died, a close relative would adopt her or him. Indeed, if a family lost a child, they would likely adopt another one, prompting C. C. Trowbridge to observe of the Menominee, "They appear to be fond of adopting children." Similarly, when the elderly became infirm their children would take special care of them.[43]

Boys and girls were simply treated as children, with no preference to either gender. As they grew of age to be helpful to the family, girls learned the skills they would need to maintain the household, while boys learned the skills they would need to provide food for the family, especially hunting and fishing. A formal education system helped children learn their roles in society. According to Trowbridge, "In every village there is an old man appointed by the Chiefs to superintend the instruction of the children. This man visits daily the different lodges of the village and assembling the young at each lodge he points out to them the course which they must pursue, and warns them of the consequences of vicious habits.

He is assisted in his labors by the parents who repeat to them at night the advice which they receive during the day from their aged counsellor."[44]

Women's economic and domestic duties included picking berries, making nets for fishing, tanning hides, building and overseeing the wigwams or lodges, cooking, and raising children. Men hunted, fished, and conducted war and diplomacy. Men and women together gathered and treated wild rice and maple sap. However, girls and women who proved skilled at hunting or fishing, or other activities in the male realm such as warfare, were respected and pursued those activities. Women could also be doctors.[45] Children and the elders were the most revered people in Menominee society because they were closest to the world beyond that of earth. Menominee society valued all of its members, supporting and nourishing the roles they played, since all were essential for survival and maintenance of an acceptable quality of life.

The most important domestic laws besides those governing family were those that governed resource usage. Since the Menominee economy had been based on cultivating their environmental riches for countless generations, perhaps for thousands of years, they developed sophisticated laws that were well adapted to the local environment as well as to the communal need. The resources consisted of those of both forest and water, and laws focused on both usage and passage. The former laws were enforced within the tribe; the latter between nations. One of the most important of these laws was firmly based in the core cultural values of reciprocity and sharing:

> The laws relating to hunting by individuals differ from those which govern the whites. If two indians hunt together, he who kills an animal gives it to his companion, who skins and dresses it and returns one half of the *flesh* to him who killed it, reserving to himself the other half with the skin. So if two hunters happen *accidentally* to meet upon the same ground, and one of them wounds an animal which is killed by the

other, he who first wounded it is entitled to the skin with one half of the flesh; but if he kill it *himself* after it is wounded by himself and another, he deprives himself of the right to the skin.[46]

John Satterlee explained why such "reciprocal treats" were important: "And the reason he [the hunter] does so is this: this very thing he was given by the guarding powers as his custom. If he does not do this, he offends, and it appears that he is not a real man, and that he is stingy." This practice causes "good feeling on both sides" and ensures "that the animal shall be entirely eaten."[47]

Hoarding food, as described in Satterlee's observation and the sturgeon war, was anathema to Menominee well-being and therefore was outlawed by the tribe's inviolable code. The legend relating how corn came to the tribe reinforces the same lesson. An older man with strong spiritual powers, a Midāēw, kept a mysterious bundle hidden in his dwelling and forbade his nephew from opening it. The young man broke into it one day while his uncle was out hunting. When the hunter learned of this he tried to slay his nephew, but instead the younger man killed his uncle. "When the old man was dead, the youth inherited all his effects, including the corn, which the man had selfishly hidden away from mankind, but which the nephew gave to the world."[48]

The strict nature of domestic resource laws can perhaps best be understood in the oversight of the fall gathering of wild rice, which generally began in mid-September. Skinner described the laws governing the harvest, which included procedural, social, and spiritual rules. The Bear as civil leader and the Sturgeon as keeper of the laws protected the rice.

According to one observer, after the camp was set up on the banks of the rice fields, "*Nanawe'tauwûk*, or police, are set to guard the rice and no one is allowed to trespass on the fields before the appointed day." These police watched the fields. When the rice was ripe, they reported the news to the tribe's leader, who in turn sent them to inform the other tribal members that the harvest would begin the next day. That night prayers and a feast were held to ensure a successful harvest. Offerings were made to both the belowground powers and the Thunderers, and the tribe's leaders instructed people in how to act. If the ceremony was properly performed, and if all individual members of the community followed proper procedures as instructed, the deities would provide for four days of calm weather for the harvest.[49]

These laws were strongly based in ceremony and ritual. They applied to an activity at once mundane and awe-inspiring the gathering of a simple harvest that supported life itself. The sacred and secular nature of the laws are inseparable, as are various components of the process of harvest: the policing, the offering of tobacco to and the request for intervention of the spiritual world, the feasting, restrictions on participation by "women undergoing their menses and persons belonging to a family in which there has been a death within a year," and the actual harvest itself.[50]

Tribal customary law shaped international resource usage as well. Individuals often had to cross other nations' territories when traveling to their hunting grounds. Waterways were public thoroughfares whose closure could be the cause of war. Like the other tribes in the area, the Menominee restricted hunting and gathering on their lands. They made it a practice to destroy the weapons of any outsiders who hunted in their territory without authorization.[51] Neighboring tribes, if they sought permission, might be granted the opportunity to "sit down upon" (*apēkon ahkīhih*) or utilize Menominee lands in times of need. Likewise, with permission, Menominee tribal members could not only pass through but hunt on neighboring tribes' lands.

Boundaries between tribes or bands were somewhat fluid and might shift, depending on the time of year, since all of the area's tribes moved around seasonally. Unlike the case with the mounds people who invaded the area, however, there is no recollection of boundary disputes breaking out in warfare, except with the Mesquakies, who arrived later. The Ojibwes fought over territorial rights with the Santees in the western part of Wisconsin, but neither the Ojibwes nor the Ho Chunks fought the Menominee. Trowbridge reported that boundary disputes had never caused war between the Menominee and their neighbors. This was confirmed later by the Ho Chunk leader Four Legs, who told U.S. representatives that the Ho Chunks, Ojibwes, and Menominee had long "hunt[ed] together as brothers."[52]

These disputes were avoided because the Menominee and their neighbors established effective diplomatic procedures that ensured peaceful relations. Negotiating and forging agreements between nations were diplomatic methods the Menominee had been practicing for centuries prior to European contact. The Menominee made both formal and informal agreements with other nations. These agreements defined boundaries, usage of neutral areas, usage of resources, trade, and codes of conduct between nations, among other issues. Over time the Menominee had established a process and practice for both negotiating and forging agreements. The process included not only negotiation but also such acts as gift giving, feasting, games, and smoking the pipe. The pipe tobacco, kinnikinnick, was made from willow bark, which when smoked has a relaxing impact on the smoker.[53] The smoke, as it rose upward, conveyed the group's good intentions to the spirit world and sanctified the process. A later visitor described it thus: They "[open] the council by lighting a pipe, and handing it to all present, each person taking a whiff or two, and passing it to the next. The mingling clouds of smoke raised by each are supposed to ascend to the Great Spirit, in token of the harmony that pervades the assembly, and to attest the purity of their intentions."[54] This process scarcely resembled the formal European treaty-making methods. Nonetheless, the decisions that resulted carried the formality of laws that were enforced both internally and externally to ensure compliance.

The basis for understanding any civilization is understanding the ways in which people behave toward other people. This is a by-product of socialization, which itself derives from a collective value system. To the Menominee, as well as to other tribes, such behavior is of primary importance. People, whether tribal members or outsiders, will often be judged more on the basis of this behavior than on other attributes.[55] In important meetings this can be more significant than the substance of the issues discussed. The Menominee term *kāēqc onāēnemaewak* — "they are acting respectfully to each other" — for example, must be understood in all its complexities to fully comprehend this way of thinking. Respect in this case is broadly defined in its physical, spiritual, and mental senses. Without this basis, a meeting, let alone negotiations or agreements stemming from the meeting, would be unthinkable. A failure of good behavior is a failure of respect, and without respect there is no basis for agreement.[56]

When a diplomatic meeting or negotiation was to commence the Menominee sent runners to the leaders of other tribes. These runners carried belts or tobacco, color-coded to signify the purpose of the proposed meetings. Red painted belts signified a call to arms for an impending or proposed war; blue signified general affairs; while a black belt with white on both ends and a white stripe painted to connect these showed "the road which is opened between the fires of two nations." This belt was used for "Commencing a negotiation or alliance with a nation not before connected with them." In addition, "All important negotiations are accompanied by belts, if to be procured, and by the pipe of war or peace."[57]

Large-scale warfare was so foreign to the Menominee that it prompted Trowbridge to remark that the tribe had never even developed a peacemaking process. There had been no need for it, at least ever since the mounds people had been driven from Menominee lands. Warfare occurred instead on a small scale, at the family or band level. Menominees occasionally joined other nations in warfare, but such decisions were nearly always made at the individual or family level. If a member of the nation felt wronged by a member of another nation and wanted revenge, he held a feast for the principal chiefs, explained how he was wronged, and passed a pipe with a red stem. If the chiefs accepted this it meant war. No notice was given to the enemy. All warriors in the band were bound by their leaders' decision to go to war. Fasting preceded war, and men avoided their wives to purify themselves. They fasted afterward as well, as Trowbridge points out:

> If victorious in battle, the warriors return to their village with the prisoners which they have taken, who are treated with great attention and kindness and particularly if females, are protected from the rudness [*sic*] of the young men. When they arrive at their village the warriors retire to a house prepared for them, where they remain separated from the women and children of the nation for four days. During this time, those who remained at home, prepare a great feast, and the prisoners are given to the chiefs, by whom they are adopted; unless some father who has lost a son in the war, begs leave to take one of them in which case the adopted prisoner supplies the place of the deceased.

Scalps were displayed at the feast; after dancing they were distributed among relatives of those killed in battle, "by whom they are preserved with scrupulous care." If the warriors were defeated, they returned to the village and were cleansed, and then a decision was made whether to reattack.[58] Significantly, these decisions were made at the local band level.

The tribe's bands were loosely linked politically but maintained strong social and cultural ties. Band affiliation defined where and with whom a person lived, while clan affiliation defined a person's relationship with the tribe's origins. Members of numerous clans might live in the same band or village.

LEADERSHIP

A late-nineteenth-century ethnographer observed that "the Menomini claim always to have had a first or grand chief, and a second or war chief, besides many subchiefs who were heads of bands or families."[59] This is essentially accurate, although band leaders were not considered chiefs and the civil leader and war leader did not rank in a hierarchical order but served different purposes and led the tribe depending on the immediate situation. One or the other may have been more influential at different times.[60] Jonathan Carver, an early traveler from New England, recognized this distinction when he observed, "They are governed by a chief who is hereditary, besides they have a chief of the warriors, and a number of other chiefs whose advice rather than authority influences public measures."[61] That advice was subject to the approval of the band members.

It was not necessary for a leader to be a powerful public speaker; leaders occasionally used orators or speakers to speak on their behalf. The Menominee based leadership positions within the clans on heredity but made exceptions when hereditary leaders proved incompetent or failed to act with the approval of the group as a whole. Thus the Menominee system of governance was both democratic, a trait little understood by the invading powers, and locally based.

The Bear clan, recognized as the original tribal clan, provided the single civil leader who presided over council when all bands came together. The tribe recognized the Bear clan as leaders during times of peace. The first Bear clan civil leader recorded by Europeans was Sekatsokemau, called Chawanon or the Old King by the British. Carron, who later became known as Vieux or Old Carron, became speaker for him after 1763. In fact, Sekatsokemau "was a traditional name for the original 'bear.' "[62]

The Thunderers provided the war leaders, acted as police to guard the rice fields during harvest, and carried the fire for the Menominee.[63] To understand the warrior class it is necessary to know the meaning of the Menominee word *gichita*, which means "warrior." This word, which defined a warrior's role, has a much broader meaning than "soldier" or "fighter." A *gichita* was (and still is) considered to be a protector of the elderly and the infirm, someone who respects and takes care of the people within his family and village, a man (or on occasion a woman) who made certain that people were provided for not only in terms of physical protection but in terms of having food to eat and a place to live.

This role included traveling ahead of the group to establish camp and build fires as well as the policing and war leadership duties more commonly associated with the word "warrior."[64]

While rules of heredity generally governed civil leadership, war leaders gained their positions based on revelations they received while fasting. Their strength was centered in the bundles they assembled under instruction from the spirits. "[T]he war power [was] vested in the owners of the war bundles . . . whose authority was limited by their reputation and personality. A civil chief was not debarred from being a bundle-owner, and hence a war-leader, should he receive the proper revelations."[65]

Although the bands retained autonomy, they occasionally assembled together to make decisions for the tribe as a whole. The leaders made these decisions, each in consultation with his own band.[66] Trowbridge described the course of events in such a meeting:

> When the affairs of the nation make it necessary to call a council, the principal chief sends a chief of the Elk tribe [i.e., clan] and sometimes one of the Wolf or Dog tribe, to give notice to the chiefs of the different tribes [bands or villages] of the time, place and business of the council.
>
> Before the introduction of wampum the messenger carried with him a piece of indian tobacco. . . . If death [were the subject of the council], the colour was black, If joyful news were to be communicated, the tobacco was painted green or pale blue, and if War was the subject, the tobacco was red.
>
> A feast is prepared and eaten at every council, and the members deliberate with the pipe in their mouths.
>
> After the principal chief has explained the business of the council, and given his opinion, the others severally express their views as the spirit moves them. The assent of the body, to any proposition is made known by a grunt from the members, which is toned in such a manner as to express the *degree* of satisfaction which they feel.[67]

As in external negotiations, process played a significant role in internal political meetings. Decisions simply could not be made without following the protocol, which lent a sober and solemn mutual respect to the proceedings. All areas of Menominee life were indeed connected: the political, the spiritual, the social, and the economic. None could function smoothly without the smooth functioning of the others. These areas were, in fact, so interconnected that the Menominee never thought of them in these distinct categorical terms. The Menominee world was one in which all parts were essential and properly shared with all others.

The most startling difference between the Menominee and the European invaders who appeared in Menominee country must certainly have been the very essence of their world-views. The Menominee culture was steeped in the values of respect, kinship, and reciprocity. The Menominee and the world surrounding them interacted in ways that were beneficial to both. The Menominee viewed the world as integrated and holistic. The European cultures, however, viewed the world hierarchically and highly valued both the domination-submission paradigm and property rights. While individual responses varied, these values generally permeated the cultures at all levels, from religious to political to domestic to commercial.

While the Menominee spiritual world was based in the people's interaction with it, in ways that were mutually supportive, Christianity demanded that man subdue the earth. Menominee religion was community specific; the objective of the missionaries who would visit them was to replace their Native religions with Christianity in one form or another. While Menominee leaders made decisions in accordance with the wishes of the people they served, with the welfare of the least fortunate being of primary concern, European leaders made decisions for or about the people they ruled. While people in the Menominee world were valued for the functions they performed within the family and community, European men were lords within their families, wherein women and children were viewed as property. For the Menominee, on the other hand, men were revered for their abilities to feed or protect, women for their craftsmanship and maintenance of the home, children as the focus of the future, and elders for their wisdom and guidance. For the Menominee, trade and commerce were used to support the village and family. For the Europeans, these things were used to acquire wealth and property in order to move to a higher rank within their society. Both the Menominee and the Europeans were shaped by their value systems, which derived from their world-views; these values and views in turn shaped their interactions with and understanding of each other.

2

Menominee Country Becomes a Trading Frontier

The first Europeans the Menominee recall meeting were French traders. Trowbridge wrote the following account of the first contact between white men and the Menominee:

> The first white people that they saw, were the [F]rench, by whom they were visited at Munnoaminee river. They were apprised of their arrival by the report of a gun, which surprised them exceedingly, but when they saw a wooden boat and the men with hats, (as they call the whites) they were struck dumb with astonishment. As the boat approached the shore the indians seized their pipes and began to smoke, to avert the wrath of these terrible *Man-ni-toos*, as they supposed them to be.
>
> Some of the crew landed and went to the lodge where after gazing at them some time, the indians made them offerings of indian tobacco, by placing it upon their heads and holding it before their mouths, during which time they continued to smoke and to implore the mercy of the *Mannitoos*. A dog belonging to the boat and a gun which they saw discharged, were treated in the same manner. At length the interpreter undeceived them, by informing them who they were, whence they came, and that they were sent to minister to the comfort of the indians by exchanging their blankets and other goods for furs and skins.[1]

This oral history may be more allegorical than factual—surely the Menominee had heard of the French before they first met them. One scholar says, for example, "Long before they saw their first French faces, [Wisconsin] Indians had at least some European trade goods."[2] Nonetheless, the story serves to describe the immense changes the meeting portended for Menominee society. This was but one of several cataclysmic events during the seventeenth century that would forever reshape the Menominee world.

At this time the Menominee consisted of several bands, including those that summered at the Menominee, Oconto, Peshtigo, and Big Suamico Rivers. Others may have summered as far north as Bay de Noc and as far south as Lake Winnebago, with possibly one more on the Fox River at Kakalin Falls.[3] When the French first arrived in the person of Jean Nicolet (who was half-expecting and half-hoping that he had found the Northwest Passage to Asia) in 1634, only the Menominee and the Ho Chunks lived along the western shores of Lake Michigan, which shielded them from intrusive contact with their eastern neighbors. Sometime before Nicolet's arrival the Mesquakies, pushed westward around Lake Michigan by the Ojibwes, arrived in the area.[4] They settled along the western fringes of Menominee and Ho Chunk land, establishing a buffer between them and the Santees. It seems likely that the Menominee invited the Mesquakies to sit down upon their land, following the custom known as *apēkon ahkihih*.

The present area of Green Bay, where the Fox River flows into Lake Michigan, was in pre-Columbian days a center of a vast trade web that included Menominee country and spread throughout much of the continent. The route from Green Bay extended north to make both eastern and western connections along what would later become major fur-trade routes. To the south it passed through Lake Winnebago before turning southwest toward Illinois and Iowa.[5] This "preexisting native network" represented the conduit by which the tribes maintained alliance with other nations and replenished a variety of material and social needs.[6] It brought people together to share news and friendships, and it also served the function of broadening a tribe's base of resources to include those available only in someone else's country.

The tribes that controlled the major portion of this trade route, which stretched from Menominee country to the new French settlement in Montreal, were the Hurons in the east and the Ottawas in the west. Through these tribes, the trade in furs, originally conducted by eastern tribes, preceded the actual presence of the French in Menominee country. Gabriel Sagard-Theodat, in a history written in 1636, reports that the Hurons, a confederacy of five tribes located on the eastern edge of what is now called the Georgian Bay in Lake Huron, traded as far as the country of the Ho Chunks, exchanging "merchandise" for pelts, paints, and porcelain.[7] This would likely have brought them into Menominee country as well.

The Hurons generally traded from the St. Lawrence River in the east to Ottawa trading territory in the west, and their trading ranged far north as well. Their control of these trade routes would make them among the most powerful tribes in the Upper Great Lakes in the first half of the seventeenth century. The Ottawas, who were more likely than the Huron to trade with the Menominee, were themselves known as great traders. Their name, Odawa, not only represents the tribe itself, which consisted of several autonomous bands, but also in translation means "to trade." They traded corn, meat, tobacco, and fishnets, among other items, and like the Hurons they traded items produced internally and served as go-betweens for other tribes.[8]

Several factors made the Upper Great Lakes an ideal area for rapid expansion of the fur trade, once the French established the demand. These included a vast forested area rich in furs, especially the coveted beaver; a magnificent transportation route consisting of rivers, lakes, and connecting trails; a method of transportation superbly adapted to water transport—the lightweight yet relatively reliable birch bark canoe; and skilled traders who already navigated the routes on a regular basis.[9] As various pressures led to a decline of the trade in the east, its focus would expand into the western Great Lakes.

EARLY FUR TRADE

The fur trade's expansion brought sweeping changes to Wisconsin's economic, political, social, and territorial landscapes. Within thirty to forty years after Nicolet's visit, the Menominee's neighbors included—besides the Ho Chunks, Mesquakies, and a handful of French—the Sauks, Potawatomis, and Kickapoos. Just to the north were the Ottawas, Hurons, and Ojibwes, and just to the south were the Mascoutens and Miamis.[10] These new peoples flooded the western shores of Lake Michigan in search of furs and in retreat from the Neutrals and the Iroquois.[11]

The Ho Chunks and Menominee resented the resulting squeeze of Algonquian tribes from both north and south, although at least for the Menominee that resentment did not include the Mesquakies, who remained as allies until as late as 1701.[12] La Potherie reports that during the latter half of the seventeenth century the Ho Chunks fiercely resisted incursions from all tribes: "If any stranger came among them, he was cooked in their kettles. The Malhominis were the only tribe who maintained relations with them [the Ho Chunks]."[13] It was, after all, Menominee and Ho Chunk territory that the other tribes invaded in the 1650s and 1660s. Despite the differences in language and culture these two nations made logical allies in the face of this invasion. The once-powerful Ho Chunks, however, were decimated by a triad of disasters: the loss of five hundred canoe-bound warriors in a lake storm, probably in Lake Winnebago; a pestilence—probably smallpox—that coursed through the tribe; and a military defeat at the hands of the Illinois.[14] Curiously, the Mesquakies, despite their recent arrival, seemed at least initially to be removed from the resulting conflict, due to their western location. Unfortunately for them this meant they were more removed from the benefits of the fur trade as well.

The center of the trade had moved so rapidly westward that Iroquois attempts to gain control of it were doomed to failure. The trade had extended too far beyond their home territory. Instead, with the Hurons largely destroyed, the Ottawas, who dwelt near the straits connecting Lakes Michigan and Huron, began to dominate the trade. By 1683, the Ottawas handled two-thirds of all pelts traded to the French.[15] In the Upper Great Lakes, Indians dealt more often with the Ottawas than with French traders. A French memoir reported that the Oumaominiecs, or the Folles Avoines (Menominee), were one of eleven nations from whom the Ottawas procured beaver to bring to Montreal, the nexus of the trade. This same memo reported that western tribes themselves "occasionally come down to Montreal, but usually they do not do so in very great numbers" because of the great distances involved and the attempts of the Ottawas to control the trade, through intimidation if necessary. Menominees themselves were occasionally known to make the lengthy and dangerous journey to Montreal as members of war parties and to trade; the few who made the voyage gained greater firsthand knowledge of the variety and quality of goods sold by French merchants and became better at bargaining back home.[16] But these travelers proved to be the exception and did not become middlemen in the trade.

According to La Potherie the Ottawas exchanged "old knives, blunted awls, wretched nets, and kettles used until they were past service" for tribes' entire supplies of beaver robes. "For these they were humbly thanked," La Potherie asserts, "and those people declared that they were under great obligations to the Outaoütas [Ottawas] for having had compassion upon them and having shared with them the merchandise which they had obtained from the French."[17]

These Indian middlemen commonly traded with other tribes only their own castoff items and with the French only furs to replace what they wanted. Though they obviously traded to their own advantage, they did not trade for profit after the manner of the French, who were apparently unable to induce them to do so. This trade before the arrival of a permanent French presence must have been unsystematic and haphazard in French terms, since it followed Indian patterns of exchange, which did not resemble French market patterns. Indeed trade, which had historically served as both a political transaction used to maintain relations with other tribes and an economic exchange, continued to do so.[18]

Indians never controlled more than those phases of the trade that occurred in the *pays d'en haut*, "the upper country." The *pays d'en haut* moved west over time and began to include Menominee country as a significant fur-gathering region in the late seventeenth century. The impetus for the fur trade flowed from the French market to the French seaports and then through Montreal to the *pays d'en haut*, while the furs themselves flowed the other direction. The French colonial government maintained its seat in Montreal, ideally located on the Ottawa River but a long paddle from the upper country. The French presence stretched from Montreal to the Upper Great Lakes and beyond with ever diminishing strength.[19]

Despite the distance, the expansion of the European trade brought more French traders and voyageurs to the *pays d'en haut*. Many of them spent more time there than in the eastern French settlements. By the latter half of the seventeenth century they began to establish a small but permanent French presence in Menominee country. As a general rule, government officials and missionaries either accompanied or followed French traders into the *pays d'en haut*. When the French established posts and later towns at strategic sites along trade routes, they also established direct contact with local tribes and bands, except for those who were remote to the posts or who were disinclined to have regular contact with the French. At best, direct contact between the French and Menominee occurred on a small scale.

Still, this French presence and the increased interracial contact brought with it deadly diseases that began to strike the Menominee and other tribes in the seventeenth century. These scourges swept through the *pays d'en haut* like wildfire, appearing suddenly and

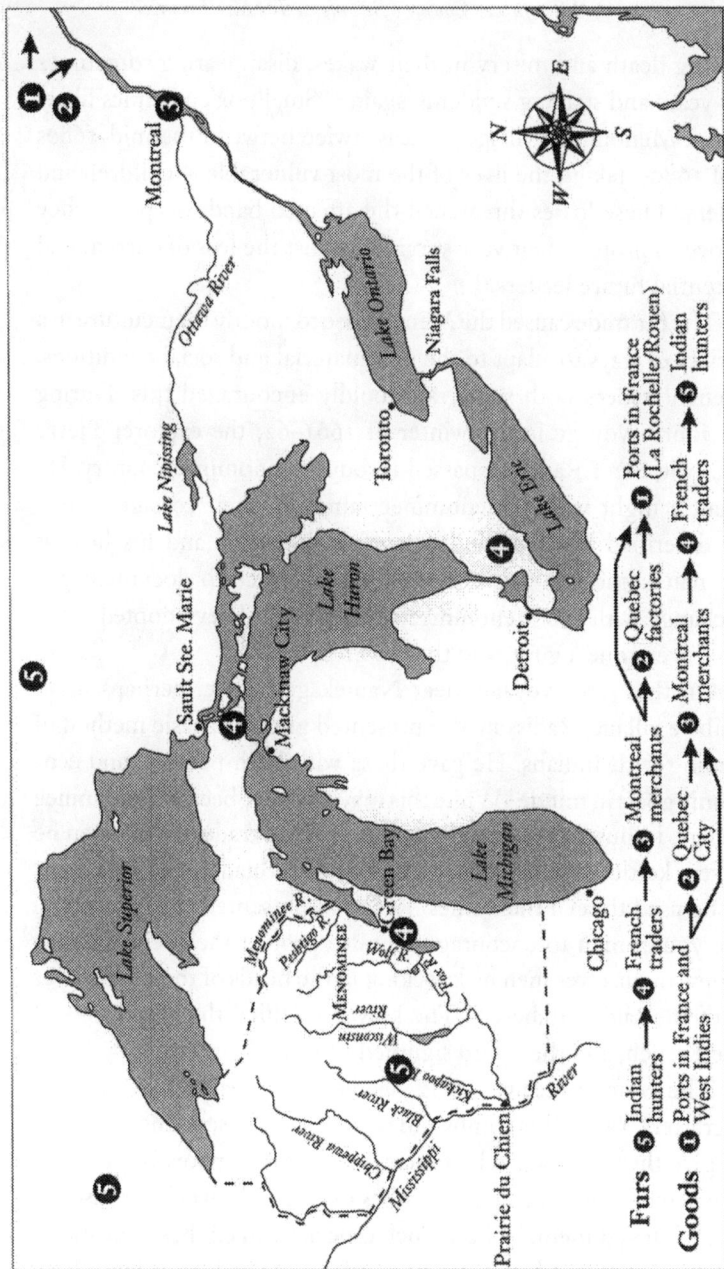

Map 2. French canoe route

leaving death and misery in their wakes, disappearing sometimes for years and striking suddenly again.[20] Smallpox epidemics likely struck Menominee villages at least twice between the mid-1660s and 1680s, taking the lives of the most vulnerable—children and elders. These losses threatened the affected bands deeply as they strove to protect their very survival against the loss of current and potential future leaders.[21]

The fur trade caused the Menominee to modify their culture in a variety of ways to adapt to the new material and social conditions. French traders both subtly and boldly encouraged this. During his fourth voyage in the winter of 1661–62, the explorer Pierre d'Esprit, Sieur Radisson passed through Menominee country. He spent a night with a Menominee family in their cottage, where he described his host as "ancient" and "witty" and his hostess as "handsome." In this earliest French source to document gift exchange with the Menominee, he reports, "They adopted me. I gave every one a guift, and they to mee."

On that same voyage, near Namekagon Lake, perhaps in an Ojibwe village, Radisson also presented gifts, the basic method of trading with Indians. He gave these with both political and economic goals in mind.[22] While this may not have been a Menominee village, it illustrates French intentions in the trade. To the men he gave a kettle, hatchets, knives, and a sword blade. The kettle was to be used to feed their allies. Radisson presented the hatchets to the young men to encourage them to protect their wives and to "shew themselves men by knocking in the heads of their ennemyes with the said hattchetts." The knives signified the mightiness of the French, and the sword signified French alliance.

The women received awls, needles, and beaver hide scrapers ("gratters") as well as combs and tin looking glasses. The awls were to give them courage when their men left to support the French. "Ye needles for to make them robes of castor [beaver], because the ffrench loved them." The French especially liked these *castor gras*, "beaver pelts that had been sewn into robes and worn by Indians fur inside."[23] Aging, smoke, sweat, and the usual wear and tear eliminated the outer guard hairs of the robes and prepared the soft inner fibers of the pelts for the hat-making industry. The other gifts for the women were "to make themselves beautiful" and "to admire themselves."

The introduction of knives, needles, and awls did not make life easier for the women but rather made more work for them. Although they lightened domestic tasks, these tools were also designed to facilitate the tanning and preparation of furs for the French market. Since women did this work, the trade increased their work load. Although the Menominee did not abandon their traditional economy for the fur trade, the men did increasingly stockpile furs for the spring trade and Menominee women prepared the hides that their men had hunted.

To the children, Radisson gave brass rings and small bells as well as goblets or mugs as symbols of French sovereignty. All of these gifts were given not out of generosity but with the hope for future returns from trade or military assistance.[24] French traders followed this pattern of gift giving among many tribes, including the Menominee.[25]

Once the indigenous people began to use French-made items, they became important producers in the French trade; yet they continued to view the trade in the traditional context of gift exchange, not in terms of profit. They gave furs to the king in recognition of friendship and alliances and accepted trade goods from the king, especially textiles, weapons, and ammunition, for the same purpose.[26] This political exchange was the first step of the trade for Indians.

The Menominee absorbed these new items into tribal life, thereby not losing their culture but changing it. For example, bells were strung on fishnets, and metal utensils supplanted those made of bone and stone. Clothing was increasingly made of cloth. They also incorporated French beads into the floral designs of their clothing.

MISSIONARIES AND TRADERS

Traders were not the only ones to attempt to modify Menominee culture. The Jesuit missionaries made it their primary purpose;

unlike French government officials and fur traders, however, they attempted to bring about a fundamental change in the tribe's world-view. The Jesuits traveled west with the trade for their own reasons, which included the conversion of "heathens" and the advancement of French culture.

The Jesuits believed the Menominee to be less spiritually de-veloped than Europeans. They viewed them as superstitious wor-shipers living outside the sphere of salvation, people who did not know the true God but could be brought to Him. They sought to substitute their own spiritual symbols for those of the Menominee and to impose their God on Menominee religious thinking. The Jesuits worked for only half a century in Menominee country before abandoning it in the early 1700s, but their presence is well documented and instructive. Although these missionaries were peripheral to most Menominee history, which went unreported in *The Jesuit Relations*, their records provide good insights into the very different spiritual worlds of the Menominee and the French as well as the first example of European attempts to profoundly reshape Menominee society and world-view.[27]

The Menominee at the time of French arrival did not have distinct divisions between the spiritual and secular aspects of their world. Neither did the Jesuits, although they were part of a larger society that increasingly did. For both groups, religion or spiritu-ality was a part of everyday life. For the Menominee, all aspects of existence derived from a spiritual foundation whose sources of power had to be honored in a variety of ways on a daily, seasonal, or annual basis. Sometimes this was the responsibility of the indi-vidual, sometimes of the family, and sometimes of the community as a whole. Unlike the Menominee, the Jesuits did not acknowl-edge multiple deities. All their efforts were expended in service to their lord, Jesus Christ. Significantly, the Jesuits' purpose was proselytization, while the Menominee world-view focused instead on keeping their own community in harmony with the powerful forces of both the natural and supernatural worlds.

Although both the Menominee and the Jesuits were profoundly

spiritual people, and although both of their religious beliefs contained dualistic world-views that encompassed good and evil, their differences were much deeper than their similarities. As one observer said of Jesuit and Indian relations in terms of religion and world-view, they interacted with a "lack of mutual comprehension."[28]

The Jesuit order, or Society of Jesus, founded in 1534 by St. Ignatius Loyola with a basis of a military-like chain of command, sent missionaries from Europe all over the world — to Asia, Africa, and North and South America. Their zealous proselytizers, well born, able, and thoroughly trained, would make any sacrifice for the greater glory of their god. In founding the order, "Loyola's intention was to shape a body of men who could serve as shock troops of the church against indifference, Protestantism, and, above all, heathenism." The missionaries underwent rigorous training, which prepared them physically, mentally, and spiritually for harsh lives in service to their lord. They viewed the conversion of the ignorant and heathen, especially children, as their properly chosen field of work. By the time the Jesuits entered the field in Menominee country, their order had over a century's experience proselytizing Indians in South America and several decades' experience in North America.[29]

The Jesuits served their lord by converting Indians to the true religion and bringing Him their souls. They used every possible opportunity to spread the gospel and were renowned for creative means of evangelism. Having learned from their failures, they developed sophisticated techniques to "gain a hearing." They became accomplished linguists, learned tribal customs so as not to offend, and became adept at transferring symbols of Indian spirituality into the language of their own spirituality. They also adapted their schedules so that their preaching occurred at annual seasonal occasions for tribes such as the Menominee who moved throughout the year.[30]

The first Jesuits arrived in Menominee country after the arrival of French traders. Father Gabriel Dreuillettes founded their first mission in Menominee country in 1658 at St. Michel near present-day Green Bay to serve the Potawatomis. Dreuillettes reported that he was near to the Noquets, the Menominee, and the Ho Chunks as well.[31] To the Jesuits "a mission was the 'substance of things hoped for.'" They considered a mission begun as soon as they baptized the first child or preached the gospel to the first adult, regardless of whether the Indians accepted the message. The St. Michel mission was relatively informal.[32]

By establishing themselves at the base of La Baye des Puants, or La Baye as the French called the body of water now known as Green Bay, at the mouth of the Fox River, Jesuits would be ready to work among Menominees and other Indians who came for the annual spring fish runs and summer camps as well as the few who may have remained on the rivers along the bay during the winter. The priests who established missions at the base of La Baye preached among several tribes at once and doubtless served the spiritual needs of French voyageurs and military men as well. Father Claude Jean Allouéz, who came west in 1665, founded the mission of St. Michael Archange, the first Jesuit mission specifically among the Menominee, in 1670 at a site on the Oconto River.[33] He visited the Oconto River band of the tribe in early May, at which time he "proclaimed the gospel to them, which they admired and heard with respect." Respectfulness was a trait of the Menominee and was formalized into their culture in both social and religious situations. Before he left, Allouéz was invited to a council of elders. They thanked him for bringing to the tribe "a knowledge of the true God." The elders told the Father, "Take heart [*prends courage*], . . . instruct us often, and teach us to speak to him who has made all things."

Understanding and creating balance and good relations with the supernatural world was of the utmost importance to the Menominee. By encouraging Allouéz to "teach us to speak to him" they seemed to be indicating an interest in pursuing yet another avenue to communicate with the powers controlling the supernatural world. If Allouéz possessed the power to do so, and was willing to share the use of that power with the Menominee, they would be willing to listen and learn. In addition, the Menominee were motivated by social obligation to host Allouéz. Storytelling played a key role in Menominee social gatherings. That Allouéz had enticing supernatural stories to tell may have made his visit even more welcome. At any rate, Menominee manners left them no choice but to host Allouéz. He viewed the introduction of the gospel among the Menominee as a grand success, although he admitted that he had difficulty understanding their language and that "they succeeded in understanding me better than I understood them."[34]

Both story and ceremony were important aspects of French as well as Menominee culture. In some ceremonial situations, the Jesuits acted on behalf of not only their lord but also their king. On some occasions all three French contingencies in the area—missionaries, traders, and government officials—worked together. On 14 June 1671, for example, representatives of King Louis XIV annexed the Upper Great Lakes region for France in a ceremony at Sault Ste. Marie. This was the first of several such occasions throughout the west on which the French conducted elaborate ceremonies with local Indians present to establish their claims among other Europeans. The Menominee were one of over a dozen tribes present at this first such function. Simon François Daumont, Sieur de St. Lusson, ran the ceremony, although the trader Nicholas Perrot, who served as interpreter for the French, in large part organized it.[35] Several priests, too, played important roles. Father Allouéz gave a speech glorifying King Louis XIV, whose "armorial bearings" were raised on a cedar pole alongside a cross that had been planted there as well. Allouéz described his king as an all-powerful captain who commanded ten thousand captains as powerful as Onnontio, governor of Quebec, whom these tribes had helped to contain the Iroquois.[36] St. Lusson followed with a speech claiming the land for the king and asking the tribes to become the king's subjects. The tribes agreed, but when this was put down to paper, tribal members ripped the document from its hiding place and burned it.[37] The French seem to have treated the event more as a public ceremony than as a treaty negotiation anyway.

At this time the population in Wisconsin's Indian villages out-numbered the approximately five thousand French living in the far-off St. Lawrence Valley.[38] The French claims, therefore, could only be put into effect using tribal alliances in the commercial as well as political and military domains. The French never actually controlled, nor did they intend to control, the land they thus claimed. The Menominee treated the French presence in terms of *apēkon ahkihih*, the Menominee practice of letting allies utilize or sit down upon their land.

After St. Lusson staked his claim, the French presence in the area became more permanent, with Jesuits, post commandants together with their men, and traders all living in or near Menomi-nee country continuously. Traders were longer-term residents, but except for Perrot, who lived in the area off and on, they left few records. Like most Frenchmen in the upper country, Perrot served numerous roles, including that of a fur trader, a soldier, and an emissary of the French government in Montreal. He spoke numer-ous Indian languages and traded and fought with the Menominee, Potawatomis, Ojibwes, Mesquakies, Miamis, Mascoutens, Iowas, Santees, Ottawas, Hurons, and Ho Chunks. Perrot is best known because he wrote prolifically, providing, besides the Jesuit accounts, the most basic written information from this period. He returned to the region in 1674 and again in 1685, and thereafter for more than a decade he moved throughout Menominee, Potawatomi, Ho Chunk, and Santee country and back and forth to Montreal. He is described as living in the area of La Baye "almost habitually" from 1665 to 1699.[39]

Perrot described briefly the Menominee's traditional methods of sustenance, which was still the vital basis of the tribal economy. "The Malhominis are no more than forty in number," he wrote.[40] "[T]hey raise a little Indian corn, but live upon game and sturgeons; they are skillful navigators. If the Sauteurs are adroit in catching the whitefish at the Sault, the Malhominis are no less so in spearing the sturgeon in their river. For this purpose they use only small canoes, very light, in which they stand upright, and in the middle of the current spear the sturgeon with an iron-pointed pole; only canoes are to be seen, morning and evening."[41]

Nonetheless, the Menominee had become increasingly involved in the fur trade. The Potawatomis had wrested control of the Baye area segment of the trade from the Ottawas. When the newly arrived French tried in their turn to displace them, the Potawatomis sent messages to several tribes in the area, though apparently not the Menominee, in an attempt to maintain control themselves. Perrot and others, fearing the Potawatomis' threat, quickly made alliances with several tribes, including the Menominee.[42]

During this tense time, in 1667, a Menominee killed a Potawatomi and another Potawatomi retaliated by killing a Menominee. This caused some Menominees to prepare to attack a nearby Potawatomi village in reprisal while a large proportion of Potawatomi men were away in Montreal on a trading trip. Perrot intervened on the side of the Potawatomis, warning the Menominee that the French would support the Potawatomis as allies and also reminding them that the returning Potawatomi traders would bring new muskets with them.[43] Potawatomi numbers and military technology combined with French alliance probably served as a strong motivating force in dissuading the Menominee attack. The Potawatomis and the French ultimately shared control of the trade in the Baye area during the latter third of the seventeenth century, and political friendship with both the Potawatomis and French traders was important to the Menominee.[44]

The Potawatomis augmented their advantage over other local nations by obtaining quality weapons. At this time guns were not yet a common part of the trade, so they dramatically increased the power of those who had them.[45] In the woods, tribes had to rely on French or Indian traders for their French-made supplies. Those tribes going directly to Montreal could trade not only for higher-quality items at lower prices but also for specific items. The Hurons, for instance, traded at Montreal in 1670–71, taking home with them only guns and ammunition, which were difficult to obtain at home.[46] Indian traders were intent upon acquiring useful goods.

The French, meanwhile, were intent upon profiting from the trade financially. Perrot, for example, living near La Baye, trapped furs, but he also used his alliances to trade for furs in trips he made to the inland.[47] The Menominee and other tribes traded their furs throughout Indian country, not merely at officially established French posts. The resultant abundance of western furs led to an even greater rush to the Upper Great Lakes area by French traders and *coureurs de bois*, the canoe men who provided the labor force for much of the transportation of furs between Montreal and the *pays d'en haut*.[48] This boost in the western trade placed an increasing emphasis on Menominee, Ho Chunk, Ojibwe, Santee, and Mesquakie territory.

RELIGIOUS INTERACTIONS

At the same time as the fur trade expanded, the Jesuits seemingly stepped up their efforts in Menominee country as well. After Father Allouéz left the area, Father Louis André served among the Menominee and other tribes in the region, beginning in 1671. He attended the French annexation of the territory by St. Lusson in an official capacity that year.

André began his service to the Menominee in spectacular fashion in April 1673, which he described in a lengthy letter published in *The Jesuit Relations*. He found the Menominee River band waiting on the banks of the Menominee River for the sturgeon to make their spring run upstream. The fish were late and had already entered the two major rivers farther south on La Baye, the Peshtigo and the Oconto, which were farther away from the mouth of the bay and the entrance to the lake. No doubt the people were in deep need of fresh fish in their diet after the winter's sustenance of dried fish and game and whatever rice was not eaten in the fall and after the spring sugar. No sturgeon had yet come to the Menominee River, and the Menominee had raised a "banner" in supplication to the sun, which they recognized as "the master of life and of fishing, and the dispenser of all things." They told André, upon his inquiry, "that it was a sacrifice — or rather, to use the expression of their language, 'an exhortation.'"

André spoke to a large part of the group, all but three elders. "After disabusing them of the idea which they had of the sun, and explaining to them in a few words the principal points of our Faith," he asked them to allow him to replace the "picture of the sun" with "the image of Jesus crucified." They permitted this, and he quickly made the switch. The next morning a bounteous run of sturgeon began. The "delighted" Menominee said to André, "Now we see very well that the Spirit who has made all is the one who feeds us. Take courage; teach us to pray, so that we may never feel hunger."

According to the father, this happenstance gave this band of Menominee a large dose of confidence in André and his religion, and many listened to his teachings. Though he asked to teach only the children, many adults came to listen as well, especially at night after they finished the work of fishing. André made such an impression that he convinced the people into "removing the black from their faces and in breaking their superstitious fast."

Indeed, with a few exceptions, he convinced a group of warriors ready to do battle not to blacken their faces or to dream of their enemies, as they traditionally did before battle: "before setting out for war, they offered no feast to the devil, nor did they dream any dreams, according to their ancient custom." André was surprised at how readily the Indians abandoned their "superstitions; for I know by experience how singularly these people are attached to them." Even the "chief juggler," as he referred to the Menominee spiritual leader, "showed that he took pleasure in my instruction." André convinced him not to seek power from the thunder, as was his practice.

André concluded by saying he could have baptized practically the entire nation but thought he should put them to the test of time. Instead, he baptized twenty-two children and two adults. Both the adults died soon afterward.[49]

Seeking power was at the center of Menominee religion. Power symbols and power objects played important roles in that religion as they did in Jesuit religion. In André's incident, at least as recorded by him, switching power symbols actually worked. Based on this success, André was able to talk individuals out of using particular spiritually based power symbols (blackened faces) and rituals (dreaming) in seeking strength from supernatural sources for events other than fishing.

Was this conversion? No—André himself did not believe it to be, so he did not baptize the adults. This represented a change in symbolism, not necessarily a change in belief. For their part, the Menominees of the Menominee River band recognized that André had access to power. After all, he had showed them a spiritual symbol that worked. The happy coincidences, divinely inspired or otherwise, of André's actions in replacing the symbol of the sun with the symbol of the cross immediately before the already late sturgeon run began probably added to the aura of the power of the French belief system. On the basis of this, the Menominee River band would at least have been interested in knowing of the French God, as the Oconto River band had been when Father Allouéz preached to its council of elders in 1670.

The Menominee were interested in investigating the power of the symbols, objects, and rituals that the French offered as an alternative. The Menominee, like other tribes, probably searched for power or ways to access power, and these French methods would have interested them. The way individuals dressed, wore their hair, and painted their faces, for example, all held elements of religious significance for the Menominee. André seemed to understand their importance, even if he dismissed it as superstition. Menominee religion reflected a highly complex cosmology, and André was offering one more manitou among many. Menominees may have believed in the power symbols and objects associated with André's spirit or manitou, but they could not have possibly given up their complex understanding of the basic forces that controlled their world.

Father André tried to reject the Menominee cosmology as superstition. He repudiated Menominee gods as demons and even specifically as the devil. He portrayed Menominee attempts to understand his religion as ready conversion to his belief system. At least, so he interpreted it for publication in *The Jesuit Relations*, which circulated among financial supporters of the missionary efforts, who would be pleased to see their money at work with such dramatic success.

Unfortunately, no firsthand record exists of Menominee thoughts in this period. Some responses are recorded, however. For example, in April 1676 an Indian man, apparently a Menominee whom André had visited while ministering to a band of the tribe, burned André's home after André had baptized one of the man's two children. Both children were then killed by another Indian. "Hast thou sense?" the children's enraged father asked André. "I think thou hast none. . . . my child was baptized and was killed."[50] André had probably convinced the man that baptism would provide some protection to the child. This would have provided an effective way to gain an audience with the man, had the baptism actually afforded the child protection. But in this case, André's ritual failed — it did not keep this man's child from being killed. It made the ritual of baptism powerless and ineffective in the man's eyes.

Unlike other orders, the Jesuits believed that baptism could be an encouragement in the process of conversion and need not occur merely as recognition of it.[51] At times, the missionaries worked even too enthusiastically for their superiors. Louise Phelps Kellogg says of Father Allouéz, for example, "His policy of baptizing children who were well, reacted so favorably that the Indians believed the rite assured their children a long life; but the Jesuit superior disapproved of this wholesale conversion of children who might soon exhibit all the marks of pagans, and cautioned the missionary against continuing such methods."[52]

Even if individual missionaries were at times unable to change tribes' belief systems, Jesuit leaders understood the complexity of their task in attempting to do so. They recognized that, although the Indians may have believed in the ritual, they did not necessarily believe in the god.

André ran into problems when his access to spiritual power turned out to be less complete than he had led the Indians to believe. André compounded his problems by telling this same man that his child who had been baptized would be happy after death. The man finally burned the priest's cabin. André blamed the devil for causing the man to act thus. "I shall not Relate here all the obstacles that the Devil raised against me," he wrote, "and how he availed himself of the effrontery of some savage to revenge himself for the prey that I Snatched from him through those baptisms."[53] The Menominee father did not view his dead child as a pawn in a battle between the Jesuit priest and the devil. He merely recognized that the Jesuit made false promises.

When the 1683 epidemic swept through the Baye area, killing many Indians, Father André, himself suffering from gout, went to live among the Menominee. "His Ailments served him more than anything else in encouraging the Christians to follow his example by patiently suffering the maladies with which God had afflicted them, and never to abandon, on that account, the faith they had Embraced," Father Thierry Beschefer reported in *The Jesuit Relations.*[54] André certainly made deep sacrifices, but his service was clearly to his god. His suffering had a higher purpose of discouraging his converts from backsliding. However, this too probably backfired. His own weakness simply illuminated for the Menominee the inadequacy of the spiritual powers that provided the father with protection.

The 1683 epidemic proved deadly to a large number of Indians from all the tribes in the Baye area, and many of them blamed the affliction not on God but on the missionaries. Once again the very survival and future of the affected Menominee bands were at stake. Neither their own powers nor those of the Jesuits could check the rapid spread of death. The mission was apparently saved only by the diplomacy of Nicholas Perrot, without whose interference the Indians would probably have avenged the ravages that the

European diseases had caused them by killing or at least driving out the missionaries.[55]

After Father André left in 1684, other missionaries served the mission at La Baye. Father Charles Albanel apparently served among the Menominee, perhaps at the same time as did Father André, but otherwise no record exists of missionary service to the Menominee.[56] By 1707 the Jesuits abandoned the Baye area mission entirely, leaving any converts they had made without priests.[57]

The Menominee reaction to the fathers, based on the meager information that exists, seems to have been a mixture of interest, acceptance, and opposition. Probably few, if any, Menominees abandoned their own religious beliefs for those of the Jesuits; but some at least probably tried to incorporate symbols and rituals of Catholicism into their system to some degree. When the priests made extravagant promises of power and protection, however, and the power failed to appear, the Menominee blamed the fathers for this failure and took action against them. Evidence shows that the priests served among the Oconto River and Menominee River bands, and when two priests served among the tribe at the same time, they probably served different bands. No Jesuit record exists of the bands they did not serve, including those that refused proselytization.[58] It must also be added that the frontier in the area of La Baye seems to have been of only minor importance to the Jesuits, who gave but little space to it in their *Jesuit Relations*.

DEVELOPMENT OF A FRONTIER

During the seventeenth century most Menominee history happened far from European eyes (see the chart, "Periods in Menominee history"). Menominee relations with other Indian nations still outweighed their relations with the French in significance. The French trade became an important factor in Menominee life, although the Menominee originally dealt with Ottawa or Potawatomi middlemen as often as with the French traders. To the French, however, Menominee country became a fur-trade frontier. The most immediate impacts caused by the French were disease, which ravaged the tribe from the beginning of French connections, and intermarriage, which brought children of traders and Menominee women almost from the time of first contact. These early French forays into Menominee country portended other serious changes whose full impact would not be felt until later.

As the seventeenth century closed the Menominee had at least several decades of direct experience with both the Jesuits and the French trade. The French trade occurred on such an immense scale that it would eventually reshape these trade patterns significantly. However, Indian country was so far from the base of French economic decision making and operations that the change was slow and incomplete. French goods began to permeate Menominee material culture and the tribal members became more sophisticated traders as time went on. In August 1695, Perrot brought about a dozen canoes full of Indians from six western tribes, including Menominee, to Montreal for the French war against the Iroquois.[59] Some of these Menominee may have received French guns and ammunition with which to fight the Iroquois. This weaponry would be a precious commodity back home and would increasingly become items for which the Menominee bargained.

Although at the beginning of the eighteenth century guns were not yet common trade items in the upper lakes country, other goods were introduced that would profoundly affect Menominee life. These included cloth, clothing, blankets, knives, hunting and hide-preparation goods, cookware, domestic wares, and vanity goods. However, before 1700 the trade had a relatively minor effect on the subsistence of the Menominee and other La Baye area tribes.[60]

The demographic impact of both the trade and missions made itself felt in the devastating diseases that swept through Menominee country in the latter half of the seventeenth century. The extent of the destruction is not known. The Menominee continued to maintain a multiple band system in the face of this; it is likely that those bands with greatest contact with the French suffered the most. Tribal attitudes toward the French were complex, based on a variety of factors: the desire for certain trade goods, political and military alliance, respect for and mistrust of the French spiritual powers, and the onset of disease.

The Menominee participated but did not become the primary movers of furs in the French economic system that was reshaping life in the Upper Great Lakes, just as they listened to the Jesuits but did not alter the basis of their spiritual outlook. Despite the harvest and preparation of furs, a time-consuming and labor-intensive wintertime task, and despite occasional visits from priests, the Menominee way of life in camp did not change drastically during this period of French contact. Other changes, such as increased pressures on their territorial range, new uses for new material goods, and occasionally devastating epidemics, slowly increased in their impact. But for the most part Menominee life continued in much the same pattern as it had for centuries. Menominee life continued to flow in seasonal cycles of abundance and dearth. The bands did not give up hunting, ricing, sugaring, fishing, and planting as the basic means of sustenance, or their belief in their complex cosmology. The Menominee may not have become dependent on the fur trade in the seventeenth century, but they were greatly impacted by it. That impact would grow in the first half of the eighteenth century.

3
Sovereign Alliances

By the beginning of the eighteenth century the Menominee and the French shared a relationship in which the two groups interacted based on mutual needs and strength. The Menominee enjoyed the benefits of both the trade and French alliance in disputes with their neighbors. To the French, Menominee country was located at one node of a far-flung empire whose remote outposts among numerous Indian nations were important both for the fur trade and for controlling expansion of the increasingly extensive frontiers of the British Empire. As the French continued to push west along inland waterways, Michilimackinac (now Mackinac) became the base for the French trade in the northwest.[1]

At the same time, the west became an increasingly important military arena for the French. This can be seen in eighteenth-century colonial primary sources, in which the French wars dominated the literature, just as Jesuit efforts dominated seventeenth-century literature.[2] The French increasingly involved western Indian nations in their war plans, as they previously had done with eastern tribes. But as with trade, French and Indian views of the purposes of war differed significantly, as did their reasons for participating in it. Although Menominee warriors frequently joined the French in battles against other tribes, nearby and far to the east, they did so only when and where it suited their purposes, and their actions in the resulting conflicts were governed by their own policy and needs, not French political desires. The colonial French were a warlike people who considered every male subject a soldier. For the

Menominee, on the other hand, warfare was personal and small-scale, far from the central focus of their culture. For the most part this remained so. During the fur trade era, small intertribal battles often involved individuals, families, or a portion of the band. These took place between Menominees and Ojibwes, or Santees farther west; between Menominees and Potawatomis, or other invading tribes; and between Menominees and the French. Most of these skirmishes were so minor that they had negligible impact on the relations between the Menominee and their neighbors.[3]

MILITARY ALLIANCES

Not surprisingly, some Menominee warriors joined the French in their late-seventeenth-century war against the Iroquois. Menominee and other tribal leaders from the Baye region traveled to Montreal to cement their alliance in a meeting on 16 August 1695. They agreed to be partners in efforts to keep peace among the Santees, the Mesquakies, and the Miamis, and they joined in a temporary alliance with a French military party heading to battle against the Iroquois. But they soon gave up this effort, over the protest of the French, and returned to Montreal for another meeting before heading home.

In that meeting on 3 September 1695, a Menominee leader pledged alliance with the French, accepted thanks from the French governor for Menominee support in the war efforts over the past couple of years, and then led his small contingent of Menominees back to their homeland.[4] Fall rice harvesttime was on the horizon, after which it would be time for the bands to move to winter camp. Both of these tasks were the responsibility of the *gichita* ("warriors") to oversee. Without securing these resources the warriors would not live to fight another year. These needs outweighed French strategic plans in their battles with the Iroquois.

By 1701, the French finally made peace with the Iroquois, which consequently caused another massive demographic upheaval that rocked the Menominee homeland as the Mascoutens, Miamis, and Potawatomis moved off toward the southwest and southeast and

the Ottawas returned east. The Mesquakies remained in Menominee country, however, and together with the Ho Chunks and
Ojibwes remained as the Menominee's closest Indian neighbors.

To formalize the peace, Governor General Chevalier de Callier
called the western nations, the Iroquois Confederacy, and other
eastern nations to Montreal to sign a peace treaty. French officers
traveled to the Upper Great Lakes in the spring of 1701 to bring
tribal leaders to the meeting, which was conducted in the beginning
of August. The leader who spoke for the Menominee tribe simply
told de Callier, "I come out of obedience to you, and to take
advantage of the Peace you have concluded between the Iroquois
and us." The word *obedience* may have been mistranslated. "I come
out of respect" better fits Menominee diplomatic practice, even if
it is less glorifying of the French.[5] The Menominee representative
then signed the document along with thirty-seven other tribal
leaders from the various nations and bands represented.[6]

Meanwhile the Menominee had continued an alliance with the
Mesquakies. While Sieur de Courtemanche had been in the Baye
area in May to round up leaders of the western tribes for the trip
to Montreal, he met with the Sauks, Ho Chunks, Mesquakies,
Potawatomis, Kickapoos, and Menominee. First he met with the
nations individually, then as a whole. The Dakotas had recently
attacked the Mesquakies, and a group of three hundred to five
hundred warriors from the Baye area nations was planning a retaliation. As part of the French peace negotiations they agreed to
refrain.[7]

Soon after, however, these alliances shifted. The Mesquakies,
who occupied the river route with a series of approximately eight
villages from the Fox River at Lake Winnebago to the confluence of
the Wisconsin and Mississippi Rivers, were increasingly in a bind.
They had developed an ever-growing need for goods produced by
French technology but were frustrated by a decreasing availability
of them. They never established themselves as trading partners
with the French, due to the isolation caused by their early arrival in
Menominee and Ho Chunk country. To their northeast the French

had established solid trading partnerships with the Potawatomis and Ottawas. In the west the Dakotas, with a larger population than the Mesquakies, had attracted French interest, which led to a growing trade despite its prohibition by French law. The Mesquakies protested by attacking and robbing French *coureurs de bois* who used the Fox-Wisconsin waterway to reach Santee country.[8]

The Mesquakies became aggressively territorial and began to enforce their control of the Fox River near Butte des Morts by levying taxes on all who used it to reach the Wisconsin and Mississippi Rivers. The Menominee and other Indian nations, as well as the French, resented this, and the resulting conflict escalated into the first French and Mesquakie war (1701–16).[9]

Control of the trade was the major reason for French involvement in the war. For the tribes, however, the war was largely about the open use of waterways as thoroughfares. Simply put, the Mesquakies broke intertribal law recognized by the local Indian nations, which joined together with the French to reopen the passage.

For the Menominee, irritation exploded into anger at what they viewed as a Mesquakie invasion of the Menominee homeland. No longer were the Mesquakies simply sitting down upon Menominee lands, but they were attempting to wrest the resources upon them from everyone else. The Mesquakie blockage of the Fox River constituted an invasion of Menominee country and a threat to the Menominee place in the fur trade and, just as important, a threat to free passage. Until they broke the Mesquakie hold on Fox River access, the Menominee fought an all-out war alongside the French and other Indian nations. When in the end the Mesquakies were nearly destroyed, the French commander, Louis de la Porte de Louvigny, accepted a peace by which the Mesquakies ceded all their lands in Wisconsin and paid war reparations with beaver skins.[10]

The Mesquakies did not leave Wisconsin, however. A brief peace was followed by the second French and Mesquakie war (1727–38), which from its inception became a genocidal attempt by the French to annihilate the tribe.[11] In 1728, when Marchand de Lignery, who had first been assigned to Michilimackinac in 1712, again came through Menominee country to fight the Mesquakies, he first stopped farther east, at his old command at Michilimackinac. There over a thousand Indian warriors, including about a hundred Menominees (probably from several bands), joined his French fighting troops for the expedition west.[12] Not all Menominee warriors took part, however.

The autonomous nature of Menominee decision making is illuminated by the following French experience in this war, which illustrates that Menominee participation in such events was determined at the individual, family, or band level. Two French leaders of the second war against the Mesquakies, in a letter to the French minister of war, mention the Folles Avoines as "our nearest allies."[13] Yet Emanuel Crespel, the Flemish missionary who accompanied de Lignery's campaign against the Mesquakies in 1728 as chaplain to the French troops, reported a skirmish in which the French fought *against* the Folles Avoines. "The whole nation consists of only this village," he mistakenly said of the Menominee village at which the French provoked the attack.[14] If indeed the French did this, it must have been a band that opposed the war or that was at the very least neutral. De Lignery, in his report of the expedition, does not mention the attack on the Menominee.[15]

In 1730 Paul Marin led a battle in which he and Menominee and Ho Chunk allies forced the Mesquakies to flee their village on Butte des Morts in a siege recognized as the beginning of the end of the Mesquakie presence in Wisconsin.[16] One story of Marin's campaign tells of how the Butte des Morts received its name. It identifies the Menominee leader who joined Marin as Aus-kin-naw-waw-witsh, leader of "a band of Monomonees that had encamped in the vicinity." Aus-kin-naw-waw-witsh offered to aid Marin in exchange for guns, ammunition, tobacco, clothing, alcohol, and the land they would take from the Mesquakies. According to the story, after a bloody victory, Aus-kin-naw-waw-witsh was rewarded at least with the alcohol and the land.[17]

The French continued their genocidal war of extermination of the Mesquakies after they had been defeated; they did not give up on the idea until they were forced to in 1737, when the leaders of numerous tribes in the Upper Great Lakes area sought mercy for their ex-enemies, the Mesquakies, as well as the Sauks, with whom much of the remnant of the Mesquakies had amalgamated. The latter had already been annihilated to the extent that their very presence in Menominee country was extremely tenuous. The French insisted on continuing their assault, but numerous tribes, including the Menominee, refused to join them, expressing disgust that the French were willing to destroy an entire people to further European commercial interests; once the Mesquakies were destroyed, they wondered, who would be next?[18]

Meanwhile, the French began to formalize their tenancy in Menominee country. They built Fort La Baye in 1717, a post that would oversee trade up the Fox River and down the Wisconsin River to the Mississippi. The French maintained the post through the duration of the French era, although its strength was initially tenuous.[19]

The building of the post at Fort La Baye brought official representatives of the French government into Menominee country. The post commandant who oversaw the fort took over roles that were played earlier by French traders, explorers, and military officers. Among other duties, he had to try to keep warring tribes at peace and in allegiance with the French—not the English; he had to control the voyageurs, making them follow government regulations; and he had to search for mineral deposits and "the western ocean," all in the name of the king.[20] He needed to be a military officer, a businessman, a politician, and, most important for maintenance of relations with the local nations, a well-received diplomat.

Wisconsin's state historian, Reuben Gold Thwaites, noted that the building of French posts, including the one at La Baye, greatly changed Indian society. "No longer could they enjoy their free life of the past," he observed. "At the command of French officers, they abandoned their old-time villages, and clustered their huts and tepees around the fur trading posts."[21] Little evidence aside from such claims supports this, however. The Menominee band system did not break up; one or several (or parts of several) bands chose to live in communities established in the vicinity of forts, but others did not. The building of a fort did not signal a new French presence in the area, even if it ushered in a new type of French presence. In fact, French and Menominee contact was so sporadic that secondhand information about the tribe was still of great value to the French back east. Father Pierre François Xavier Charlevoix paddled by the mouth of the Menominee River where a Menominee village was located in 1721, but he did not stop. His few recorded observations, perhaps gleaned from his guides, shaped not only French but later historical understandings of the Menominee. "The entire tribe is comprised of this Village," he reported incorrectly, "which is not very populous." He also remarked that the Menominee subsisted on wild rice and were "fine-looking men, and among the most shapely in Canada."[22]

Many voyageurs merely outfitted themselves at the post before trading inland. The trade was conducted not only at the French forts but at outposts established by traders in the woods and at Indian villages. Perrot, who had established himself along La Baye before the French built a post there, had traded and trapped inland during the winter. Whenever traders with goods met Indians with skins and furs, trading was likely to take place. Voyageurs traded in the interior, and Indians paddled canoes to the forts, which like La Baye were centrally located on important fur trade routes.

Even before the founding of the fort at La Baye, an independent and illegal French trader ran a good traffic in furs there as early as 1706, and the Baye area "swarmed with [illegal] *coureurs de bois*" previous to that time. During the first war with the Mesquakies, the fur trade, which had declined in profitability due to overproduction and declining needs in France, underwent a revival. Prices rose, causing traders' canoes to pour west from Montreal up the Ottawa River to Michilimackinac, La Baye, Kaministiquia, and points west.

COMMERCIAL ALLIANCES

The fur trade reshaped Indian life in the Upper Great Lakes to a greater extent in the eighteenth century than during any other time. It brought permanent change to the Menominee. Throughout the first half of the century the beaver population in the Baye area declined precipitously. This had a dual impact on the Menominee, since beaver were not only an important trade item but a food source as well. This change caused the Menominee and other Baye area tribes to expand their territory westward. Some Menominee bands began wintering in the Mississippi River area while others moved into territory abandoned by the Mesquakies along the Wolf River and in central Wisconsin.[23] This expansion created the opportunity for an increase in the Menominee population and in the number of tribal bands that existed during the eighteenth century.[24]

At the same time, the trade had an important impact on the tribe's material culture. Three fur trade items stand out above all others: textiles, alcohol, and firearms. By the eighteenth century, textiles became the cornerstone of the trade, with clothing, buttons, thread, and tools such as awls making up over 65 percent of the goods traded in La Baye. In sheer volume this far topped any other trade item.[25]

Alcohol—the French brandy and later the British rum and the American whiskey—could be obtained for credit or furs. If on credit, the bill would be paid in furs. Although Perrot rarely mentioned it a hundred years earlier, by the end of the eighteenth century alcohol was a staple of the trade. Previous to the introduction of alcohol, the Menominee dismissed fermented foods as unhealthy. When the first French adventurers rolled their kegs ashore the Menominee were loath to drink. The young men refused, tradition says, even though the traders drank. The tribe finally chose the oldest men, who were most knowledgeable and also not much longer for this world, to undergo this trial. They drank heavily and finally passed out. The Menominee, thinking them killed, began to mourn. But the elders awoke, still intoxicated, and began to dance and sing. When asked how it felt to be dead, they described the odd feelings and the effects of drunkenness on their thoughts.[26]

The Menominee viewed alcohol as a mood enhancer, and many quickly accepted its use, relying on the sporadic supplies of traders who often traded them the vilest brandy.[27] They might give away the first dram or two, which made it easier for them to bargain sometimes an entire winter's stock of furs in exchange for the alcohol. This brought large profits for the traders.[28]

The traders and Frenchmen attached to various posts drank, often to excess, and even in the American period alcohol was part of the daily rations given each soldier at the fort at Green Bay. Already in the 1650s the Jesuits believed alcohol in the fur trade to be enough of a problem that they began to call for its prohibition.[29] Yet alcohol flowed into Indian country on a regular basis, even into the twentieth century.[30]

By the eighteenth century French law forbade traders to sell brandy to Indians. The law, however, permitted each voyageur to carry four jugs of brandy into the *pays d'en haut*, and posts could be stocked with up to 160 times that amount. No doubt traders smuggled even more into the interior to trade with the Indians.[31] The French system brought alcohol also to the Menominee, where Indians living in the vicinity of the fort had greater access to it than did those in the interior, who got it only when they traded the winter's furs for goods or redeemed credit. Although most Menominees only rarely if at all consumed alcohol, it led at times to disaster.[32] The tragic consequences of intemperance have haunted the tribe since the introduction of alcohol.

Firearms also brought profound changes to Menominee life. These were slightly more durable goods than alcohol, although ammunition had to be constantly replaced and the firearms broke often. Firearms changed methods and accuracy in hunting and affected the balances of power in warfare. Also important were the other goods exchanged in the trade such as domestic wares, hunting and warfare tools, and vanity items.

Of perhaps greater significance than the goods, the French trade brought to Menominee country a system of credit, the economic basis for the trade, which profoundly affected the tribal economy. The French extended credit for tools of the trade and for necessities such as food, cloth, and cookware. At the end of the winter, the Menominee traded furs against their debts. (Local non-Indian traders did the same as the trade developed.) This extension of credit meant the Menominee could afford to spend more time pursuing the trade and less time on individual survival. This system changed the nature of Menominee trading, which had a centuries-long history based on barter systems, and it also changed Menominee and other tribes' hunting patterns to a market orientation. The hunting of fur-bearing animals began to occur on a commercial basis.

Great profits flowed to the French government through these forts or trading posts, and initially the governor appointed commandants for these posts based on their skills in dealing with Indians and finances as well as their positions in the army. The tribes had some influence in the appointment process. For instance, Governor Beauharnois appointed François Lefebre, Sieur Duplessis-Fabert as commandant at Fort La Baye in 1727, after the Indians served by the fort rejected his first choice.[33] The governor knew the French cause would be advanced if not only he but also the Indians trusted the post commandant.

The French government recognized the post's primary purpose to be profit. The commandant knew this also and kept tight control of the trade. The government sold licenses to trading firms that outfitted the traders who operated out of the posts.[34] The government paid for the post and its personnel as well as gifts for Indians. The post commandants used the latter as diplomatic tools.[35] Although the governor trusted the post commandants, he also knew they profited from the trade. As Kellogg tells us, "The commandants connived at every means to increase the profits, and usually accepted the office expecting to enrich themselves in a brief term of service."[36]

Menominee country played a relatively minor role in the French fur trade but at times could assume both strategic and economic importance. Mackinac and Detroit brought in more revenue than did the post at La Baye, although the latter post did bring healthy profits to the traders and the commandants and an annual fee for the crown.[37] The importance of the route for which the Menominee and French battled the Mesquakies lay not only in the furs obtained from Menominee and Mesquakie country but also in access to the Mississippi River and Ojibwe and Santee trade in what is now west and northwest Wisconsin and eastern Minnesota. Indeed, outlays of goods were large enough that the traders relied on credit from the Montreal merchants from whom they procured trade goods or with whom they formed partnerships. Trading had become a big business, and wide-ranging partnerships were now sending their tentacles into Menominee country.

By the 1740s, however, the minister in Paris believed that the posts were becoming an expensive burden, so he decided to monopolize the trade at them, leasing them out to the highest bidders and requiring the bidders to fully support the posts financially. The minister hoped this system of monopolization, which was consistent with economic policy in Paris, would cut costs and increase government income.[38] The minister believed that gifts to the local Indians, for instance, cost the government too much, and he apparently rebuked Governor Beauharnois for this. Beauharnois understood, however, that without liberal gift giving French hopes for alliance would fail. Gift giving in trade had political, economic, and social significance to the Menominee and other tribes. It institutionalized the kind of generosity practiced by individuals and families, serving the broader purposes of cementing alliances and showing respect to others.[39] "I am really mortified," Beauharnois wrote to the minister, "that you are sorry to see the expenses for the Savages increasing every year." Beauharnois predicted that this change in policy would harm the trade in the long run by angering the Indians. Unfortunately for French policy, the minister in France decided to fully monopolize the trade at the posts at the same time Governor Beauharnois promised the western Indians, including Menominees, at a meeting in Montreal that the French would do the opposite.[40]

In the summer of 1742, Beauharnois promised the tribes increased competition after they had reported to him that they got better prices for furs when more than one store operated at a post. For this reason, Beauharnois feared that "as soon as the Savages learn the posts are to be disposed to the highest Bidder, they will all go over to the English."[41] Indeed, the tribes could trade with the English, whose trade goods were generally recognized as better and, on top of this, less expensive. The British traded goods of higher quality than the French in exchange for fewer furs. For example, the British traded a blanket for one beaver fur, while the French demanded two; and the British traded eight pounds of powder for one beaver, while the French demanded four.[42] In 1749, eighty Menominees in ten canoes brought seventy packs, presumably of furs, to trade with the British in Oswego.[43] Only the political alliance and institutionalized gift giving saved the French a place in the trading arena.

At this point, either at the minister's request or in anticipation of the minister's request, Beauharnois replaced La Baye's post commandant, Joseph Marin, who was well respected by the local tribes, with Sieur de Lusignan.[44] A Montreal trading firm then purchased the lease at La Baye. That firm charged high prices for goods. As Beauharnois had predicted, this action alienated the local tribes.[45]

The French fur trade declined, and voyageurs refused to pay for licenses to trade in the interior. When the lease came up for renewal at La Baye in 1746, no one was interested.[46] At this point, the government sold the rights to trade at La Baye to two individuals from Mackinac. One of them, Augustin de Langlade, together with his son Charles, paid a thousand francs for the rights. They built a warehouse and in 1765, along with Pierre Grignon Sr., moved to the post, where they established the permanent settlement that eventually became the city of Green Bay, a town inhabited increasingly by French and mixed-blood people involved in the trade in one way or another.[47] Charles de Langlade was the mixed-blood son of Augustin and an Ottawa woman. He served the French as an Indian agent and interpreter until 1754. One of his most important assignments at the end of the French era consisted of raising Indian armed forces to fight alongside the Europeans in their imperial wars.

In 1747 the monopoly system broke up, and experienced traders returned to La Baye, but the trade, which had implicitly supported French government officials in the *pays d'en haut* all along, now directly supported the post.[48] By this late date in the French period, well-established systems controlled the trade between Montreal and the upper country. The traders sold goods to Indians on credit and in turn redeemed their debts when they brought these same furs to the merchants from whom they had borrowed.[49] The line of credit did not stop here, however; it continued all the way back to the shippers in France, sometimes through an additional middleman at a factory in Quebec City (see map 3). Although individuals profited from the trade, including traders and post commandants, the largest profits flowed through the big companies in Montreal and to the French port cities of La Rochelle and, to a lesser extent in later years, Rouen.[50]

Between 1749 and 1756 French officials profited from an increasingly corrupt trade in Wisconsin. At that point, the new governor, Vaudreuil, appointed a corrupt nephew, Hubert Couterot, as post commandant.[51] Despite this diplomatic bungling, the Menominee maintained an alliance with the French.

The Menominee alliance with the French was partly social, as Menominee women in some cases married or had children with French men. The small town of La Baye that grew around the fort had a population of mixed Indian and white blood, or métis as one observer described it. For twenty-two of the twenty-seven heads of household in Green Bay between 1740 and 1756, "one or both parents were at least one-eighth Indian."[52] Some of those people were Menominee or part Menominee, but it is not known how

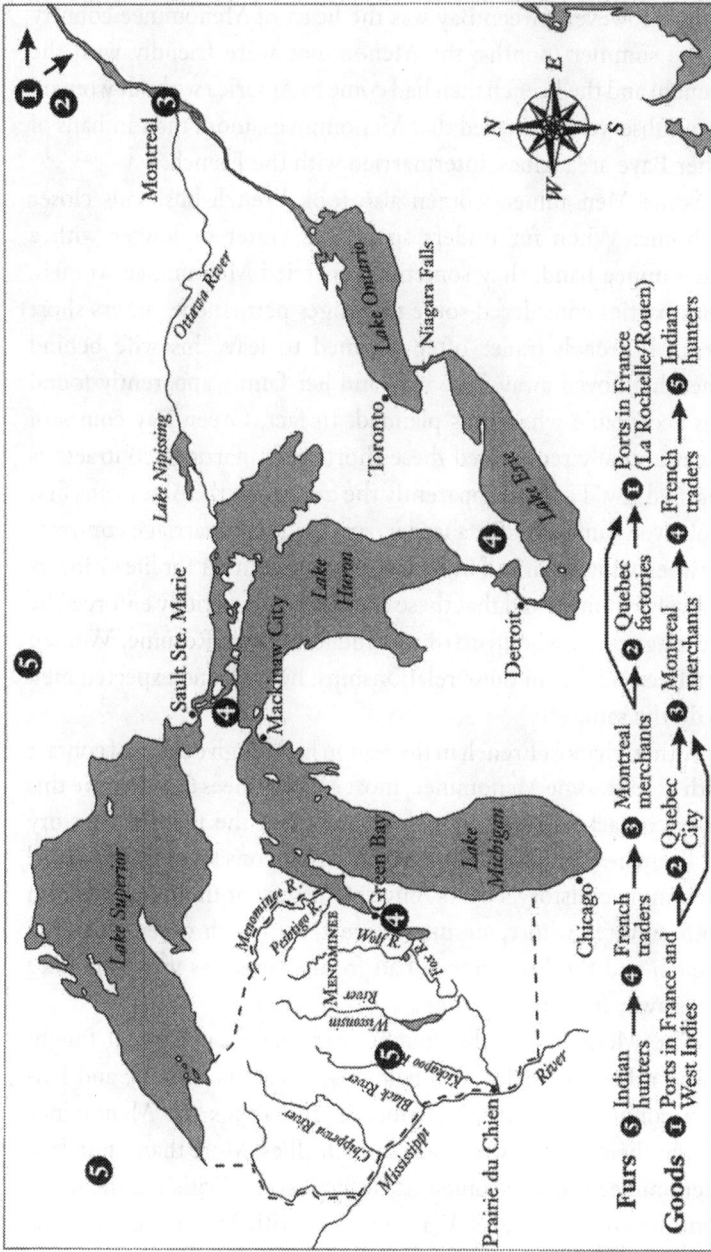

Map 3. French fur trade: Lines of credit

Furs ⑤ Indian hunters → ④ French traders → ③ Montreal merchants → ② Quebec factories → ① Ports in France (La Rochelle/Rouen)

Goods ① Ports in France and West Indies → ② Quebec City → ③ Montreal merchants → ④ French traders → ⑤ Indian hunters many. However, Green Bay was the heart of Menominee country in the summer months; the Menominee were friendly with the French; and the French men had come to America without women. Later observers remarked that Menominees, more than Indians of other Baye area tribes, intermarried with the French.[53]

Some Menominee women also took French husbands closer to home. When fur traders spent the winter or longer with a Menominee band, they sometimes married Menominee women. Both parties considered some marriages permanent, others short term. A French trader often planned to leave his wife behind when he moved away. The wife and her family apparently found this acceptable when thus planned. In fact, Green Bay courts of law eventually recognized these short-term marriage contracts as codified law. This was apparently the case when the Americans first took over. James Biddle, a trader, reported that marriage contracts between white men and Indian women were either for life or for six or twelve months and that these contracts were strictly enforced by the magistrate, who in 1818 was Judge Charles Reaume. Women practiced fidelity in these relationships, he said, and expected men to do the same.[54]

Although most French in the region had a high degree of contact with at least some Menominee, most Menominees did not have this close contact with the French. Here again the recorded history of French-Menominee interaction, and consequently recorded Menominee history, covers only the history of those people from both cultures who came into contact with each other. Both the French and the Menominee had frontier areas as well as culture areas away from the frontier.

The Menominee who fought with the French often fought under a French leader who had close social, economic, and kinship connections with the tribe. In the 1750s the Menominee fought their last war with their French allies. More than a hundred Menominee warriors joined battle against the British in the intercontinental Seven Years' War, traveling with Marin and Langlade in the summers of 1757, 1758, and 1759. The French conducted their North American warfare from Montreal, to which some Menominee warriors traveled during those years. Since most Menominee bands and people still lived remote to the Europeans, many of the Menominee warriors doubtless stayed home. For the most part, we do not know which Menominee leaders made the decision to ally with the French or for what reasons. We do know, however, that Old Carron and his son Glode, both prominent leaders within the tribe, were with the French in Montreal.[55]

The Menominee bond with the French was soon to become tenuous, however. Couterot enraged the tribes to the extent that the local Menominee band attacked the fort at La Baye in May 1758, killing eleven Frenchmen and plundering the storehouse. Couterot barely escaped with his life. Unfortunately little is known of the causes of this event, so we are forced to speculate. Since Couterot knew nothing of Indian diplomacy, he could have done any number of things to upset the Menominee. Perhaps he allowed unfair prices by not controlling the fur traders; perhaps he failed to be generous in gift giving.[56] A year later, on 17 May 1759, the Menominee became involved in the French justice system over this event. When Langlade brought a thousand Indians to Montreal during the war with England, the Menominees in the group included "two of those most culpable in this murder" of Frenchmen at La Baye. The Menominee presented these two men to Governor Vaudreuil, who returned them to the tribe for justice. The Menominee killed their two tribesmen on the spot, apparently using Menominee customary law to satisfy French justice.[57] The Menominee continued to fight alongside the French but increasingly distrusted them.

BRITISH ALLIANCES

The Seven Years' War ended with the British displacing the French as the European representatives in the Upper Great Lakes. After replacing French political institutions, the British began to create alliances and build forts where the old French posts had been. The last three forts to fall to the British were Detroit, Michilimackinac, and La Baye.[58]

Lieutenant James Gorrell arrived at La Baye in mid-October 1761 and observed that "there was but one family of [Menominee] Indians in the village" nearest the fort, the rest having gone to their winter hunting grounds. Gorrell immediately set his men to work in building Fort Edward Augustus. Between October and the first official British meetings with the tribes in May, "Some few men of the different tribes or nations of Indians came at different times to know how they would be treated, and were agreeably surprised to find that we were fond of seeing them. . . . They asked for amunition, which I gave them at different times, as also sent flour to some of their old men, who, they said, were sick in the woods."[59]

The Menominee had suffered great hardship during these years of transition, losing people not only to warfare but to disease. Those who fought alongside French soldiers in the east in 1757 brought a devastating smallpox epidemic to the tribe.[60] The Menominee leaders in their first meeting with Gorrell told him that "they were very poor, having lost three hundred warriors lately with the small pox, and most of their chiefs in the late war." Gorrell counted 150 Menominee warriors. The other British census made in this time period, Sir William Johnson's 1763 enumeration of the tribes in the northern district, included 110 "Meynomeny" men and 110 "Folsavoins" men in the count, which may have meant two bands of Menominee.[61]

The Menominee's first meeting with Gorrell occurred on 23 May 1762. The Ho Chunks were present as well. Although Charles de Langlade served as Gorrell's Indian agent, Charles Gautier, another French resident of the area, served as his interpreter until 1763, when Gorrell replaced him with Thomas Carty, who spoke English (Gautier did not speak English). Gorrell gave the tribes belts of wampum to signify alliance and friendship. "The French, in their time," Gorrell observed, "always gave them belts, rum, and money, presents by which they renewed their peace annually."[62] He had brought one belt for each tribe but learned he needed two, three, four, or more, because the tribes had several "towns." He apparently had dealt with only two Menominee villages, both located in the vicinity of the fort at Green Bay, because those are the only two he counted in a census he made.

Through Gautier, Gorrell informed the Indians that since the English had vanquished the French, King George, "my master and your father," had sent him "to keep the best order and administer the strictest justice amongst you." He also brought a trader with him and told the Menominee and Ho Chunks to treat the traders honestly and to report to him if the traders treated them unjustly. The Menominee "expressed great satisfaction that the English traders were coming among them, and seemed desirous that they should continue to come, as they found by experience that the goods were half cheaper than when the French were amongst them." They also requested rum and a gunsmith. Gorrell promised to supply the latter but not the former.[63]

The Menominee leader who welcomed the British to Fort Edward Augustus was Sekatsokemau. He led the tribe during the entire time the British claimed control of the Old Northwest, living until about 1821. He is said to have died at about a hundred years of age, which means he would have been almost forty years old when Gorrell arrived. On a British war document from 1778 he is recognized as "Chawanon," a name signifying "southern," perhaps because he was recognized as a leader of the southern bands. He was also referred to by the British and early Americans as the grand chief or the Old King. Sekatsokemau was head of the Bear (*awāēhsāēh*) clan, a hereditary position that included the civil leadership for the tribe.[64]

Sekatsokemau himself was not an accomplished public speaker. His chief speaker, Old Carron, was half-Indian and half-French-Canadian. Carron was born in approximately 1700 near Montreal and lived until 1780. He had moved to Menominee country and married a Menominee woman long before the British arrival. Carron himself was a prominent leader within the tribe. He fathered a number of sons who later became prominent Menominee leaders as well.[65] As they did with Carron, the tribe normally recognized those who married in as tribal members if they participated in Menominee life. The Menominee have habitually welcomed individual outsiders into their tribe; for example, the French men who did not leave their wives behind or did not move to the French town of La Baye often became part of the tribe, as did their children.[66] Outsiders could even become involved in the leadership of the tribe. The Menominee adopted other Indians, as well as Euro-Americans, recognizing tribal affiliation by participation within the society rather than by race or ethnicity.

When Sekatsokemau welcomed the British to La Baye, through Old Carron's voice, he reminded them that they were building on Menominee land. As other tribal leaders had done in the past, he invoked the time-honored practice of *apēkon ahkihih*. Sekatsokemau generously invited the foreigners to use Menominee land but made it clear that the Menominee still considered the land their own. Gorrell himself stated that the English fort stood on Menominee lands. In effect, the tribe granted the British use rights but did not convey to them any actual property.[67]

In hindsight Sekatsokemau's welcoming proved a significant strategic move in which the Menominee consciously maintained ownership of the land. This strategic move was not calculated in Western terms, with the idea that property was central. Instead the decision and action stemmed from a tribal cultural tradition in which land was imbued with spiritual life, including what Euro-Americans would consider both living and inanimate components. This land was a part of the Menominee world, spiritual and physical, which the tribe in this instance had no reason to relinquish. The Menominee expected their generosity in sharing the use of these resources with their new allies to be reciprocated somehow within the context of the alliance. Although most tribes refused to accept the British and many joined in the attacks orchestrated by Pontiac throughout the lakes region, the Menominee welcomed the British as they built their fort, in part because of the recent problems they had encountered with the last corrupt French commandant, Hubert Couterot.[68]

By this time Europeans finally controlled the middleman's role in the fur trade, and the European trade in the west had already entered a phase that Kellogg has called "the heyday of the fur trade" in Wisconsin.[69] Though the British claimed title to Wisconsin only from 1763 to 1783, they dominated the European end of the fur trade there from 1760 to 1815. During those years, "The British regime in Wisconsin was essentially a vast commercial enterprise controlled by Montreal traders," but it left few long-term marks on the area's historic landscape.[70] Many French traders and habitants remained involved in the western commerce and kept an important French cultural presence, even if their national allegiances shifted to Britain and later to the United States. The terms of French surrender permitted French-Canadian habitants who lived in the area to work the fur trade with the same advantages as British subjects. In Montreal, the same old French traders helped the British to learn the ways of the Wisconsin trade and gained most of the contracts in the early years.[71]

The British stay at Fort Edward Augustus ended after the Ojibwes captured Fort Michilimackinac on 4 June 1763. The fort's commander, Captain George Etherington, ordered Lieutenant Gorrell to leave the Baye area and help him to "open the road which the Chippewas have shut up."[72] Menominees helped Gorrell escape. Menominee leaders accompanied Gorrell and his men all the way to Montreal, for which eight Menominee leaders were presented with certificates, and traders were sent back to Green Bay. The British never officially returned to Fort Edward Augustus, however. Although it held strategic importance in the upper country, the post fell victim to international political affairs.[73]

The trade concession at the site had been granted to the Marquis de Rigaud-Vaudreil and his wife on a lifetime basis, but they returned to France after the war. The French refused to give this up to the British in the peace treaty, but the marquis sold the claim to a Londoner, William Grant. Grant both married into "the former nobility of New France" and sent an agent to press his claim and levy tribute. The traders in the Bay area refused to deal with Grant's representative; the only way out for the British was to abandon the post.[74]

In the summer of 1764, the British held a General Council meeting with their Indian allies at Niagara, New York. The British superintendent of Indian affairs, Sir William Johnson, called the gathering "the largest Number of Indians perhaps ever Assembled," some two thousand members of both eastern and western tribes.[75] About one hundred Menominees arrived together with a similar number of Ottawas, probably on the evening of 12 July.[76] Though the British were most concerned with affairs in the east, they also needed to maintain peace in the west to gain control of the fur trade in the wake of French departure. On 15 July, Johnson met with all of the Menominees in attendance, among them six chiefs, including Carron.[77]

The Menominee leaders began the meeting by describing the diplomatic protocol with which they regularly opened such discussions. "Our Fathers ... desired us, when we spoke with our Brethren, and wanted anything to smoke a Pipe with them first." They brought out their specified pipe and smoked it with Johnson, then gave it to him as a gift "as a Token of their Regard, or Sincerity." They reminded Johnson of their rescue of Gorrell the previous year, emphasizing the dangers and difficulties involved, and hoped that the English would repay the Menominee in some way. Johnson informed them that he indeed had positive reports regarding the Menominee, that he was pleased so many had come to see him, and that he would talk to them another day.[78]

On 17 July Johnson again met with the Menominee leaders, who hailed from two villages east of La Baye. They informed him that they spoke on behalf of all the people in their two bands, young and old. They reminded Johnson of their friendship and asked him to allow them to begin trading again. They brought furs.[79] Johnson made a lengthy speech in which he emphasized the English position that trading had been disrupted because of the Ojibwe attacks at Michilimackinac. "All we wanted was to keep the Posts, which we took from the French, in Peace, and Quietness, and to carry on a fair Trade at them with you for our mutual Advantage," he told them. So long as the Menominee and other Indians would ally themselves in peace and friendship with the English, he continued, they would reestablish trading at the post at Michilimackinac, which had been interrupted by warfare.[80]

Johnson agreed to ask traders to reestablish relations with the tribes, and he set trading prices for goods and furs. He also determined what items could be sold. These included blankets, clothing, kettles, knives, rum, and various silver articles, including earbobs, armbands, and crosses.[81]

On 21 July Johnson again met with Menominee leaders, thanking them for their alliance. "I have allowed you a Trade here," he told them, "and you will for the future, if you behave well, be indulged with a plentiful one."[82] On 1 August Johnson presented a certificate of commendation to Sekatsokemau in thanks for Menominee help in saving the British officers from Fort Edward Augustus and in escorting them to Montreal in 1763.[83]

Before they left, the Menominee requested the British to reoccupy the fort, and Johnson himself apparently made this recommendation to London.[84] Again the next summer in a conference at Michilimackinac, Menominee leaders requested reestablishment of the British post at La Baye.[85] But despite the desires of the Menominee and other Bay area tribes, it never reopened. The Menominee continued to traffic with the British fur traders in the region, however, and eventually formed military alliances with them as well.

Traders remained in the La Baye area, but the British pursued their policies from the top of the lake, at Mackinac, which became the western center of the British trade.[86] These policies amounted to profiting from the fur trade and containing the advances of the expansionistic and increasingly independent-spirited Americans.[87] As was the case with the French, British traders, many of whom were French Canadians, had closer relations with Indians and greater impact on Indian-white relations than any other colonials. They effectively limited American relations with the tribes.[88]

In addition, both liberal gift giving and familiarity gave the British an advantage in the trade over the Americans, who, to compound their weakness, offered goods of obviously inferior quality. The British wanted to retain access to the fur trade, while Indians fought to maintain control of their lands and consequently their ways of life, which varied from tribe to tribe. Despite these differing goals, Indians formed alliances with the British against the Americans during the whole of the British tenure in the Upper Great Lakes and even beyond. Many of the British traders continued to be familiar faces in Menominee country, where the change was especially slow. In 1767, only five British traders received licenses for La Baye; the rest went to the same old French Canadians. As late as 1774, French traders still received four times as many licenses as their British counterparts, although most served British firms.[89]

By the time of the American Revolutionary War, "the fur traffic had become big business," but the greatest profits in the trade increasingly flowed through the route to the west of Lake Superior and not through La Baye. In the long run, this far western trade simply proved more enticing to the British.[90] In the short term the American Revolution meant little to the Menominee, who continued to trade solely with the British. When Zebulon Pike passed through the territory a quarter-century afterward, Tomau, the second son of Vieux Carron and one of the tribe's primary leaders, recollected to him

> that near the conclusion of the Revolutionary War his nation began to look upon him as a warrior; that they received a parole from Michilimackinac, on which he was dispatched with 40 warriors; and that on his arrival he was requested to lead them against the Americans. To which he replied: "We have considered you and the Americans as one people. You are now at war; how are we to decide who has justice on their

side? Besides, you white people are like the leaves of the trees for numbers. . . . No, I will return to my nation, where my countrymen may be of service against our red enemies, and their actions renowned in the dance of our nation."[91]

Tomau refused to enroll the forty warriors under his charge to fight against the Americans during that war.

During the American Revolution some Menominees maintained neutrality.[92] For a variety of reasons, other bands chose to ally themselves with the British, who not only remained generous in gift giving but regularly held councils with the Menominee and other Baye area tribes to maintain alliances.[93] The British used these alliances to encourage Indians to join them in battle. Most of England's Indian allies, among them the Menominee, needed little encouragement, and many fought the Americans without even consulting the British.

Meanwhile, Charles de Langlade had become established among the Menominee at La Baye. In 1777 and 1778, he led some sixty Menominee warriors, including Carron, in a unit under Captain Arent Schuyler de Peyster, the Mackinac commandant, on a foray for the British to the east. However, a number of Menominees turned back before reaching the eastern battlefields. Meanwhile, other Menominees were parlaying with the Americans in Virginia, though no alliance apparently came from these discussions. The Menominee may well have viewed this war as a civil war. By late 1778, however, even British threats to cut off the fur trade could not draw most of their western tribal allies into the war. In fact, their agent, Charles Gautier, had to be rescued by Menominees and Ho Chunks who still sided with the British when he made an unsuccessful appeal among the Sauks and Foxes, who it may be recalled included long-time Menominee enemies.[94] In 1778 Sekatsokemau was again awarded a British certificate, this time by Sir Frederick Haldimand, the governor general.[95] Several Menominee leaders and a small number of warriors continued to support the British through the end of the war with the Americans.[96] But by the time the American Revolutionary War was settled, the Menominee had lost interest in the fight itself.

The Menominee shifted alliances with the European powers rather easily, primarily focusing on ways to maintain trade relationships. The European trade goods changed Menominee life, but in many ways the Menominee were able to maintain control. The tribe adapted quickly to cloth and blankets, which were made into clothing and used for protection from the elements; domestic cookware and utensils, which changed the way of food preparation; vanity goods; and tools used to advance the fur trade. The systems introduced by the French—one of exchanging alcohol, illegally and in large quantities at a rendezvous or payout time, the other a system of credit—also had lasting impact, but the Menominee had less control over these. These systems would prove to be a much larger long-term threat to Menominee survival.

Through the various wars in which the French became embroiled and the uncertainties of the trade, Indians from the west increasingly traveled to Montreal for commercial and diplomatic purposes and to fight in colonial wars, a practice that the British later also encouraged after the political and military elimination of the French in Canada.

These legacies, together with the Frenchmen who decided to remain behind and the people of mixed blood, were soon all that was left of the French "empire" in the Upper Great Lakes. The British victory in the Seven Years' War of the 1750s and 1760s changed the identity and to some degree tactics of the European invaders of Menominee country. But their tenure was even shorter lived. By the time of American arrival on the scene, the Menominee were beginning to understand both the permanence and the growing threat of the Euro-American presence, and they reacted accordingly.

4

Diminishing Fur Trade
and Illegal Treaties

In the peace of 1783, which officially ended the American war of
cession from England, the United States claimed Wisconsin and
other areas south of the Great Lakes. Beginning the next year,
the United States began to establish regulations governing the use
of the land and the rights of Euro-Americans who would move
onto it. Congress authorized and specified the process for land
surveys in the area in 1785 and in 1787 passed the Northwest
Ordinance, which established basic American law governing the
territory. Americans did not immediately move to Menominee
country, however, nor did the British leave.

At the same time, the Menominee tribal population began to re-
cover from the disease and warfare of the 1750s. With a population
surge during the 1780s, the number of the tribe's bands increased
and the tribal territory continued to expand.[1] Hunting lands that
the Menominee shared with other tribes extended inland as far
as the Mississippi River where it borders on present-day Iowa and
upstream into the heart of Minnesota, where the Menominee were
allowed to hunt on land disputed by the Ojibwes and Santees.

By the 1780s all of these tribes had long experience in negotiating shared land use arrangements. The trader John Baptiste
Perrault, who had established a post along the Red Cedar River,
in the winter of 1787 described this process.[2] He traded with the
Ojibwe, Santee, and Menominee hunters in the region, though
parties representing the different nations usually came in at different times. In November, while several members of the Lac Court

Oreilles Ojibwes were trading at his post, twenty-eight Santees arrived unexpectedly. Their leader, whom Perrault called le Petit Corbeau, made a gift to the Ojibwes and said, "My brothers, we have taken the liberty of approaching your lands for awhile. You know that the deer seeks the thick woods for The winter, and that upon it depends the life of our women and children. We hope therefore that you will bear with us for a Couple of months On the upper waters of that branch of your river, and we will retire as soon as we have acquired provisions for our spring." One of the Ojibwes responded in the affirmative, "Hunt peaceably on our lands here till the month of march, when we beg of you to withdraw.... The master of life has given to all the Indians the land to live on in peace." This undoubtedly reflects negotiations in which Menominee hunters struck similar bargains with both sides.[3]

As this instance indicates, the Native nations still held the balance of power in Wisconsin and their customary laws governed interactions. Indians allied themselves with the British because the British trade was better than the American one and because the British supported the creation of an Indian-controlled territory in which Indian country and its trade would remain undisturbed and would serve as a buffer between the United States and Canada.[4] The British recognized as well as the Indians did that American farming communities, which were slowly expanding westward, would destroy the fur trade, the major British interest in the area.

The British therefore worked hard to cement their alliances with Wisconsin tribes in a variety of ways throughout their tenure in the area. Their methods included gift giving, provision of supplies for those who aided the British and for their families, and generous support of trading posts.[5] Sir John Johnson, British superintendent of Indian affairs, decided in late 1786 to convene the western nations (i.e., those in the Upper Great Lakes region) for an elaborate and expensive council in Mackinac in the summer of 1787 to ensure that the alliances would remain strong.[6]

In preparation for that meeting, in October 1786 Johnson ap-

pointed John Dease as the new manager of Indian affairs at Michilimackinac. He also sent a trader, Joseph Louise Ainsée, to meet with
the western nations to convince them to bring their representatives
to Michilimackinac the next summer. Ainsée met first with the
Menominee in the Baye area. He presented them with rum and
trade goods and invited them to send representatives to accompany
him to Michilimackinac. Among the goods he traveled with were
those of symbolic importance, including medals, flags, and uniform
jackets, which he called "chiefs coats."

After this meeting with the Menominee, Ainsée traveled west.
He went to St. Anthony's Falls (present-day Minneapolis), where
he held an eight-day meeting with the Ojibwes, Sioux, Mesquakies,
and the Menominee who wintered in that area. Each village promised to send "six men of the principal village chiefs and also war
chiefs" the next summer. Ainsée then traveled down to Prairie du
Chien, where he met for four days with the Mesquakies, Sauks,
Sioux, Ojibwes, and the band of Menominee that wintered there.
Here he was met with more skepticism but did enlist some allies.[7]

The trader Perrault spent two days at the Prairie du Chien
meeting, where he observed the tribes negotiate peace among
themselves. He described it thus:

> The custom is for the allies to present themselves in Columns,
> one in front of another. This took place at la prayrie [Prairie
> du Chien], in the presence of all of us others. The scioux
> presented themselves in the same Line; The sauteux [Ojib-
> wes] and the fol-avoines in another; the sacs and the renards
> [Mesquakies] in a third. These three Lines formed three
> triangles. Then an orator from Each of the Confederates,
> with Each one their attendant, placed themselves in the
> center of the three triangles, each holding in his hand the
> Pipe of peace, Having chanted a moment and then made a
> genuflexion, which he repeated three times. The one who
> held the Pipe was the son of le vieu français, called lapon,
> a man Brave and warlike. He brought to the sioux the pipe,

lighted it, and presented it. Each one took a draw of the pipe, but it happened that one young man, a sciou refused to accept the Pipe. This arrested the ceremony a moment. Then a chief of their Band went to him and said to him, "Why do you do this? Do you not know that this place is sacred? You ought to reflect before refusing." Then the young man accepted it and the ceremony Proceeded.

When each Band had performed It's [sic] ceremonial, they all joined hands. Shouts of joy followed, and they retired, Each one to their camp.[8]

Treaties among Indian nations were both solemn and joyous occasions, replete with ceremony and agreements. Whether for determining land usage or for resolving conflict, they were imbued with sacred authority. Breaking these agreements was serious and a valid cause for warfare if the problem was not resolved. The British viewed the Michilimackinac meeting in the summer of 1787 as a treaty. One hundred and ninety-six Indians of nine tribes, including the Menominee, attended.[9]

During the first week of July 1787, Dease met with tribal leaders in small groups to discuss the future of the trade in the west.[10] Then on 11 July he met with the entire group in council. All parties agreed to abide by a general peace in the region, and the British agreed to send Ainsée back to the interior to trade during the next year. Both the belts that symbolized agreement and the written proceedings were stored in the post at Michilimackinac. Dease provided the Indians with rum and provisions and then headed southeast to Arbre Croche, on the eastern shore of Lake Michigan, to meet with the Ottawas for the same purpose.[11]

The situation on the eastern side of the lake was far different than that to the west. The Ottawas reported they were in desperate need of aid from the British: "our Lands are exhausted, [our] hunts are ruined, no more Animals remain to call us out to the Woods, the only resource left to us for subsistence is the cultivation of these sandy plains, and what we can procure from the water."

Dease provided the Ottawas with fishing equipment, including nets, abundant clothing, guns, and ammunition in addition to the rum and provisions.[12]

Perhaps because of experiences like these the British could clearly see the future of Indian country in Wisconsin if they failed to establish an Indian-controlled territory. However, whatever the intentions of agents in the interior, diplomats in Europe always traded away these demands early in the negotiation process. Time and again the tribes were bitterly disappointed at the failure of the British to fulfill promises regarding support of tribal territorial sovereignty.[13]

After Jay's Treaty of 1794 the British concentrated official efforts away from the frontier. They abandoned their forts in the American territory within the next couple of years, including at Mackinac, retreating across the border to posts such as the one at Drummond Island on Lake Huron. However, they still maintained relations with Indians in the Old Northwest through the fur trade and gift giving. It was generally traders, and not British government officials, who supplied the tribe with gifts, including the medals and flags that represented alliance in trade and politics. It was also generally traders who interacted with the local Indian nations.

While large-scale trade partnerships became increasingly common elsewhere, in the area between Lake Michigan and the Mississippi River traders tended to make small-scale and short-term partnerships. The major traders, both French and English, learned Indian languages, married Indian women, and raised their mixed-blood children. These included Pierre Grignon (son-in-law of Charles Langlade) and several of his sons, including Pierre Jr., Louis, and Augustin; Jacques Porlier, who originally came to the area to tutor Grignon's children; and Jacob Franks and his nephew John Lawe, both Englishmen.[14] All of these people would be important traders among the Menominee for years and, in the case of the Grignons, for generations to come. Augustin Grignon is a prime example of the slowly changing face of the trade at La Baye. A son, grandson, and great-grandson of the town's founders

(Pierre Sr. and the Langlades), he remained a trader among the Menominee until after the treaty-making period with Americans ended in 1856.

Because Menominee and Indian country in Wisconsin became marginal to the large trade profits, the trade there remained distinctively local. There was no large concentration of a single type of profitable fur but instead a multiplicity of fur-bearing animals in preagricultural Wisconsin. Lists from the early nineteenth century show a stunning variety of furs and hides being sold. Deer, beaver, and muskrat provided the majority of shipments, but bears, lynx, cats, martens, fishers, foxes, minks, otters, raccoons, skunks, and even swanskins were all shipped east.[15] Besides these, traders shipped castor (from beaver glands) and deer tallow.[16]

AMERICAN ARRIVAL

The Americans began a serious assessment of western lands in 1806, when the U.S. military commissioned Zebulon Pike to explore the section of the recently purchased Louisiana Territory that lay along the Mississippi River. In March Pike visited Tomau's band of Menominee in the first recorded social and trading experience between Menominees and Americans. Tomau's band wintered near the Mississippi River in what is now central Minnesota, just south of Little Falls. Pike spent a month at a fort in the vicinity of Tomau's sugar camp. This was in the heart of British fur-trading country as well as borderlands disputed by the Ojibwes and Santees. Both of those nations were still on good terms with the Menominee, whom they allowed the privilege of hunting there during the winter.

Pike and Tomau visited each other's camps more than once during this month. On 13 March 1806, Tomau went to see Pike and invited him to repay the visit at Tomau's camp. On 18 March, after spending the previous night in the woods with but one blanket and no shelter, Pike and his men arrived in Tomau's village. Famished on their arrival, they were treated with typical Menominee hospitality. They were invited into Tomau's lodge, where Pike was given "the best place in the lodge." Tomau pulled off Pike's leggings and offered him dry clothing; then they were fed. They began by drinking maple syrup, then, given the choice among elk, deer, swan, or beaver meat, Pike selected the latter, and a luscious soup was prepared. Finally, as they settled down to sleep, Tomau, since he had observed that American men slept with as many as six different Indian "wives" during a winter's stay, offered to provide Pike with the company of a woman. Pike, being happily married, refused. Pike reciprocated the hospitality when his newfound friends visited his camp by feeding them, which nearly depleted his food supply.[17]

Menominee generosity even extended to adversaries but did not signal capitulation by the tribe to their adversaries' wishes.[18] Although Pike and Tomau were friendly, the Menominee still preferred to trade with the British. When Pike demanded that the Menominee give him the king's medals and Union Jacks provided to the tribe by British traders, they reluctantly gave up the medals but not the flags. Soon after Pike's departure the Union Jack flew again in Indian country, as Indians continued to trade with British traders who remained in the area.[19]

Pike visited not only Tomau's band but also the village of Shawanoe, an older Menominee leader who wintered in the Northwest with his people. After his journey, Pike reported the St. Croix River valley to be inhabited by "Fols Avoins" and Ojibwes.[20] By this time Menominee country included perhaps a dozen villages scattered from the site of present-day Milwaukee to the Menominee River and along the Fox River and Lake Winnebago during the summer months; in the winter the bands moved inland, ranging across south central Wisconsin from Prairie du Chien in the south to Mille Lacs in what is now central Minnesota in the north.[21]

Pike's tour through Menominee country portended a threat to Menominee resources, which the tribe recognized—their word for Americans translates as "the Great Knife," with an implication of "people coming at you with knives."[22] Like other tribes in the area, they began to recognize American avarice for land and resources.

Though the Americans first claimed Menominee country in 1785 and created the Northwest Territory in 1787, they failed to establish an official presence until after the War of 1812. Meanwhile, the alliances between tribal nations and the British, though weakened, did not break. The British were many tribes' best hope of an ally to thwart American advances; British promises provided hope and British traders peddled higher quality goods. In the War of 1812 many Menominees sided with the British, who at least paid lip service to protecting tribal resources. The Americans had fought their Revolutionary War in part to establish their rights to expand across the Appalachian Mountains into Indian country, and they were doing so rapidly. Not surprisingly, when war broke out between the Americans and the British, who had the support of most of the tribes, the British government appointed Robert Dickson, the most influential British trader in Menominee country, as its Indian agent for tribes west of Lake Huron.[23] By the time of his appointment he had already raised forces among Indians. Together they captured the new American fort at Mackinac without a shot being fired. After his appointment he returned to Prairie du Chien, La Baye, and Mackinac to recruit Indians to fight in Ohio and Pennsylvania.[24]

The outcome of the War of 1812 would have a significant immediate and long-term impact on the tribes in the Upper Great Lakes. In the Treaty of Ghent, which ended the war, the British agreed to leave Wisconsin. According to Kellogg, the American-British treaty "forever laid at rest the plan for a neutral Indian state, which would have condemned Wisconsin to remain a wilderness reserved for Indians and fur bearing animals exploited by traders for their own profit."[25]

This treaty destroyed the political basis of Britain's alliances with Wisconsin's Indians, but the economic basis remained. The British continued to trade higher quality goods than those of the Americans and for better prices. Despite American attempts to control the trade using legal and political methods, Menominees and others continued for years to cross the border to trade with the British. They still made the long trek to exchange gifts with the British at Drummond Island, but after 1815, when the Americans first officially established an Indian agency and government trading post at the renamed town of Green Bay, they exchanged over the protestations of the Americans, who desired that the tribes become entirely free from any potential British influence.[26] Even Tomau, who had originally refused to take sides between the British and the Americans, and who had met on friendly relations with Pike, was so distraught at the thought of these changing relations with the British that he caused his own death from alcohol poisoning in a fit of depression in 1817 on Mackinac Island. A trader provided him with an entire three-gallon keg of brandy, which he consumed alone over a period of two or three days, angry and depressed about the shifting political landscape.[27]

Like the French, the British had essentially treated the Menominee as allies, in both the fur trade and imperial struggles. Their post commanders relied on traders to serve as Indian agents and interpreters. While they certainly exploited the tribe's resources, and while they referred to the Indians as subordinates in official documents, they were not powerful enough to control them, only to form alliances. The Americans were different.

When the Americans permanently arrived in Menominee country in 1815, their first goal was to contain the British. The Americans wanted to eliminate the British military and fur traders and eventually replace the latter with their own traders. As had their French and British predecessors, the United States established forts in Menominee country to gain control of the fur trade and to gain access to Indian nations. At Michigan governor Lewis Cass's recommendation, the United States established agencies at Green Bay, Fort Wayne, Chicago, and Michilimackinac to "encircle the Country to which access from the British dominions is so easy."[28]

On 20 June 1815, Cass warned the acting secretary of war, A. J. Dallas, that the United States must establish forts at Green Bay and Prairie du Chien if it hoped to stop British smuggling of goods for the fur trade and to control the river route between the places.[29] On the same date, President James Monroe approved the establishment of an Indian agency supplied with troops and a trading factory at Green Bay, and Dallas appointed Charles Jouett as the agent. Jouett was told to report to Governor Cass for instructions and to communicate with the War Department through Governor Cass.[30]

This line of command lasted through the territorial period in much of Menominee country. The Office of Indian Affairs in Washington was part of the War Department; territorial governors in their role as superintendents of Indian affairs reported directly to the secretary of war. Ranked below them was the local Indian agent or subagent, who reported to the governor and ran an agency or subagency established to oversee local Indian affairs. In theory, Indians dealt with this official in day-to-day affairs but dealt with officials higher up during important occasions such as treaty councils. At this time Wisconsin was part of Illinois Territory, but the post personnel at Green Bay were requested to report to Michigan's governor. Fort Howard was built at Green Bay in 1816, after which army troops moved in.

Between 1815 and 1820, the Menominee lived in the vicinity of four agencies, Green Bay, Prairie du Chien, Michilimackinac, and Chicago.[31] Since Menominee bands lived throughout what are now Wisconsin and the Upper Peninsula of Michigan and moved with the seasons, they reported at different times to one or more of these four agencies. In an 1819 census, for instance, approximately 830 Menominee are listed in Colonel John Bowyer's Green Bay agency, but another 270 are listed as living only seventy-five miles from Jouett's Chicago agency. The numbers include children. Menominees under Jouett's jurisdiction were situated on the Illinois River; probably some of them became part of the mixed Menominee-Ho Chunk-Potawatomi groups in the Milwaukee and Rock River areas. The Menominee at the Chicago agency disappeared from the records after 1819.[32]

At the same time, other Menominees were under the jurisdiction of the Prairie du Chien agency. An 1821 census shows 500 Menominee warriors at Green Bay and 160 Fals Avoines men and 330 women and children at Prairie du Chien.[33] The latter agency was charged with overseeing the affairs of Indians who traded at the Mississippi, which included Menominees.[34] Some Menominees also lived in the vicinity of Michilimackinac, as they had since at least the seventeenth century.[35]

Upon establishing a post in Green Bay, the Americans forced the area's French and mixed-blood residents to swear an oath of allegiance to the United States and soon required traders to hold American citizenship or else face confiscation of their goods.[36] During and after this period of steady decline of the fur trade in Menominee country, the character of the trade became increasingly impersonal. As the U.S. government intervened, the importance of generosity in the trade rapidly vanished, making trade an economic transaction increasingly on American and decreasingly on Menominee terms. "[T]he young American Republic had neither the means nor the disposition to spend adequate sums for gifts," one observer wrote, because Americans believed gift giving would cause dependence and weakness.[37]

Besides lacking generosity, the United States brought mediocre goods to the trade. According to James Lockwood, an early American in the area, any inferior trade items were referred to as "American," denoting the low stature of American manufacture among both the British and the Indians.[38] Nonetheless, the American government attempted to control the trade, for a time permitting it only at government forts and generally only by traders who were federally approved. These traders, concerned primarily with making a profit, often cheated Indian customers purposefully, even when they were hired by the federal government to provide promised provisions.

Federally authorized trade contracts were highly coveted. Though they often went to those with some political clout or connections, the federal government insisted on cutting costs wherever possible. Matthew Irwin, a trader at Green Bay in 1816, reported to the secretary of war that lengthy instructions he received from Mackinac contractor James Biddle on how to make a profit despite a low contract rate included "issuing condemned provisions, to the Indians, . . . issuing provisions, in barrels, which were issued at more than they would weigh, . . . reducing whiskey both for troops and Indians, and . . . giving the Indians much less than the provision returns called for."[39]

The U.S. government opened a trading factory at Fort Howard in an attempt to provide local Indians with fair prices on goods. But the government did not extend credit, nor did it use alcohol as a trade item (though it sanctioned its use by traders).[40] So in reality the trading factory posed little threat to local traders. A far greater threat to them was John Jacob Astor's American Fur Company (AFC), which gained the monopoly in the Great Lakes region. For trade with the Menominee, Astor's agents hired some new clerks and traders, but for the most part he incorporated Green Bay traders into his system. His company decided which traders dealt with which of the tribe's bands simply by assigning trade territory to each post. In 1816 Astor shipped $150,000 of goods for the trade into the Great Lakes and shipped $600,000 of furs out.[41] By comparison, in 1819 the fur sales of the U.S. government factory in Green Bay totaled a mere $151.97.[42] Few independent traders succeeded during this time, as Green Bay became an increasingly unprofitable outpost.[43]

During this period the Grignons, Lawe, and Porlier, all key traders among the Menominee, lost their trading licenses and their furs. In 1817 they were all forced to sign on to sell their furs to Astor's company. This uneasy partnership with the AFC lasted officially until 1834.[44] Since Green Bay brought little profit, Astor and his deputy, Ramsay Crooks, wasted little energy on developing the trade there. They even allowed other AFC traders to take over trading locations originally worked by Green Bay traders. According to Jeanne Kay, "the policies of the American Fur Company toward the Green Bay traders—specifically high markups and curtailments of trading territories and goods—ensured their failure."[45]

The Green Bay traders, used to wintering as far away as the Mississippi, continued to do so for only a short time. In 1821, Augustin Grignon traveled to the upper Mississippi, probably near what is now Winona, Minnesota, with the Menominee.[46] Crooks had encouraged him to do so but thought he would be trading nearer to what is now Minneapolis, at St. Anthony Falls, where he would not be a threat to Joseph Rolette, the AFC's trader based at Prairie du Chien. Two years later, after physical intimidation by Rolette, who was backed by Crooks, the Green Bay traders made an agreement with the company to confine their trade to the Green Bay watershed and the upper Wisconsin.[47] This agreement meant trading with different bands of Menominee in some cases and caused a change in trader policy. In 1818, John Lawe had been instructed by his uncle Jacob Franks to try to lure the Menominee to the upper Mississippi to trade, probably because it would be easier to trade without licenses and there were more fur-bearing animals there. By 1823, however, Louis Grignon wrote to Lawe and Porlier and Co. that he was attempting to keep some Menominees on the Fox River, in his own restricted territory, although some had already departed for Rolette's territory on the Mississippi.[48]

In 1824, when Governor Cass of Michigan announced the locations of licenses to be issued from Indian agencies, the eight sites allocated to Green Bay were in a much reduced area of the traders' previous terrain. They ranged from Bay de Noquet in the north to Milwaukee in the south to the portage of the Wisconsin River and the upper Wisconsin River in the west.[49] The Menominee had not yet been restricted in their movements, and different bands continued wintering in the interior of Wisconsin and up the Mississippi River. Traders with whom they had long allied themselves, however, were restricted from entering these areas. The Menominees wintering at the Mississippi, for example, traded at Prairie du Chien, and those bands living remote distances from the trading fort probably traded with Rolette at Prairie du Chien or with sanctioned traders in the interior rather than with the Green Bay traders who used to follow the tribe into its winter trading grounds.[50] Those bands wintering on the upper Mississippi traveled the Fox-Wisconsin waterway to the Mississippi and then paddled upstream, directly past Prairie du Chien. Tomau's band wintered on the upper Mississippi but traveled as far east as Drummond Island in the summer. Rolette, being on the Mississippi, worked for the AFC's western division and, like many of the new traders, lacked the social ties to the tribe that the Green Bay traders had developed and maintained, in some cases through marriage and raising families.[51] The new traders were driven in their relation to the tribe solely by profit. While profit was a prime goal of the Green Bay traders as well, they had also served as friends and allies to the Menominee, as they would continue to do.

FIRST TREATIES

Green Bay lost its strong connections with the Menominee nation as non-Indians moved west and the fur trade waned. Immigrants flowed steadily into Menominee country, circumventing the shield of isolation that Lake Michigan had provided; many came to farm, others to exploit resources such as timber, water, and minerals. These were not only white newcomers—Indians from several New York tribes also came to settle on Menominee land. At this most inopportune time, as the Americans and eastern Indians began attempting to purchase parts of Menominee country, Sekatsokemau and several other of the tribe's elders passed away, making the Menominee's task of responding to the invasion even more difficult.

These deaths, together with Tomau's death, led Keesing to say that the Menominee underwent a leadership crisis, or a "dispute . . . concerning the title to the head chieftaincy," in which young leaders with less control of the tribe emerged. The continued multiplication of bands to as many as eighteen in the early nineteenth century caused dispute over hereditary leadership or at least, as Keesing put it, over the "supreme leadership" of the tribe. Oshkosh, Sekatsokemau's grandson, was direct heir, but Tomau, Carron's son, was "virtually head chief of the tribe" during Sekatsokemau's old age. Tomau's son, Josette, and Oshkosh thus both became eligible for the "chieftaincy." But the established leadership did not all pass away. During this time, indeed until his death in about 1834, Kaushkananiew remained the tribe's orator, the public speaker during meetings with foreign dignitaries.[52]

The unsettled state of Menominee leadership initially manifested itself when several Menominees signed their first treaty of so-called friendship with the U.S. government in St. Louis on 30 March 1817. This was one of several treaties of friendship that the United States negotiated with tribes in the Northwest following the War of 1812. The Treaty of Ghent stipulated that "The United States of America engage to put an end immediately . . . to hostilities with all the Tribes or Nations of Indians with whom they may be at war . . . and forthwith to restore to such Tribes or Nations respectively all possessions, rights and privileges" that were theirs in 1811. This was only required if the tribes "shall agree to desist from all hostilities against the United States."[53] Between 1815 and 1817, the United States dispatched William Clark, Ninian Edwards, and Auguste Choteau to negotiate what in many cases amounted to boilerplate treaties with tribes in the Old Northwest and West, "re-establishing peace and friendship between the United States and said tribe."[54]

The treaty with the Menominee called for friendship between the nations and reaffirmation of Menominee cessions to Great Britain, France, or Spain. In actuality, the tribe had made no prior cessions. The tribe also refused to recognize the signers of this treaty as legitimate leaders of the tribe. Colonel Bowyer wrote to Governor Cass on 22 July 1817, "I have taken the liberty of enclosing to you the Copy of a treaty made at St. Louis with the Menomenee Tribe of Indians. The fellows who have Signed this treaty, have no influence or character with the Indians, and I am confident this treaty has been made without the knowledge of the principle chiefs, and of nine tenths of the nation knowing or even hearing of the transaction."[55]

Unfortunately, documentation fails to show the circumstances surrounding the negotiation of this treaty, so we do not know why the tribe did not recognize the signers as legitimate. Two of the signers, Weekay and Makometa, both show up in later documents. Perhaps Weekay was the father of the Thunder clan leader Wéka, founder of the Weka settlement.[56] If Weekay, known in English as Calumet Eagle, was a Thunder clan leader, the tribe would not have recognized him as a legitimate treaty negotiator, since Thunder clan members were not sanctioned as diplomatic negotiators. Of course, his signing does not imply anything more than his attendance and perhaps an agreement to his understanding of what was written in the document, so he may not even have been involved in negotiations. We know nothing of the interpreters the government used at this negotiation, so we can draw no conclusions regarding their accuracy.

The focus of Menominee-American treaties soon changed from friendship pacts to land cession. The bands under the jurisdiction of Prairie du Chien never ceded land in that area, nor did the Menominee in the Mackinac or Chicago jurisdictions cede land in those areas. Instead, attempts were made to get the Green Bay bands to cede territory. Bowyer negotiated the first treaty that proposed the purchase of Menominee land, but again the tribe failed to recognize the treaty's signers as its representatives. Secretary of War John C. Calhoun charged Bowyer in May 1818 with gaining title to the land around Green Bay for the needs of the garrison. Calhoun instructed him to report which Indians owned the land and whether they would be willing to sell it. Bowyer responded in October that he would attempt to negotiate a deal with the Menominee the next spring when they returned from their hunts. He anticipated few problems since they only fished and gathered rice in the area and such a cession would not interfere with that.[57]

When the Menominee returned from their hunting in May 1819, Bowyer held a council asking if they would sell twenty-five or thirty square miles of land. "The next day," he reported, "they told me they could not at present think of disposing of any of their lands, that I was not the first white man that had asked their Nation to Sell their lands . . . and [they] did not like to leave the graves of their forefathers." Bowyer reminded them that they could no longer use those lands for hunting and that he had helped them with provisions from the fort. They acknowledged these points but refused to sell the land. But, according to Bowyer, it was only four chiefs whom the British had appointed who refused to sell; the next day, eight other chiefs who had always been friendly to the United States agreed to sell the land. He did not name any of the Menominee people involved but added that he had issued about a thousand rations of pork, flour, and whiskey to the Indians during the negotiations.[58]

Calhoun responded, "The Department is not desirous of obtaining a cession of this tract of country, unless it can be purchased for a small consideration." He also warned Bowyer that the United States spent too much money on rations during treaty negotiations and that he should issue no more than necessary should he make a treaty, which he finally negotiated in June 1820.[59] Bowyer negotiated the treaty with "two Menominee youth left behind" after the tribe had left the area "to follow the usual summer cycle of planting and hunting in other areas of the [Menominee] nation." The tribe's leaders returned to the area immediately upon hearing of this treaty and executed the leader of the two youths.[60]

There are apparently no extant copies of that treaty. Its terms caught even Governor Cass, who thought that Bowyer had far exceeded his authority, by surprise.[61] Cass informed the secretary of war in the fall of 1820, after Bowyer's death, that the Menominee had ceded a portion of land "extending forty miles up the Fox River, and twenty-five or thirty miles on each side of that river."[62] This was perhaps eighty times more than the twenty-five to thirty square miles Bowyer had originally proposed.[63] The latter had followed instructions to keep the price low; he suggested paying eight hundred dollars, apologizing to Calhoun that since it was to be divided among more than one thousand Menominees this amount was "as little as I could possibly offer for it."[64] This proposed payment for over 1 million acres amounted to more than 12.5 acres per penny, or less than eighty cents to each Menominee.[65] This was a sign of things to come.

The Menominee protested angrily that this treaty had cheated them. In 1820 Aus-kin-naw-wau-wish, one of the tribe's speakers, told the Reverend Jedidiah Morse, who had been commissioned by President James Monroe to conduct a study of conditions in all of Indian country, "We disapprove of what has been done by the Agent, and of the conduct of those of our nation, who treated with him, and sold our lands without our consent." He spoke for Mau-cau-tau-bee (son of Tomau), Sekatsokemau, and Aiometah, the Menominee's "three principal chiefs."[66] Morse reported that "Nearly all the *real*, acknowledged, chiefs of the nation were strongly opposed to the sale of this land, which they very justly considered, as the most valuable part of their territory."[67]

Governor Cass also opposed the treaty, because with the extinguishment of Indian title the land would be "thrown open to every adventurer, who may choose to enter it," and these people would be beyond the control of American law. As early as 1820, furthermore, Indians removing from New York wanted to purchase that same land.[68] That year a deputation of eastern tribes led by the missionary Eleazer Williams started out toward Green Bay but received word in Detroit of Colonel Bowyer's treaty. The deputation "conceived that the govt had *anticipated* them, and got possession of the best tract of land," Morse wrote to Calhoun. They wondered whether this was done with the knowledge of officials in Washington. Morse encouraged them to continue on their trip and stressed that the government intended to act with their welfare in mind.[69]

The New York tribes had been in an increasingly untenable position. By the 1810s government policy, missionary activity, and land speculators conspired to pressure New York tribes to vacate their lands and move west. The Ogden Land Company, for instance, "gained preemptive rights to Indian land in western New York" in 1810, and after 1815, this company increasingly pushed to gain title to that land, which could only be accomplished by removing the Indians living on it.[70] They therefore increased pressure on all of the Six Nations of the Iroquois to leave New York.

After Illinois became a state in 1818 the coveted Fox River country became part of Michigan Territory. Reverend Morse supported David Ogden's desire to remove the tribes from New York, and his tour of Indian country included the evaluation of the Fox River area for the eastern tribes. Some New York tribes were interested in moving, especially the Christian Oneidas under the direction of Williams and a group of Stockbridge and Brothertons who had previously moved from the east to Oneida lands. Williams eventually urged some of the St. Regis Indians to become involved in the negotiations also. The Munsees were among the New York nations involved as well.[71]

When they heard news of the treaty made by Bowyer for purchase of Menominee lands, the New York nations "contacted New York congressmen and 'friends of the Indian' in the east," who convinced President Monroe "to cancel the treaty."[72] Monroe therefore never submitted Bowyer's treaty to the Senate for ratification. Calhoun informed Cass when this was done, adding that a delegation from New York would again make the trip west to negotiate for lands. He then encouraged three Oneidas, including Cornelius Beard and John Anthony Brandt, to make another trip west. As it had done the year before, the federal government supplied rations for the journey.[73]

The United States planned for the Fox River to become an Indian-controlled agricultural state. Yet "the fundamental flaw in the design was [that] the New York tribes predicated the state on acquisition of Menominee lands."[74] In the summer of 1821, Cass appointed his personal secretary, Charles C. Trowbridge, to accompany a group of Indians from New York State when they went to Green Bay to attempt to purchase land from the Menominee.[75] Trowbridge, whom Cass had apparently appointed to guard the interests of land speculators in New York, accompanied the delegation from Detroit to Green Bay to help bring about the treaty on behalf of the U.S. government.[76] The two resulting treaties of 1821 and 1822 exchanged millions of acres of land for a few thousand dollars of goods.

The New York delegation included deputies representing the Oneidas, Onondagas, and Senecas of the Six Nations, as well as the St. Regis (Caughnawaga), the Stockbridge, and the Munsee nations. The St. Regis people were made up mostly of Mohawks but also of people of other Iroquois nations.[77]

Though Trowbridge had accompanied the tribal delegates as an official federal representative, he believed the treaty did not require Senate ratification, since it was made between Indian groups. However, Samuel C. Stambaugh, an agent at Green Bay a decade later in 1831 and 1832, believed that since Trowbridge was not a duly assigned treaty commissioner, the treaty was not even legal.[78]

The government's attempts in this negotiation can best be described as a series of errors. First, Trowbridge's party arrived just after John Biddle, the Green Bay agent, had left for Chicago to participate in a treaty-making convention there. Second, Biddle had taken his interpreter with him, which left Trowbridge and his crew in a state of "very great mortification." Nonetheless, a substitute interpreter was apparently found, probably among the French or mixed-blood people living near Fort Howard, and local Menominees were invited to meet with the delegation. The interpreter did not speak the Menominee language but rather Ojibwe, which was considered the traders' language in the area. The Menominees came to the house in which the delegation had situated itself, accompanied by some Ho Chunk tribal members.

On 8 August 1821, the deputies from New York delivered a speech to the Menominee, urging them to invite their chiefs to parley. Accidentally, the interpreter invited both the Menominee and the Ho Chunks. Trowbridge had wanted to avoid dealing with the Ho Chunks because of their reputation for unwillingness to sell their lands. The invitation could not have diplomatically been withdrawn, however. Eight days later the leaders of the two tribes met again.

The Menominee initially refused to sign the treaty, but the Ho Chunks were not so reticent.[79] Stambaugh later reported that one of the Indian leaders of the New York delegation bribed the Ho Chunks to sign the treaty: "A Winnebago Chief took a great fancy to a *uniform coat* on the back of *Solomon N. Hendricks*, and upon condition that the Winnebago would sign the Treaty, Solomon presented *him* with the coat."[80] The Ho Chunk leader Four Legs remembered it differently, however, saying that both they and the Menominee intended only to permit the eastern tribes use of the land, not ownership, and that the Ho Chunks supported the results of the negotiations only on that basis.[81]

After the Ho Chunks agreed to sign the treaty, the Menominee signed as well. The treaty, concluded on 18 August 1821, called for the New York Indians to purchase 860,000 acres of land from the Menominee and Ho Chunks. In exchange, the Green Bay tribes agreed to receive two thousand dollars— five hundred in cash and fifteen hundred in goods.

The Menominee decision to sign was made by individuals, not by the tribe or even its representative leaders. Although the treaty purported to represent the Menominee nation as a whole, nearly everyone involved agreed later that it did not. In the period of eight days in which the negotiations proceeded, the Menominee would have been unable to gather leaders representing all bands. (As late as 1849, after the tribal land base had shrunk considerably, the agent estimated that three weeks would be necessary to gather the tribe.[82]) Oshkosh was nearby in 1821, but he could not attend on account of family illness, so he sent his brother to speak for him. Oshkosh's brother, speaking to the delegation on 17 August, stated that he saw no reason for the Menominee to sell land to the easterners, since the Menominee land was so small and the easterners claimed to have fine lands in their own country.[83]

Later American treaty commissioners learned that two of the six Menominee who signed the 1821 treaty were not considered principal chiefs by the tribe and that three others were considered war leaders.[84] The latter would have been Thunder clan leaders, who lacked the authority from the tribe to treat with the U.S. government. Only one legitimate Menominee leader signed the treaty. Signatures of two or three civil leaders from each of the more than a dozen bands would have been needed to properly complete the proceedings. One witness familiar with the Menominee language later testified that the interpreter failed to explain to the Menominee that they had sold their land.[85] Tribal members believed the tribe had agreed to share the land with the easterners, under the long-standing system of *apēkon ahkīhih*.

Governor Cass sent Secretary of War Calhoun a copy of the treaty and observed that the New York Indians would probably soon begin moving west from New York to the Fox River area, where they could form a useful barrier against the British or the western Indians. Calhoun urged Cass to aid in the migration in any way he could but without incurring further expenses. Calhoun then wrote the Stockbridge leader, Solomon U. Hendrick, that President Monroe had approved the treaty on 9 February 1822, "which is all the ratifications that is necessary" in a treaty between Indian nations.[86]

Hendrick apparently wrote to Calhoun that some of the Six Nations disliked the terms of the treaty because not enough land had been ceded and that it was too far from Green Bay. Calhoun then authorized the easterners to negotiate for more land to be purchased outright. "The country the Six Nations have or may acquire from the Menomeenees and Winnebagoes, will be held by them in the same manner as the Indians who previously owned it." The government would also provide rations to this deputation. Calhoun then wrote to the government's subagent in New York and included a statement to be read to the Indians. He emphasized that the president "thinks that it would be better for the respective tribes of the Six Nations to dispose of their lands in Newyork" and to move to land purchased from the Menominee and Ho Chunks. He added, however, that the president "by no means intends to adopt any measures for the removal of the Six Nations, or any part of them, nor will he suffer it to be done, without their free assent."[87]

Some Menominees and the New York Indians signed a second "treaty," more preposterous than any of the previous treaties, on 23 September 1822. The terms of the 1822 treaty between the eastern Indians and the Menominee, if interpreted as a land sale, were the most penurious of any treaty in Menominee history.[88]

John Sergeant Jr. signed this treaty as a witness and an "Agent on the part of the government of the United States." The Green Bay agency's official interpreter, Richard Prickett, absent at the time of the 1821 treaty, apparently provided his services at the 1822 proceedings.[89] Yet Prickett, though the official interpreter, did not speak Menominee! Stambaugh reports that in this treaty the Menominee agreed to cede 6,720,000 acres of land in exchange for three thousand dollars in goods.[90] This amounts to approximately 22.4 acres per penny, or, if the two thousand dollars in goods from the 1821 treaty are included, approximately 13.4 acres per penny. Some of this land, which covers most of northeastern Wisconsin, is the richest and most valuable in the state. According to Stambaugh, "the country, claimed to have been purchased by the New York Indians, and for which the Menominies received $5,000! would have sold to the United States, at the lowest price ever paid for Indian lands, a sum exceeding $500,000 dollars!"[91] In other words, this land, according to Stambaugh, was worth over one hundred times more than it cost. President Monroe partially approved the 1822 treaty on 13 March 1823, first granting six hundred thousand acres to the New York tribes, then, after being pressured by Thomas Ogden, modifying the amount to two million acres.[92]

The issue was hardly resolved, however. Nearly a decade would pass before the Menominee would be able to get out from under these shameful treaties, which had been initiated by the preposterous American treaty of 1820. In the process, the Menominee would learn lessons in negotiating with a duplicitous U.S. government that would prove valuable in future dealings.

5
Menominee Resources under Siege

At first glance, judging by the astonishing amount of lands ceded in the three treaties of 1820, 1821, and 1822 and the paltry sums received for them, it would seem that the Menominee simply failed to understand the American concept of land value. But actually they were not even trying to understand the American system. They were simply making agreements, as they long had done, based in the tribal customary laws of the region. In the case of the first treaty, the tribe's leaders punished those who misrepresented them, killing one. As to the next two treaties, the Menominee never thought they sold the lands. As gracious hosts, they offered to share their lands with the New York Indians, albeit reluctantly, as they had with the Mesquakies, the French, and the British. The Menominee probably understood the gifts they received from the easterners as the offerings of gracious guests who were visiting them on their land. What the Menominee failed to understand was the far-reaching impact of the new American system and the strength by which it could reshape the Menominee world. Just as the Menominee understood little of the American system, the Americans understood little of the Menominee view, but the American, not the Menominee, system became the basis for the law to which the Menominee had to adapt.

The New York Indians, or Wabonockies as the Menominee called them, slowly but steadily moved into Menominee and Ho Chunk country, whose people began to realize that the newcomers believed they now owned the land.[1] This sense of ownership surprised and angered the Menominee and Ho Chunks as well as the non-Indian and métis residents of Green Bay. The Menominee responded angrily, twice almost resorting to war in the hope of "driving the Wabonockies into the bay."[2] Green Bay citizens who regularly dealt with the Menominee, in trade and as interpreters, testified that the Menominee had been told in negotiations that the eastern Indians wanted only to share their lands and that no proper interpreters had presided.[3] On 16 June 1824, the Menominee, led by Oshkosh and Josette Carron as well as others, presented a petition of protest to their duly appointed agent, Henry Brevoort. They insisted that, although the tribe's leaders had informed the eastern Indians that their land was too small to sell, the easterners had met with some Menominee men, none of whom were principal chiefs, "and purchased or pretended to purchase a part of the Menomonie's country" from people without authority to sell.[4]

Green Bay citizens feared they would lose their landholdings, which they maintained by permission of the Menominee, although the government had previously determined these agreements to be just. These people, mostly of French-Canadian and métis background, began petitioning the president as early as February 1823, claiming the Menominee had been cheated in unfair land dealings. They argued that the 1821 and 1822 treaties abused Menominee title to the lands.[5]

In September 1824, a representative of the Indians from New York delivered a supply of goods, as was called for in the treaty. The principal leaders of the Menominee held a council with him and "refused to receive any of the goods, alledging that they had made no sale of their lands." The next day, however, other Menominees, presumably those who had originally signed the treaties, accepted the goods. Again the tribe's leaders decided to appeal to Agent Brevoort.

They gathered together with non-Indian inhabitants from Green Bay outside the fence of the agency house. But Brevoort refused to hear them, instead sending a note that said, "When I wish a number of Indians Collected I will send my Interpreter, to let them know." If they wrote down their speech he would consider reading it and responding to it. He accused the Green Bay inhabitants of bringing the tribe to see him; they denied it, saying the Indians had gathered on their own.

Finally, twenty-two Green Bay residents, apparently under the leadership of the future governor, James Duane Doty, bypassed the agent and sent a protest to the president of the United States, claiming that the Menominee did not consider the land as sold. Describing the agent's actions, they stated their belief that the Menominee had been treated unfairly by both the U.S. government and the New York Indians.[6]

All of this disagreement led to a series of treaties negotiated between 1825 and 1832 in which the federal government attempted to resolve the dispute by encouraging the Menominee to legally cede land to the New York Indians. Meanwhile, more white migrants began to settle in Menominee country, and corporate interests began to recognize the potential for accumulating wealth there. The American frontier and presence surged inexorably westward, into the Menominee homeland. Treaty negotiations thus began to encompass more than disputes between Indian nations, including also boundary resolution and land cessions to the United States.

In the 1825 treaty in Prairie du Chien, the U.S. government established borders between the Sioux, Ojibwes, Sauks, Mesquakies, Iowas, Ho Chunks, and others. The Menominees who attended were unable to make decisions on behalf of the nation, so Menominee borders and land claims remained undetermined.[7]

Meanwhile, in a treaty of January 1825, the Six Nations, St. Regis, Stockbridge, and Munsees sold some of the land they had supposedly purchased from the Menominee and Ho Chunks to the Brothertons, another displaced tribe from the east. The Menominee "had looked upon their strange neighbors as humble petitioners," Colonel Stambaugh later wrote, " 'praying for a small piece of land for some of their people to rest upon, who they said were crowded out of the State of New York by the White Man,' But they now found out that they had been deceived—that the '*Notoways*' were not only claiming their country, 'but were selling it, at a speculation, to other Tribes.'"[8] This loss of land was the primary Menominee concern at treaty negotiations during the 1820s, but it was not the primary federal concern.

1827 TREATY

The U.S. government pursued three goals in the 1827 treaty: to determine borders between the Menominee and Ojibwes in the west and north, to settle the dispute between the eastern Indians and the Menominee and Ho Chunks, and to create borders between the Americans and the Menominee. The War Department sent two treaty commissioners, Governor Lewis Cass of the Michigan Territory (from which Wisconsin had not yet been carved) and Colonel Thomas L. McKenney, the Indian Bureau's first commissioner, to represent the United States' interests in meetings held at Butte des Morts in August 1827. Cass opened the negotiations on 6 August and declared, "We want . . . that they [Menominee and Ojibwes] may know their own country, and that there may be no dispute between them, nor between their children, nor between their childrens children." However, the boundary concern between the New York Indians and the Menominee needed to be determined for different reasons: "Now our people [Americans] have settled in the country, and we are anxious that boundaries be established between them and the Indians," Cass explained.[9]

Regarding boundaries, Four Legs, a Ho Chunk leader, said on 8 August, "We do not need any line." He explained how the Ho Chunks, Menominee, and Ojibwes had always understood their boundaries as follows:

The Father of Life, made the Earth for the Indian to roam upon — that the Chippeways and Menomonies and Winebagoes might wander where they pleased. Since the time that we can first remember, the fires of the Chippeways and Menomonies and Winebagoes have been one fire. We have always held each other by the hand. We appeal to the ancient traders to say whether they have not at all times hunted upon our lands, and whether they have not found us hunting together as brothers. And we hope, that we, the Menomonies, Chippeways and Winebagoes will continue to live together like three brothers, as we have hitherto lived.[10]

Nevertheless, the treaty created an official Menominee-Ojibwe border in the northern and western part of Menominee country, signaling the end of the tribes living together as brothers and paving the way for easier negotiations for the United States in future land cession treaties with both tribes.[11]

Regarding the New York tribes, the Menominee continued to insist that they had not sold any land. Oshkosh told Governor Cass, "From the time that the stranger Indians first came here, we have no knowledge of having ever ceded any part of our country to them." Josette Carron, another Menominee leader, agreed, adding, "This is the answer the Menomonie nation makes to all the treaties which have been read here."[12] Four Legs supported the Menominee contention. He started with a solemn oath, which indicated the sincerity and veracity of his testimonial, then described what had occurred:

> I will tell you what has past between our brothers from the East and us. I will tell you the truth. What I say, I say before the Great Spirit who is the Father of Life, as well as the Heaven above us, as the Earth upon which we stand.
>
> They said, "our Brother! It was at the request of our Great Father, that we have come here to meet you. We are here on your lands. Our Brothers! Winebagoes and Menomonies! We are poor. We ask you to take pity on us. We are not masters of our own land; neither of the waters within it nor of the trees on it. We ask of you therefore, the charity to let us sit upon your land here!"
>
> Father! When they first came, they asked for a small piece of land, sufficient for them to put their children on that they

might live. They and the Menomonies were assembled at the first visit, and that Menomonie Chief who has spoken to you was hesitating for two days—so much, that he did not know what answer to make.

They said, "Menomonies, Our Brothers! We hope you will give us what we ask. We ask you to lend and not sell us, a small piece of land. Do this, in charity to our impoverished situation."

Father: It was long before the Menomonies would consent; but we, the Winebagoes, interfered and said, "What harm can it do, to grant their request, since they only want to borrow the land, and not to buy it." It was not a sale, nor a gift, but it was a loan. We had too little ourselves to be willing to sell it. The New York Indians told us, that we should not regret the loan, nor the Charity we had yielded them. If they had Sugar Camps, our children should occupy them in common.[13]

This issue proved too difficult for resolution in the 1827 agreement. Article 2 stipulated that a decision would be deferred and that the Menominee and Ho Chunks agreed that "the whole matter shall be referred to the President of the United States, whose decision shall be final."[14]

The treaty resolved the third issue, land for the United States, by granting a stretch of the Fox River from south of its confluence into Green Bay to the Grand Kakalin, where Augustin Grignon had claimed land.[15] This encompassed two hundred thousand acres on "a very valuable tract of land," Cass and McKenney wrote to Secretary of War James Barbour on 11 August 1827 (see map 4).[16]

Cass and McKenney ignored Menominee land possession rules to justify the granting of an "American Reservation," as they called it. They told Secretary Barbour that the United States claimed the land because the Menominee had already ceded it to the French and the British years earlier. The major problem, they continued, was to determine exactly where the boundaries lay:

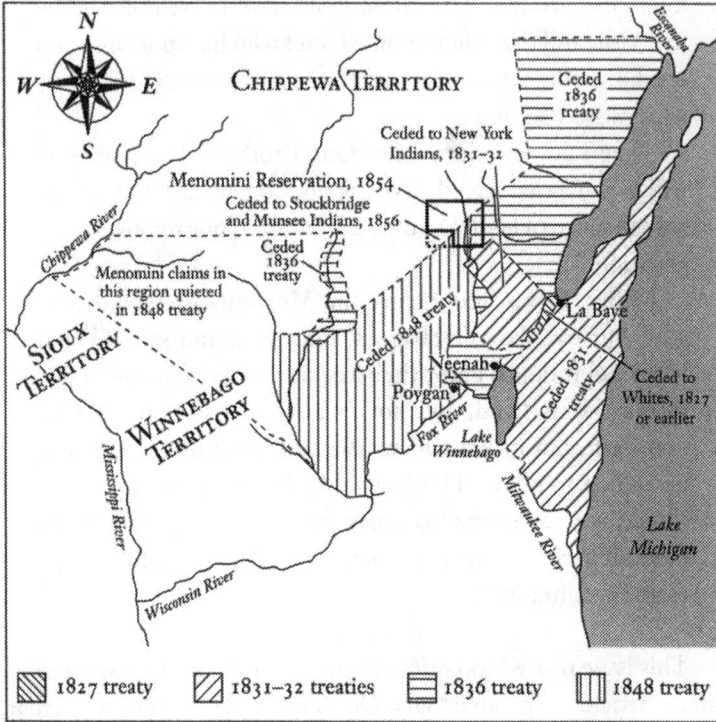

Map 4. Felix Keesing's Menomini land cessions

Our right is derived from that of French and British governments, and no documentary evidence exists of its extent. It is
well known, that the French authorities, when in possession
of this country took possession of such land as was wanted
for their purposes, without the formality of a treaty. They
merely declared to the Indians, that their Great Father, the
King, desired such a piece of land and after distributing Such
presents as they thought proper, they took possession of it. In
this manner, their right, as well of jurisdiction as of soil, was
acquired, and it was doubtless in this manner, that possession
was obtained of the country upon Green Bay. The Settlement
was So remote, that it is not probable the British ever took any
important Step respecting it, and to this day the question of

jurisdiction is unsettled, and the boundaries of the reservation
left to be determined by Such facts and recollections as have
Survived the period of the Settlement.[17]

The French and British indeed had claimed sovereignty over
the land in relation to Europeans but recognized that the land still
belonged to the Menominee. The claims had been made for the
purpose of keeping other Europeans off of the land but were not
intended to remove the land from Indian control. The French as
well as the British lacked the strength to do so. To the Menominee
the Europeans were "sitting down upon" the land in the same way
as the Wabonockies did in the early 1820s and the Mesquakies had
done 150 years earlier.

For this valuable land the Americans paid a very small price.
An amount of $15,682 in goods, purchased from local traders,
was distributed on the spot to all the Indians gathered at the pay
grounds. This reward was divided among all of the tribes present —
including Menominee, Ojibwes, Ho Chunks, the New York tribes,
and others — for their liberality in dealing with each other. The
commissioners had promised these gifts in advance when they
invited the various nations to attend the treaty. Despite official
disapproval of the policy, the United States had found the necessity
of offering inducements if any tribes were to attend such negotiations. The rations distributed to the Indians during the meetings
included 116 barrels of whiskey. The tribes viewed the gifts in the
same way as those made at other treaty gatherings. In addition
to the gifts, the treaty called for money to be granted annually
by Congress to be shared among the tribes for education: $1,000
annually for the first three years and $1,500 annually thereafter.[18]

These costs cannot be considered as payment for the two hundred thousand acres of Menominee land, not only because the commissioners divided these monies among the several tribes present
but also because the commissioners believed this was European
land to which the United States had a legitimate previous claim.
The Menominee therefore did not cede that land. The federal
Indian agent, Colonel Stambaugh, confirmed this in a detailed

letter to the secretary of war in 1831, when he stated that the Menominee had sold no land to the government and had not received any annuities.[19]

Meanwhile, Governor Cass finally resolved the issue of legitimacy of Menominee leadership as far as the United States was concerned in 1827, when he and McKenney appointed Oshkosh as the head chief and Josette as second chief during the treaty proceedings at Butte des Morts. "The Menomini have since abided by this decision and thus the old hereditary right has been acknowledged," Keesing later concluded, although some Menominees dispute this.[20]

Cass told the Menominee in his opening remarks at the negotiations, "We have observed for some time that the Menomonies have been in a bad situation with respect to their Chiefs. There is no one to whom we can talk, as the head of the nation. If anything happens, we want some person who has authority in the nation to whom we can look. They appear to us like a flock of geese without a leader. Some fly one way, and some another. Tomorrow at the opening of the Council we will proceed to appoint a principal chief for the Menomonies. We shall make inquiries this afternoon and select the proper person. We shall give him the medal and expect the Menomonie nation to respect him as the head man."[21]

Colonel McKenney the next day said to the Menominee that their Great Father "wants one mouth, that he may hear more distinctly, and one pair of ears to hear through, and a pair of eyes to see for him." He continued, "Take care how you act in this matter. When his [the Great Father's] white children are wrong, it is the duty of your people to speak through your mouth."[22] When the Menominee made no immediate decision, Cass made the appointment.[23]

Though the tribe abided by Cass's decision, not all tribal members liked it. Oshkosh, though a member of the Bear clan and grandson of Sekatsokemau, was not a band leader himself, and a part of the tribe believed Waukechon to be the rightful leader of the nation as a whole.[24]

The autonomy of the Menominee bands caused this tension. Each band had several male leaders, whom the United States designated as first, second, and third chiefs. The bands and the tribe met in council to pass major decisions. The Menominee recognized numerous leaders at once but made decisions democratically in open council meetings. All bands had to ratify an agreement before the tribe recognized it as binding.

The process of involving all bands in treaty negotiations proved extremely cumbersome, especially because the United States often announced these proceedings on short notice and occasionally left bands out of the decision-making process on purpose. This process worked against the Menominee system. The Menominee chief Mau-cau-tau-bee, in 1820, had pointed out to Reverend Morse that a council of adult male members of the tribe had to accept decisions regarding land cessions if they were to be acceptable to the tribe as a whole.[25] Without consensus, there would not be widespread support for these decisions.

As many as seventeen individual Menominee village sites, each the home of distinct bands, existed by the 1820s, ranging from Mackinac in the northeast to Prairie du Chien in the southwest, from Chicago in the southeast to the upper Wolf River in the northwest. Menominee hunting grounds and winter encampment sites extended even farther. The seventeen village sites included seven along Green Bay (including one at the fort), four on the Wolf and Fox Rivers (the upper Wolf, Keshena Falls, Lake Poygan, and the present Winneconne-Fond du Lac-Oshkosh area), three on the Wisconsin River (at Portage, at "River's Mouth" or Prairie du Chien, and one in between those two), and three others in the vicinity of growing American cities (Chicago, Milwaukee, and Mackinac).[26]

Besides dealing with a new government that largely failed to understand the tribe's geography and sociopolitical makeup, the Menominee had to do so in a foreign language, which further complicated matters. By the early treaty-making years, the Menominee had developed political savvy in regard to language but only after costly miscommunication. Few U.S. agents learned the Menominee language, instead relying on mixed-blood or non-Indian interpreters to communicate with the tribe for them.

Accurate communication was more important to the Menominee, who had more to lose, than to the United States. Besides official interpreters, the Menominee often brought their own interpreters to important proceedings, beginning at least as early as the 1820s. Oshkosh himself knew English, but even so, he always brought an interpreter with him to official councils. This way he was able to feign ignorance if it suited his purpose and, more important, to seek clarification of points that he did not clearly understand.[27]

For the most part the interpreters whom Oshkosh and the Menominee hired were from among the traders who had long affiliated themselves with the Menominee nation and traded among them. These traders were changing their commercial affiliations and were working for companies with pure profit motives, but the traders continued to live among the Menominee and travel with them. In the early 1820s AFC agents or traders affiliated with the company firmly established their new trading areas in proximity to the home villages of the various Menominee bands. John Lawe, as part of his Green Bay Company agreement, traded with northern Menominee bands, as his territory covered the Green Bay and Wolf River watersheds, which included Shawano Lake.[28] Porlier and the Grignons traded on the watersheds of the Fox and Wisconsin Rivers.[29] Augustin Grignon eventually set up a permanent post near present-day Kaukauna, an officially sanctioned site on an important rapids between Green Bay and Lake Winnebago. Porlier also traded with a Shawano Lake band of Menominee, which indicates that the traders' areas overlapped.[30] This overlap was unavoidable, given the Menominee's seasonally mobile lifestyle. Menominees regularly traded as far south as Milwaukee, Wisconsin, and Davenport, Iowa.[31] Some Americans, including Daniel Whitney, Robert Irwin Jr., and William Farnsworth, who came to trade at Green Bay, independently became involved in the fur trade. Though they did not move to tribal villages to do so, even they established some social connections with tribal members.[32]

1831 AND 1832 TREATIES

In 1830 the War Department made an unsuccessful attempt to resolve the conflicts between the Menominee and Ho Chunks on the one side and the New York Indians on the other. Secretary of War John Eaton sent three commissioners, Judge James McCall, General Erastus Root, and John T. Miller, to Green Bay to try to resolve the issue. The secretary, however, failed to give them power to make treaties. Although over seventeen hundred Indians attended a council with these three men in late August, they could not reach agreement. The negotiations were interpreted into Ojibwe, which the commissioner assumed the Indians all knew. The Menominee demanded an interpreter who spoke their language, naming one of the Grignons as a possibility, but the commissioners did not appoint him since he required eight dollars a day to perform the service.[33] The Menominee and Ho Chunks agreed to allow the New Yorkers two hundred thousand acres of land, which the Menominee still insisted they had never sold to the easterners. The New York tribes refused to accept the offer, saying it was not enough. The commissioners finally left Green Bay having resolved nothing but having spent War Department rations on thousands of individual meals.[34]

In 1830, Colonel Stambaugh brought a Menominee delegation to Washington to negotiate a treaty, with the support of Governor Cass but with the initial disapproval of the secretary of war. Oshkosh disapproved as well, reportedly staying behind because he knew a treaty would not be valid if negotiated without him.[35] The party reached Detroit in November and went from there on to Washington. The parties signed the treaty on 8 February 1831 and signed an amendment to it on 17 February in which the Menominee agreed to sell five hundred thousand acres to the eastern tribes and approximately 2.5 million acres of land to the Americans. This included their land on the eastern shore of

Green Bay, all the way to the northern tip of the peninsula east of Green Bay, to present-day Door County, and south all the way to the Milwaukee River, east of Lake Winnebago. The southern boundary of this cession coincided with the southern boundary of the Green Bay agency's jurisdiction.[36]

In exchange for the land, the 1831 treaty provided for agricultural, domestic, and educational funds. In fact, the money set aside for these funds totaled more than half of what the Menominee received for this land sale altogether. The total the tribe received from this sale amounted to almost $160,000, with the payments spread over ten years. But over $85,000 was specifically earmarked for farming, mills, housing, and education expenditures.[37] In the treaty, "the President of the United States, as a mark of his affection for his children of the Menominee tribe," agreed to employ five farmers for the Menominee for ten years on their land west of the Fox River and five women for the same period of time to teach the Menominee women housewifery. The federal government also agreed to spend $10,000 to build houses for the tribe (and $3,000 to build houses for the five farmers and their wives). The United States agreed as well to build a gristmill and sawmill on the Fox River for the tribe, to provide a good miller "subject to the direction of the agent," and to run at least one blacksmith or gun shop. Beyond this, $8,000 in clothing was to be delivered to the tribe within six months, along with $1,000 in flour and provisions, with the cost of transporting these to be figured as part of the money set aside. Finally, the tribe would receive an annual payment of $6,000 for twelve years. Schools would still be funded under the 1827 treaty, with a small additional sum appended here.[38] All these expenditures cost the United States five cents per acre. This was the first actual sale of Menominee lands to the United States for payments.[39]

Colonel Stambaugh, the federal agent to the tribe, also served as the federal negotiator of this treaty. He inserted a clause in the treaty that allowed the federal government to extinguish title to the rest of Menominee land when other eastern Indians should be removed to the area, commenting in a letter to the secretary of war that the Menominee would not need more than one-third of their remaining land once they became farmers, which he envisioned happening sometime during the nineteenth century.[40]

Meanwhile, the Menominee became embroiled in war with the Sac and Fox under Black Hawk. Some of their old enemies, the Mesquakies, were now part of this group. The Sac and Fox were fighting desperately against the United States to retain their homeland south and east of Menominee country. Menominee involvement in the war was not so much related to the Americans as to a long-standing dispute with the Mesquakies, whom they identified with the Sac and Fox. This dispute had escalated in 1830 when a Menominee-Sioux coalition killed eight Sac and Fox leaders. In July 1831, the Sac and Fox retaliated by attacking a Menominee band living near Fort Crawford in Prairie du Chien. Twenty-five Menominee were killed, over two-thirds of them women and children, and another six were injured. The band leader Carron lost his wife, children, and brother in the attack. The Menominee planned to retaliate but were held off by U.S. officials who hoped that a peaceful restitution could be made. Tensions rose throughout the spring of 1832 until the United States initiated military force against Black Hawk.[41]

Colonel Stambaugh organized two Menominee companies at Green Bay to join the war in July 1832. Stambaugh had been relieved of his duties as agent before the treaty delegation had left Washington DC in March 1831.[42] Nonetheless, Secretary of War John Eaton instructed Colonel Stambaugh to return to Menominee country with the tribal delegation. "They have objected to go back with any but yourself," Eaton wrote, "with you they feel a security, which they represent can be felt with none other, and have expressed earnestly a desire that you may be permitted to accompany them back to their native forest."[43] Stambaugh, though not reappointed, served for over a year as the de facto agent, until the War Department appointed Colonel George Boyd to the position in April 1832.[44] Consolidation of the Sault Ste. Marie and Michilimackinac agencies, and assignment of that new jurisdiction to Henry Rowe Schoolcraft, had left Boyd jobless. After Boyd's appointment, Stambaugh continued to do the work of the agency, because Boyd refused to move into the agency house after hearing reports of the far-off fighting between the Menominee and Sac and Fox.[45]

That settlers and the U.S. military were forcing Black Hawk's people out of their homelands was of little concern to the Menominee, who had failed to receive restitution for the twenty-five murders of 1831 and were eager to join the United States Army in its war against Black Hawk. The Menominee's orator, Kaushkannaniew, requested that Boyd appoint Stambaugh to remain with the Menominee during their campaigns in the American war against Black Hawk and his people. The two Menominee companies organized under Colonel Stambaugh's command were captained by Augustin Grignon and George Johnston and numbered some three hundred Menominee warriors, including civil leaders such as Oshkosh, Komanekin, Aiometah, and Kaushkannaniew and war leaders such as Carron. They served until 28 August 1832, but most of the action they saw consisted of mop-up duty chasing down a dispirited, disorganized, and increasingly diminished fighting force that was largely defeated on 30 July, just ten days after the Menominee took arms at Green Bay and before they reached the front.[46]

Upon their return home the Menominee were shown the modified 1831 treaty and were asked to ratify it in council. The treaty, which granted half a million acres to the eastern nations, failed to satisfy the Menominee. They sent a delegation to Washington DC to lobby for changes that were written into the agreement. The Menominee leaders, "having taken time to deliberate and reflect on the proposition . . . did in the most positive and decided manner, refuse to give their assent" to the Senate modifications, "which would have pushed them back upon the Wolf river 'on lands of decidedly inferior quality.' "[47] This refusal resulted in negotiations for a new treaty, which were held in late October 1832.

The Menominee wanted to clarify which lands they intended to sell and which they intended to keep. Colonel Stambaugh had pushed the government to compromise, based on the financial cost to the United States.[48] More important to the Menominee, they were losing the full support of Stambaugh, previously their stout ally. They learned this when the Brothertons had ignored the 1831 treaty entirely and moved onto land east of the Fox River, though the Menominee had ceded none of that. The Brothertons settled into some of the Menominee's best sugar bush, or maple stands, against the recommendation of Stambaugh. Yet Stambaugh urged the Menominee to allow them to stay, even though he recognized the injury this would cause to the Menominee sugar lands. Some of the Menominee wanted to take up arms against these illegal squatters and drive them out, but Stambaugh convinced them that after the Senate ratified the 1831 treaty all would be settled. The Brothertons refused to move and claimed the land based on the invalid 1821 and 1822 treaties. This problem continued to plague the Calumet band for several years, despite the addendum to the 1832 treaty that purported to resolve this issue.[49]

The Menominee, a largely nonagricultural tribe, mattered little to the government, which did not wish to support Menominee nonagricultural pursuits. Perhaps Stambaugh asked this band of the Menominee to give in because he believed the tribe as a whole had more than enough land and that the loss of maple sugar lands might help wean them "from their wandering habits," as the treaty put it. Yet the Menominee still believed the resources of the land to be theirs.

The Menominee view of the land's status and value differed from that promulgated by their federal representative. Stambaugh's observation that the land ceded would have been of little use to the Menominee reflects only one side of the story. On 23 October 1832, during the meeting with Michigan territorial governor George B. Porter and Agent Boyd, the purpose of which was to negotiate alterations in the 1831 treaty, Kaushkannaniew, in his role as speaker, said "The forest is our life, and . . . we do not like to part with it—or any of our land as we said to you before."[50]

At these negotiations the Menominee made clear that they were willing to make concessions for their allies, the United States, but refused to do so for the New York Indians, to whom they referred as dogs because "they have no ears" and "when we give them a piece [of land] they want more." The change that the Senate had written into the treaty at the instigation of the eastern tribes moved the boundary line of the cession to include land around Little Chute on the Fox River. This served as an important passageway, a portage and trading ground on which Augustin Grignon's trading establishment was located. If the Menominee lost control of that land they feared the northern bands would be split from the southern ones and that they would lose a significant footing in their ability to trade.[51]

Though this dispute over the boundary line was the immediate basis of Menominee dissatisfaction, there were other problems with the treaty as well. The tribe had three major concerns at this negotiation: the loss of this piece of land; the trespass of the eastern tribes and American settlers on Menominee resources; and the fact that they had received nothing for the lost land, which they did not believe they had sold. The Menominee angrily pointed out that, though they had permitted the eastern nations to farm on Menominee land, they had never granted them usufruct rights to the resources. The intruders had not only invaded the Menominee sugar bush but had cut timber and had hunted Menominee deer.[52]

In fact, the Menominee had reserved usufructuary rights on the ceded lands according to the 1831 treaty. The treaty stipulated that the Menominee "shall be at liberty to hunt and fish on the lands they have now ceded to the United States . . . with the same privilege they at present enjoy, until it be surveyed and offered for sale by the President."[53] As Stambaugh had stated, *he*, not the tribe, inserted the clause that provided the president with the right to sell the land. The Menominee only knew that they retained the right, certainly not agreeing that they were obliged to give it up one day.

Consistent with their long-standing practice of *apēkon ahkīhih*, they viewed the use of the land and its resources as bound by different sets of customary law. They may have given up the land, but the resources on it they still viewed as theirs. The statements of tribal leaders in the negotiation process show a clear desire on the part of the Menominee to maintain use rights for fish, game, and plant foods, although the treaty as written specified only hunting and fishing.

Kaushkannaniew described problems with the eastern Indians from the area of the Grand Chute all the way to Wolf River: "They hunt on our land and kill our deer:—Have they any right to do so? [W]e are becoming angry. . . . [T]hey have killed a great many of our deer. . . . Was this their agreement? No—They were to cultivate the land—This is what they wanted land for, they said:—not to hunt deer on."[54] These abuses of their hospitality angered the Menominee.

Penaitenaw, a Menominee River band leader, described similar theft of Menominee resources by a non-Indian trader and entrepreneur in the north of Menominee country. William Farnsworth had dammed up the Menominee River, cutting off the all-important supply of fish. "Did we ever sell all the fish?" Penaitenaw asked. "[T]his man says, he owns all the fish in that River and all the cranberries—We never sold all these. . . . [A]ll I wish is that the channel on the River may be left open, so that the fish can go up and down: and that we may catch them as heretofore, to subsist on."[55]

The land was an equally important issue to the Menominee. Kaushkannaniew recollected precisely which land the Menominee had agreed to sell at the 1831 negotiations in Washington. They had agreed to it grudgingly and granted this amount and "not . . . a step more." They also insisted on the protection of rights that they had granted to some of their traders.[56]

It was primarily for these reasons that the Menominee rejected the amended treaty. Though Governor Porter requested them to change their minds several times over the next few days, Menominee leaders stood firm. At one point, Kaushkannaniew described in anger the Menominee decision-making process and why they remained unmoved.

> You do not seem to know us — We do not change our mind so soon as this — We have already told you that when we have any thing to do, we consult together and decide; and when done, so it must be — We have also told you that we do not care . . . whether [the New York Indians] are pleased or not. — We will not do any thing for *them* — We would not take all the money our Great Father has, nor all the good things you have offered, to give the *N.Y. Indians* any more of our Land — You tell us that if we do not agree to do something now by which a settlement will be effected the Treaty will fall to the ground; and we will lose all the advantages secured to us by it — We say, no matter, let it fall to the ground — We will not do any more — We are willing to do what is right — [W]e will do nothing more.[57]

As they did with other negotiations, the Menominee treated this one as sacred, opening the meetings by sharing a pipe through which tobacco was offered to Māēc Awāētok. In the face of Menominee insistence, Governor Porter had no choice but to accede to Menominee demands for a change in the text of the treaty. His instructions had been first to attempt to get the Menominee to agree to the amended treaty, but if that failed he was "to endeavour to procure their assent to the best practicable terms short of those proposed by the Senate."[58] The compromise they reached called for the substitution of two hundred thousand acres of the original five hundred thousand–acre cession to the New York Indians, which allowed the United States to claim two hundred thousand additional acres.

Porter's next task was to get the eastern tribes to agree to the changes, which they first refused to do. Samuel Beall, an attorney acting on behalf of those tribes, attempted to stall the process because its settlement would have ended a lucrative contract that had apparently remained his sole source of income during the dispute between the eastern nations and the Menominee. When Beall was found out by Governor Porter, the leaders of the eastern nations divided, some signing the newly amended agreement. This finally led to the end of the decade-long dispute between the Menominee and the New York Indians.[59]

In the 1831 and 1832 treaties the Menominee also ceded a large portion of land to the United States, as described above. Kaushkannaniew explained the reason for this, pointing out that the Menominee had sold the land east of the river because, although it was their land, the Potawatomis had already sold some of it and were receiving annuities while the Menominee were receiving nothing. He said, "We know what we agreed to. We sold [pointing to the map] all on this side of the River [the East side] and the Lake, because the Potawatomies had already sold a part of our land on the same side and got a heap of money and annuities—and we got none of it. We did not wish any more of our land sold by them, and we agreed to sell it ourselves to our Great Father."[60] They did not necessarily even fully view this treaty as a land cession; it was partially preemptive and partially an attempt to gain some restitution for land already improperly purchased by the United States. In addition, they did not view usufructuary rights as sold.

The 1832 treaty created a compromise that produced what the federal government believed to be "the best practicable terms, short of those proposed by the Senate." The Menominee thus modified the Senate's modification before the 1831 treaty became law.[61] The Menominee had learned difficult lessons in their dealings with the federal government and the New York tribes in the 1820s, but the lessons were well learned. Because of the problems that developed from these experiences, the tribe was willing to have federally appointed "chiefs" deal with the United States, especially since the "chiefs" already had some accepted leadership roles within the tribe. They hired their own interpreters at important proceedings. They began to solve the mysteries of the American belief system. These lessons would be sorely needed in the years to come, as changing economic conditions caused a drastic shift in the political landscape and as a flood of changes swept through Menominee country in the decades immediately following the 1831 and 1832 treaties.

6
"Civilizing" Influences

As the fur trade dwindled, the land rush began; loggers, farmers, and miners flooded into the region west of Lake Michigan and demolished America's frontier in pursuit of a livelihood and a place to live. With them came federal Indian agents and missionaries to mediate between races and cultures and, at least theoretically, to minister to the needs of the Indians whose lands and resources were being usurped and who now had to share their homes with these unwelcome intruders. These outsiders and the things they brought with them proved far more destructive than the fur trade to the Menominee economy and political autonomy and undermined the tribal social structure.

As the Americans displaced Menominees and Ho Chunks from the territory, they resettled the land themselves. This required an official attitude of disregard for tribal sovereignty. In 1830 the population of Michigan Territory numbered thirty-one thousand; in the next decade it grew sixfold.[1] In 1832 Black Hawk was captured and the Ho Chunks "were removed from the Fox River Valley and established north of the Wisconsin" River.[2]

Ironically, one of the most powerful events symbolizing tribal sovereignty occurred in 1830. Oshkosh was put on trial in federal court for killing an Ottawa Indian. Future governor Doty defended Oshkosh for following Indian customary law by killing the man in retaliation for his killing a Menominee. The court recognized that Oshkosh had followed Indian law, and since only Indians were involved it dismissed the case as outside of federal jurisdiction.[3]

Instead of signaling a clear delineation of political separation, however, this event marks the end of an era in which the United States dealt with Menominees as equal powers and the beginning of an era of significant dispossession of Menominee land and resources.

This process began with treaty making. Not only did the Menominee and the territorial or state and federal governments work hard for their own interests in these transactions but so did speculators, loggers, settlers, traders, and missionaries. Federal officials often showed more sympathy to special interest groups than to Indians selling their lands. Treaty negotiations were often complex political contests, and some or all of the parties involved sometimes failed to understand the true meaning and ramifications of them until many years after the actual treaties became federal law.

The Menominee treaties of the 1820s through 1840s purported to convey real estate from the tribe to the federal government or other parties and in effect did so. Treaties are much more than land sales, however; they are also legal statements of tribal rights retained in exchange for the loss of portions of the homeland. Some of these were short-term rights, some longer-term rights. Long-term rights included hunting, fishing, gathering, land use, and education rights, for example. As part of the short-term exchange, the United States agreed to provide annuity goods and services to the Menominee in their homeland to be disbursed by federal agents. These were necessary provisions because the Americans swept across the Old Northwest like an army of locusts, laying waste to the land's resources in their wake.

LOGGING, MILL RIGHTS, AND TREATY PROVISIONS

Lumbermen led the way into Menominee country, cutting trees that built the city of Chicago both physically and as a lumbering center and that provided wood for the fences, farms, and railroads of the westward expansion into the prairie.[4] The entire northern tier of the Lake Michigan shoreline, including significant portions of both Michigan and Wisconsin, provided a valuable target for the loggers. The northern two-thirds of Wisconsin, which included much of Menominee country as well as parts of Ho Chunk, Ojibwe, and Santee country, contained 18 to 20 million acres of north woods forest that had grown in ideal conditions over thousands of years after the glaciers had receded. This magnificent forest stretched across the Upper Great Lakes, extending from New England to Minnesota and northward into Canada. Between 50 and 80 percent of the timber in northern Menominee country was pine, mostly white and Norway, with hardwoods mixed in. Twenty-nine varieties of timber grew there, whereas a smaller area of Menominee country along the Fox River and southward was predominantly maple.[5]

Wisconsin's forest became known as the pinery because initially only pine trees, some of which grew to gargantuan heights, proved profitable to the lumber industry. Pine was ideal for the growing building trade because it provided soft yet sturdy and readily worked wood. Lacking the density of hardwoods like oak and hemlock, pine also floated easily on water and remained the only feasible wood to lumber until the advent of the railroad.[6]

Logging began slowly because until the mid-1830s Indians still held title to much of Wisconsin's land. For the most part in these early years, tribes leased or sold logging or milling rights to non-Indians who agreed to provide the tribe or band with some goods or payment on an annual basis. This was usually done with the sanction of the Office of Indian Affairs, or Indian Department, and the War Department. Although these agreements were often abused by the lessees, the tribes continued to make them, but they insisted that the conditions be honored on both sides.[7]

The Menominee leased mill rights to individuals on the waterways over which the tribe had full claim. In 1827, for instance, Colonel Ebenezer Childs and Judge John Arndt purchased rights from Menominee leaders to build a mill and dam on Menominee land for three barrels of flour a year. The contract had been signed by Arndt and three Menominees in August 1826 and called for a meager fifteen-dollar annual payment. Arndt agreed to provide the tribe with any lumber it needed and to grind any grain Menominees brought him. In exchange, Arndt was permitted to cut the timber necessary to build and run the mill. The site was probably on the small Pensaukee River just south of the Oconto River in ancient Menominee territory.[8]

In 1831 the tribe leased a mill site on the upper Wisconsin River to Daniel Whitney for ten years for $67.50 in annual supplies of flour, tobacco, pipes, and corn. Albert G. Ellis, who more than a decade later would become the Green Bay Indian subagent, Robert Irwin Jr., and Charles Grignon in partnership leased a site at Little Chute on the Fox River between the Bay and Lake Winnebago for eight years in exchange for annual payments of powder, lead, flints, tobacco, pipes, and flour. In both cases the payments were to be made annually in September and the contractors agreed to provide lumber to the tribe or to the U.S. government at a reasonable price.[9]

The traders John Lawe and Louis and Augustin Grignon soon joined the lumber business, signing a lease with eleven Menominee leaders in 1835 for the site of a mill on the Waubunkeesippe, or White Wing River. This was to operate for twelve years "upon the same condition that a Similar grant was made to Powell and Grignon upon Wolf River."[10] The tribe also permitted two men, William Farnsworth and Charles Brush, who both had supplied and provided help for the Indian agent at annuity time, to build and run saw and gristmills on the Menominee River.[11] Other contracts and agreements may have been concluded for rivers such as the Oconto and Peshtigo.

This small-scale logging, though relatively innocuous at first glance, presaged the loggers' successful attempts to reshape the area's economy from the 1840s into the 1900s. The loggers could not begin to do this, however, until the Americans legally and politically redefined the landscape. The Americans did this through land purchase treaties and the stationing of agents in Menominee country. Beginning with Colonel Bowyer the United States had begun to locate agents in Menominee country, although for decades the agents refused to move to Indian land, even when ordered to by their superiors. The agents were required both to fulfill the terms of treaties made with the tribe and to pave the way for further concessions. They drew meager salaries, as did their assistants and employees, and many were on the lookout for ways to supplement their incomes, often at the expense of the tribe. Mismanagement, corruption, and fraud characterized the actions of the agents during most of the years before the Menominee settled on a reservation.

George Boyd, appointed to oversee the Green Bay agency in 1832, was arguably the worst of numerous incompetent or corrupt agents to represent the federal interests in the guise of fulfilling legal responsibilities to the Menominee. A failed businessman and a political hack, Boyd was able to shape and prolong a career largely because he was a brother-in-law to John Quincy Adams and because he served in a bureaucracy with low standards for its employees and little oversight of those living and working far from the center of the government in Washington DC. As his biographer observed, "Remote from the inspection of his superiors and shielded by his ties to the Adams family, Boyd did not have to demonstrate a high degree of competence."[12]

Boyd was described in the *Collections of the State Historical Society of Wisconsin* as "truly one of the government's most faithful employees," whose "integrity bore the scrutiny of various administrative changes during his thirty-five years of official life." This description, however, comes from the husband of Boyd's granddaughter.[13] The slightest glance at the evidence proves otherwise. Boyd used his position to his own, his family's, and his friends' financial advantage, cheating the Menominee time and again. He was the most blatantly corrupt of the prereservation agents to the tribe, several of whom left unsavory records. His record worsened as time passed; he may have begun to lose his faculties. Henry Rowe Schoolcraft, who oversaw some of Boyd's finances for the Office of Indian Affairs, wrote to Commissioner Crawford in December 1840, "The negligence and imbecility of the old gentleman are becoming, every year, more apparent."[14]

As the Green Bay agent, Boyd oversaw the federal assumption

of its responsibility in regard to first the 1831 and 1832 treaties and later the 1836 treaty. With the 1831 treaty the federal government made bold attempts at "civilizing" the Menominee. The civilizing goals are clear from the terms of these treaties. The United States expected the Menominee to become sedentary farmers and to receive a Western-style education. Stambaugh, the treaty negotiator, let the tribe determine where it wanted the public services to be provided. Menominee leaders chose Winnebago Rapids on the Fox River west of Lake Winnebago. Stambaugh viewed the land set aside for the tribe as agricultural.[15]

To begin the actual physical improvements called for in the treaties, the federal government hired farmers along with their wives, even before homes were built for them. Animal shelters were built first; it was not until 1834 that William Dickinson received a contract to build houses and the mill.[16] In 1835 he apparently subcontracted at least part of the work to Daniel Whitney, who for $6,900 agreed to build twenty houses, two farmsteads, two dwellings for traders, two schools, an interpreter's house, and a blacksmith shop. The treaty called for the houses for the Menominee to be built "as soon as the Indians agree to occupy them."[17]

Agent Boyd did not know exactly how to proceed with the farmers. The treaty said they were to be men "of established character and capacity" who would "assist the Menomonee Indians in the cultivation of their farms, and to instruct their children in the business and occupation of farming."[18] At the 1832 treaty negotiations Kaushkannaniew had caustically observed that farmers would be of little help to the Menominee: "these farmers will eat up all the Flour and give the Bran to their Hogs — We never will get any thing of what they raise." Governor Porter responded, "we will not send among you such . . . Farmers as you describe — We will give you honest men."[19]

Kaushkannaniew's prescience proved more accurate than Porter's assurances, however. A contemporary visitor described one of these men of "established character," Nathanial Perry, as a man "who is said to be lazy and who when he wants to have the garden of one of the farms hoed, after waiting a week there doing nothing, made a bee and treated the Indians to whiskey while they hoed a garden on a sunday."[20]

Boyd's real dilemma regarding the Menominee agricultural country, as he called it, was what portion of the work done on the farms should benefit the tribe. If the farmers hired Indians to help with the labor, they would split the grain with the Indians, but he feared the Indians might be unwilling to share this grain with the whites. However, if the farmers cultivated the land alone, they would be unable to raise enough grain to share with the Indians.[21] Boyd apparently did not understand the farmers' role as serving and instructing the Menominee, although he knew that they were being paid with money derived from tribal land sales.

According to one contemporary observer who visited the Menominee agricultural settlement at Winnebago Rapids, houses were built for the farmers while huts were built for the Menominee, who, however, preferred living in their wigwams.[22] Instead they stabled the horses in the new huts or let traders live in them.[23] These houses were not all completed when the tribe signed a new treaty in 1836, selling the land on which they were being constructed.[24]

This method of treaty payment by making physical improvements was inordinately unfair to the Menominee because it was contradictory to the tribe's band system of social organization. The farms, the mills, and the missions were all built on fixed sites. To the extent they benefited the Indians (and many Menominees believed they provided little or no benefit), they benefited only those bands living in the vicinity of the facilities. In fact, several Menominee bands did not remove from their ancient village sites until their removal to the present reservation, so most received nothing of the treaty money earmarked for so-called civilization and improvement.[25]

Even Agent Boyd recognized that the Menominee money spent under the 1831 treaty benefited only those bands that lived in the Green Bay–Lake Winnebago area and those that may have joined them there. The northern bands did not receive these government-provided services. They did not move to the agricultural settlement or send their children to the schools. They received only their share of the annuity cash, $6,000 divided among 2,345 Menominees, or $2.55 apiece each year.[26]

The mills, too, for the most part failed to benefit the tribe. During the 1831 treaty negotiations, Colonel Stambaugh told the Menominee that both gristmills and sawmills would be built with treaty money the following year. Mills were a subject in the 1832 treaty negotiations as well. Kaushkannaniew insisted that the tribe would prefer money for its lands. "We do not want these mills," he told Governor Porter. Kaushkannaniew recognized that the tribe would pay for construction of the mills and also for employment of the carpenters and millwrights. Porter insisted, however, that "your Great Father knows better than you do what will be for your good."

The mills were built, but not for several years. The government delayed construction while Governor Porter, who also served as the superintendent of Indian affairs in Michigan Territory, decided how best the mills could serve not only the Menominee but the Stockbridge, Munsees, Brothertons, and American settlers. The gristmill's location at Winnebago Rapids would benefit all these people but only the southern Menominee; the northern bands lived too far away to use the mill.[27] Menominee needs remained largely unfulfilled; instead, the pattern of non-Menominee people benefiting from the tribe's timber resources continued. The sawmill built on the Fox River with tribal money as part of the Menominee agricultural experiment cut little timber and served primarily to provide economic speculation for white businessmen and politicians after the 1836 treaty.

MISSIONARIES

Missionaries spent tribal money as well, often on people the U.S. government identified as Menominee, using a biological definition, but whom the Menominee considered American, using a cultural definition. More than a hundred years after the Jesuits abandoned the area, by the 1820s and 1830s Christians again began to feel the need to evangelize the Menominee, along with other tribes in the western Great Lakes region. Both Episcopalians and Catholics ministered with some effect among several Menominee bands, converting children and adults, attempting to convert others, conducting church services, and establishing schools for Indian children. These groups vied for Menominee souls and government money.

Before the reservation years, the federal government contracted out its educational responsibilities as established in treaties to religious institutions and oversaw the programs with little intervention or direction from the federal agent. The commissioner of Indian affairs stated the federal philosophy regarding tribal education succinctly in a letter to a man who had written him inquiring about a teaching job: "as a general rule, it is deemed preferable to confide the application of funds provided in treaties for education of Indians, to Some organized Society, and to leave to its managers the employment of instructors."[28] The government did precisely this in the Menominee case, turning over the tribe's education money first to the Episcopal mission in Green Bay and then to Catholic teachers and missionaries, even above the protests of the tribe's leaders, who ironically had been appointed by the federal government to communicate the tribe's needs and interests.[29]

In October 1821, Major John Biddle, the federal Indian agent at Green Bay, suggested to Governor Lewis Cass that a school should be established in Green Bay for the children of "mixed origin." Most of these were children to Menominee women and French men. Biddle thought such a school might have a positive influence on the Indians in the area.[30] Missionaries soon founded two such schools in Green Bay, one Episcopal and one Catholic. The Episcopalians, who had helped negotiate treaties in New York to bring the New York Indians to Menominee and Ho Chunk country, began work among the Oneidas and the Menominee in 1822. Then in 1825 and 1826 they established a mission in Green Bay.[31]

The main work done by Episcopalians among Menominees,

however, began with the arrival of Rev. Richard Fish Cadle in 1829. In 1830 Cadle, together with his sister Sarah B. Cadle, opened a school on land given to the Episcopal Church by the federal government to serve children of Indian blood. By 1831 he had approximately fifty students, nearly all of mixed blood from the Green Bay community. Their parents were apparently part of the nontribal settlement in Green Bay, which consisted largely of families of mixed blood, rather than any Menominee settlements nearby.[32] Cadle's Catholic rival, Father Samuel Mazzuchelli, a Dominican, said with disdain, "Some Indian children of Canadian fathers, and sometimes half a dozen full-blooded Indians were kept at the mission, principally because of the food available there."[33] Cadle charged a reasonable price — thirty dollars a year to those who could afford to pay it and nothing to children of indigent parents. He expected no payment at all from parents of full-blood Indian children.[34] All children had to have some degree of Indian blood to be admitted. He would teach them all reading, writing, arithmetic, and geography. The girls would also learn housekeeping, sewing, knitting, spinning, and weaving skills, and the boys would learn farming.[35]

Cadle's school coalesced well with the plans of the federal government. As part of the 1827 treaty with the Ojibwe, Menominee, and Ho Chunk Indians, the United States had agreed to pay fifteen hundred dollars annually for the education of those tribes and the New York Indians in Wisconsin for "as long as Congress think proper." Cadle's mission received this money in the early 1830s. The mission was, in his words, "designed peculiarly for the benefit of the Menominees." In 1834 the War Department voiced concern that all of this money went to serving the Menominee rather than benefiting the other tribes.[36] Even if this education can be considered a benefit, it did not benefit the Menominee tribe. It benefited a few individual Menominees but for the most part served people of Menominee background who were not considered Menominee by the tribe's bands. The basis of Menominee identity was cultural, not biological, in the tribe's view. The Menominee accepted people of mixed blood, and sometimes with little or no Menominee blood at all, as tribal members if they acted as such, before the federal government forced strict definitions. However, people who did not actively participate in tribal life were not considered Menominee unless they returned. These would include the families of most of Cadle's students.

The education money from the 1831 treaty too went to the Episcopal Church in the early 1830s, probably in part because the federal agents were sympathetic to Reverend Cadle and also because the commissioner of Indian affairs so decided. At the 1831 treaty negotiations, Colonel Stambaugh had urged the Menominee to send their children to Cadle's mission.[37]

Though Stambaugh did not convince the tribe, his cynical reasoning had a chillingly appropriate logic. He told the Menominee that Cadle was correct in telling them that the president wanted "to see your children educated like the children of good white men." He mentioned the large amount of money the treaty would set aside for that purpose and urged the Menominee to take advantage of the opportunity: "How proud the menominies will be when their children can read and write; can calculate the prices of what they eat and wear, of the furs they have to sell, and the powder and ball they have to buy. You will then be able to protect yourselves from being cheated and abused by bad traders who may get into your country, or by faithless agents who unfortunately are sometimes sent to live among the Indians Tribes."[38] In retrospect this was probably the best argument that could have been brought in favor of the tribe sending its children to government-sponsored schools: to learn to cope with unscrupulous government agents and traders.

Meanwhile, the Catholics, like their Episcopalian cohorts, arrived in the Green Bay area in the 1820s, establishing a mission to serve the mixed-blood French and Indian population there. They too established a school for children of mixed blood and Menominee children. They also used this as a base to travel among several bands of Menominee in attempts to convert them.

Father Mazzuchelli was the first Catholic since the Jesuits to preach extensively among the Menominee. His memoirs give us insights into his religious and ethnological beliefs, as well as his methods of conversion and preaching. Mazzuchelli, like the Jesuits before him, worked over a large area of the Upper Great Lakes, only part of which surrounded Green Bay. Like many nineteenth-century Catholic missionaries who served among the Menominee, he hailed from Europe. Mazzuchelli and others like him born in Milan knew the American Midwest as "mission country." After being ordained in 1830 he began his first assignment at Mackinac Island. For the next thirty years he served various parishes of Indians, people of mixed Indian and French blood, and traders and trappers, many of French-Canadian background. His service area included the Menominee until 1835. According to one twentieth-century observer, he "thrived on the competition" with Protestant missionaries on the frontier.[39]

The Episcopal Church won the competition for government funding throughout most of the 1830s, but the Catholics won the competition for Menominee conversions, probably for several reasons. The earlier experience with the Jesuits may have played a minor role, but more important, the tribe's white business associates and allies, who both preyed on the Menominee and aided them, for the most part consisted of French-Canadian Catholics. Mazzuchelli went directly among various bands to proselytize. He reported that the Protestants' stricter rules also harmed their chances at conversion. Protestants required Indians to assess the truth of Scripture before allowing conversion and therefore attempted to convert Indians primarily by distributing Bibles to them. Catholics, on the other hand, only required the abandonment of vice and the belief in doctrine, not an analysis of Scripture.[40]

Father Mazzuchelli first visited Green Bay from his base at Mackinac in the fall of 1830 and returned again in May 1831. He preached daily among the one thousand French Canadians living there, as well as among the Indians, especially Menominees and Ho Chunks. In the fall of 1831 he returned again, this time spending two months instructing and baptizing Menominees, "where the harvest had been so abundant," in his own words. He believed American Indians' intelligence to be as fit for religious instruction as anyone's. Otherwise, he reasoned, the Messiah would not have commanded his Apostles to bring all nations to the Lord. At the same time, he also believed Indians to be in dire need of transformation, since all tribes "lack . . . the sciences, the arts, education, social order, conveniences, luxuries, and whatever else distinguishes a cultured from an uncivilized people." He believed that since Indians in Wisconsin did not live in permanent homes they had not formed societies.[41]

Mazzuchelli believed Indians to be "superstitious rather than flagrantly idolatrous." He knew from confession that they understood morality and recognized good spirits and evil spirits. But because they lacked familiarity with the Gospel, he believed they remained in a state of darkness. He failed to recognize Indian religiosity as anything more than unenlightened superstition, as can be seen in his description of an Indian religious ceremony:

> These [medicine] men are believed to possess superior power exercised by means of equally potent objects, generally nothing more than a snakeskin, a bird's beak, a tortoise shell, the head of a night bird, a root, a piece of wood carved by themselves, the flesh of some animals or the first ripe ears of corn, the people meanwhile dancing around a caldron and chanting during the whole time it is on the fire. After this, they offer part of the contents to the good or bad spirit and then put it back into the caldron. Then they eat all the meat or the sacrificial grain. During this ceremony the medicine man repeats some strange meaningless words as an invocation to the spirit.

Since Indians lacked what Mazzuchelli called human learning, he believed the priest could successfully provide religious instruction: "All the mysteries of faith and the sublime teachings of the Savior seem to shine forth with full splendor in those souls not yet corrupted by the pride of human learning, which without religion has never succeeded in improving the intellectual condition of savage tribes."[42]

With these beliefs providing the basis for his work, Mazzuchelli labored to convert and instruct Menominees, as well as other people living in the area. At Mackinac, Mazzuchelli taught Ojibwes, Ottawas, and Menominees (those who had affiliated with the Mackinac agency rather than those who remained along the shores of Green Bay and Lake Winnebago) to sing in Latin and in "Indian." Since all three tribes spoke Algonquian languages, they could communicate with each other to some extent. Mazzuchelli eventually published a songbook in the "Indian" language, perhaps a mixture of these Algonquian languages.[43]

Mazzuchelli apparently did not speak Menominee. He described how he conducted confession through an interpreter, commenting on the ready availability of mixed-blood people in Green Bay who could serve as interpreters for Menominees. The penitent brought his or her own interpreter to confession. Since mixed-blood people in the Green Bay area tended to be Catholic rather than Protestant, this gave Catholic missionaries unfamiliar with the Menominee language a distinct advantage over their Protestant counterparts.

For the Indian school, Mazzuchelli hired Rosalie Dousman as an instructor in 1831.[44] This was undoubtedly the most propitious decision he made for Catholicism's future among the Menominee. Dousman's fluency in French, English, and Menominee served the Catholic Church well. She and her daughters taught in Menominee schools for the next several decades, providing a greater continuity than the priests would provide. The Dousmans moved where the Catholic bands of the tribe moved after treaty land sales, eventually living on the present reservation. Thus, for priests who did not speak Menominee, these women were able to provide translation and serve as go-betweens. When malicious or merely incompetent priests served among the Menominee, the Dousmans served as buffers, gaining the admiration of many Menominees as well as U.S. government officials.

In the winter of 1833 the bishop sent Father Mazzuchelli to live in Green Bay, assigning Mackinac to another priest. Mazzuchelli served Green Bay's French-Canadian settlers that winter but recognized his major assignment to be to the Menominee. Mazzuchelli found that the ritual and ornamentation of the Catholic Church attracted the Menominee, and he believed it helped convince them of Catholicism's spirituality. Feast days proved extremely popular, commonly attracting up to two hundred Indians. Of course, feasting had long been an important part of Menominee spiritual and social life. Mazzuchelli estimated that by January 1834 over six hundred Menominee had been baptized by himself and two Redemptorist predecessors, one of them probably the Reverend Samuel or Simon Senderl.[45]

Mazzuchelli's key to success lay in his method of conversion. While Christian Indians attended church, which when he traveled often consisted of a rapidly built and disbanded Menominee bark house, "pagan" Indians had to be converted in their own huts by the missionary. "In truth it is not the lost sheep that runs after the shepherd, but rather the shepherd who runs hither and yon in search of the lost sheep to bring it back to the fold." The best times to do this were in those seasons when Menominees lived near the mission: in the winter when several bands lived near the shores of Green Bay or Lake Winnebago, where they fished through the ice; in sugar-making season when the bands camped out at their favorite sugar bush; and in farming season when the agriculturally oriented bands brought in their crops. During hunting season the bands moved from place to place in search of game, so proselytizing then was too difficult.[46] As a consequence, Mazzuchelli's successes, and in the long run those of the Catholics, though significant, remained limited primarily to southern bands that made their homes in the earliest ceded lands and included less than a majority of the tribe. Mazzuchelli did not visit Menominee bands that lived in areas other than the vicinity of Green Bay, such as Shawano Lake or Prairie du Chien.

Mazzuchelli traveled by sleigh to the winter fishing sites, going from hut to hut with an interpreter, where he "sowed the seeds of conversion." In one case, he found a woman and her four children on the verge of starvation, and "without delay the basket of provisions for the journey was opened and the poor woman and her children made to eat all its contents." The next Easter, in 1834, she and her children and her formerly intemperate husband all came to the church in Green Bay to be baptized.[47]

But most conversions occurred less dramatically. The priest and interpreter explained Christianity as the one true religion that "gives true consolation in this world." They also told the potential converts that Christianity's ultimate goal was to allow the Christian "to enjoy after death the companionship of the Great and Good Spirit to whom they sometimes offered sacrifices." He added that the Christian religion overpowered the malevolent spirits that the Menominee referred to as demons.[48] In this way, Father Mazzuchelli presented Catholicism as a logical extension of their own religion rather than in contradistinction to it. Although he viewed their religion as nothing more than superstition, he acknowledged their understanding of morality, which was more similar to his understanding than were their religious practices. He insisted only that they did not understand God well enough, and he implied that they could gain God's favor more readily by converting to Christianity.

In most cases conversions did not happen immediately. Instead, those Menominees interested in the priest's message would, after a period of weeks or months of consideration, approach Christian Menominees, who would teach them the catechism and prayers. Only after this would they "present themselves for baptism." Father Mazzuchelli was astute and honest enough to observe that "The Christian Indians were actually better adapted to making converts and more resourceful than the Missionary himself." In one case, at the winter fishing village at Lake Winnebago, a zealous convert took over Mazzuchelli's proselytory argument to a number of Menominees. The argument lasted all night, as the Christian responded to numerous challenges to his religion. Father Mazzuchelli fell asleep during the argument. Two months later, from this visit, fifty Menominees presented themselves for baptism.[49]

Father Mazzuchelli, though he did not respect their religion, respected the Menominee as people. He converted Menominees out of concern for their souls. Many of his converts came from among those who disdained traders because of the brandy they plied or from among those who gave up alcohol to improve their lot in life. Father Mazzuchelli's compassion and his low-profile approach helped him in his attempts to convert Menominees. That he did not seek to gain anything himself or to exploit the people he visited also caused comment from Menominees, even those who apparently never converted.[50]

Another reason for Mazzuchelli's successes could well have been the sometimes overwhelming forces bearing down on Menominee society. The destruction of their resources and initial sales of their lands, both of which induced malnourishment and starvation, were compounded in 1834 and 1835 when epidemic disease again coursed through Menominee society. Both cholera and smallpox struck the tribe in those years and struck it hard. As much as one-fourth to one-third of the Menominee population died from these diseases, once again — as in the 1600s and 1700s — striking at the weak, ravaging the sense and structure of family and community, and causing survivors to seek desperately for answers.[51]

Although his figure of six hundred Menominee converts (which would represent nearly one-fourth of the tribe at the time) may be an exaggerated number, Father Mazzuchelli indeed sowed the seed for Catholicism among several Menominee bands.[52] His aggressive yet at the same time almost passive style, in which he argued his beliefs only long enough to pique the interest of potential converts, who then learned more about the religion from fellow Menominees, led to his successes. His choice of Rosalie Dousman as schoolteacher added to the initiative that brought a large portion of the Menominee to the path that led to Catholicism.

Nonetheless, despite these factors, the majority of Menominees continued to follow their traditional spiritual ways. Nearly all of those who became Christians were Catholic. Still, tribal monies dispensed by federal officials went to support the Episcopal, not the Catholic, mission school.

Tribal leaders well knew that missionary efforts, as well as the agricultural efforts of federal officials, were paid for by the Menominee. They recognized that money from the government was not a gift but a partial payment to the tribe for lands sold. After Governor Cass's appointment of Oshkosh and Josette Carron and after Governor Porter's appointment of Aiometah as officially sanctioned tribal representatives to the federal government, these leaders regularly and with effect attempted to hold federal officials responsible for their treaty-based obligations. If the U.S. government hoped to more easily control the tribe through these appointees, it failed. The appointed chiefs acted in the tribe's interests, at times earning the wrath of federal officials but helping to ensure Menominee survival on tribal terms. Agent Boyd complained of this very problem, saying at one point that because of Oshkosh's "very exceptionable conduct . . . I would respectfully recommend that He be removed from his situation as first Chief of these people, and that another be appointed in his stead." Boyd noted that Oshkosh "always *boasted* that he is not the Chief of the U. States Government, *but the Chief of the Traders*." Aiometah, too, needed replacing, Boyd recommended.[53]

At an 1834 meeting between several Menominee leaders and Agent Boyd, at which the Menominee were trying to make arrangements for a typically late federal annuity payment, Oshkosh brought up the subject of money for the school. According to Boyd, Oshkosh said, "if any portion of this money be paid to the Mission here, he would employ a lawyer, or as the Indian language expresses it, a Judge to go to Washington immediately, and protest against such proceedings, to the President." Oshkosh meant the Episcopal mission, the mission to the Menominee that received tribal money at the direction of Commissioner of Indian Affairs

Elbert Herring. Boyd reported to Secretary of War Lewis Cass that he had threatened Oshkosh "that if he dared to consult with a white man, touching the distribution of the fund set apart for the Mission here, by your authority and direction, that I should immediately report him thro' you, Sir, to his Great Father the President of the United States with an earnest request that he should be degraded from the rank which he at present so unworthily holds in the Menominee Nation."[54]

Boyd ignored the real issue: how Menominee money was spent and to what extent it benefited the tribe. Those Menominees who did not take up farming, who did not send the children to the mission schools, or who did not move into the houses saw the money from the sale of their land spent on these "improvements" anyhow and had no recourse.

Though Boyd was probably frustrated by the actions of the commissioner of Indian affairs as well as tribal objections and requests, he chose to blame tribal leaders rather than his superior for the ensuing problems. He especially blamed Oshkosh as head chief. Boyd was wrong about Oshkosh's allegiance being to the traders but was correct in his assessment that Oshkosh opposed federal plans. Oshkosh counted on the Catholic French-Canadian and other Bay area traders for advice, used them as interpreters in official councils, and in turn gave them business, but he acted in the tribe's, not the traders', interests.

A month later Boyd wrote to Commissioner Herring in a letter that indicates that the issue had not yet been resolved but that the government still favored the Episcopal mission. He asked how he should respond to the tribe's request that a portion of its education funding be given to the Catholic Church, which received nothing. The federal orders set aside no money for the tribe's priest, Father Mazzuchelli.[55] Mazzuchelli, in his memoirs, angrily discussed this circumstance, blaming Agent Boyd rather than the government in general, which he said "protects the rights of individuals, whatever their religion." Mazzuchelli could not understand why the Catholics did not receive the Menominee education money from the government. He claimed the tribe in council had requested it be disbursed that way. He needed that money to pay for buildings he had erected for the congregation. Mazzuchelli said that Boyd, "against the express will of the Indians, chose to give that annual sum to the Protestants of the Anglican sect." Not a single Menominee had converted to the Episcopal sect, Mazzuchelli claimed. "The agent himself, the Anglican minister, and all the Protestants in the neighborhood were witnesses that the Menominee had not become Protestants but Catholics; on each Sunday morning everyone saw them going to the Catholic church, not to the sectarian meetings."[56]

Agent Boyd, however, noted that the Menominee rejected the bill submitted by Mazzuchelli, totaling $1,083, for services rendered from 1831 through 1834 and for building materials. "The whole Chiefs of the Menomonee Nation of Indians assembled in Council say that they know nothing about the within paper, and refuse to pay this account," Boyd wrote of the bill.[57] No mention is made of how he presented this bill to council, so we have no way of knowing whether the tribe was rejecting *all* religious payments at the time or whether it was rejecting *further* payments beyond those stipulated in treaties. Boyd had already distributed the latter to the Episcopal mission, which the tribe had protested. Boyd wondered, though, whether it wouldn't be judicious to send some of the education money to the Catholics if enough Menominee children attended their schools.[58]

The Christian battles for both treaty money and Menominee souls throughout the 1830s and 1840s displeased tribal leaders, who thus voiced disapproval of the federal support of the Episcopal mission and school with tribal money. That support, however, was all that kept the mission open. The other Episcopal missions in the Northwest served children of white community members, so this was the only one actively serving Indians, whom the Episcopalians considered especially heathen and therefore needful of salvation. One Episcopal visitor to the area, Rev. Jackson Kemper, voiced his church's hopes and fears regarding the Green Bay mission:

If we give up this school we not only afford a triumph to its enemies the traders and the R[oman] C[atholics] but we abandon a station of great importance. Is it nothing to have rescued more than 200 ch[ildren] from degradation and vice and ignorance and death — to teach them the arts and feelings of civilized life and the principles of the Gospel? * * * Many of these chld are real Inds born in our ch, but who wld be ignorant of knowledge and our language were it not for this school. And many born heathen exhibit by their conduct and writings an evidence of the Gospel upon their souls. Here, in this mission the Ch is exerting herself and has an opportunity of doing good to heathen. If we give up this, we abandon the only post we have among the heathen.[59]

Despite these statements of support from church officialdom, and despite financial support from the federal government, this post lacked the future for which Kemper had hoped. It also lacked the numbers of which Kemper bragged. In 1833 Reverend Cadle had pleaded with Governor Porter to encourage the Menominee to send their children to his school, but this apparently helped enroll few or none at all.[60] In 1834 Agent Boyd reported the school would serve to educate six children, only two of them Menominee.[61]

The Protestant failure had several causes. First, Reverend Cadle needed an interpreter to teach the children, which the agent requested the commissioner of Indian affairs appoint, but he never got one.[62] He could hope for but little success without effective communication. In addition, parents withdrew their children after some of Cadle's instructors whipped several children, forcing them into the hospital, and then humiliated them by cutting off their hair for offenses deemed minor. Corporal punishment of children was unheard of in the Menominee world. These actions also hit the Green Bay press, and public outcry rose further when pamphleteers published tracts denouncing each other over the issue.[63] Fiscal shortages were another problem; Cadle worked without pay for over two years before he retired in 1834. But observers also said he

was unfit for the job, being too sensitive to deal with hard-edged
and usurious traders and businessmen.[64]

After Kemper's visit Cadle finally resigned. The Reverend Henry
Gregory, assigned to a site on the Fox River south of the town
of Green Bay, arrived as Cadle's replacement in January 1836,
where he found that no house had been provided for him.[65] He
also did not speak Menominee or any Algonquian language. He
too wrote to the commissioner of Indian affairs requesting an
interpreter for the school. In November 1836, the commissioner
informed Gregory that the government would not provide one:
"All applications heretofore made for allowance for interpreters to
Indian Schools having been refused, I am constrained to decline
complying with your suggestion on the subject." Gregory apparently reported directly to the commissioner of Indian affairs rather
than to a religious board.[66] The house Gregory had been promised
was probably never built, because in 1836 the Menominee sold the
land on which he had established himself. In May 1837, citing the
litany of problems he had faced, Gregory wrote the commissioner
of Indian affairs to resign from his post. These reasons included
the failure of the government, probably in the person of Agent
Boyd, to pay Gregory's salary since June 1836.[67]

After the 1837 annuity payment, the Menominee rejected their
education money altogether over anger at the Episcopal mission. Writing to the commissioner of Indian affairs, Boyd blamed
Oshkosh and Aiometah. Aiometah's action especially angered Boyd:
"He is entirely under the direction of the Catholic-Priests — and
has done more than any hundred other men of his Nation to defeat
the intentions of the Government, in relation to every thing like
education, farming, andc. for the benefit of their Nation." The
government provided the treaty money to the Episcopal mission
again that year to counteract what the commissioner referred to as
the unwise judgment of the tribe.[68]

One of Gregory's successors, Solomon Davis, expressed a concern for the state of Menominee culture similar to that of Reverend Kemper. Davis saw no value in the way Menominees lived.

To him, the Menominee way of life needed changing, purpose enough for missionary efforts. He complained that the boarding schools currently used were inappropriate because 90 percent of Indian children returned home "to that indolence of mind and body which is characteristic of the Indian, and which totally unfits them for usefulness."[69] So although the school taught farming and attempted to "civilize" Indian children in white terms, the attempts ultimately failed. The changes he hoped for could not be achieved in Green Bay. Davis proposed that, to be successful, the Episcopal Church needed to take its mission to tribal land and work directly among the Indians rather than expecting the Menominee to come to Green Bay. It never happened. Interestingly, Cadle had made this same suggestion seven years earlier, in 1834, but could not do so since the location of the school had been decided upon by the church's executive committee.[70]

The number of children served in the school ultimately changed little during these years. An 1836 report showed thirty-two of seventy-two students to be Menominee.[71] But by 1841 a mere ten Menominee children, all from three families, attended the school, which the minister intended to close "as soon as existing obligations will allow this desirable measure to be carried into effect."[72] The Menominee as a whole simply saw no reason to send their children to the Protestant school.

Meanwhile, Father Mazzuchelli's successor, Father Theodore Van den Broek, a Dominican from the Netherlands, served among the Menominee from 1832 until 1846 but with far less success than Mazzuchelli. Van den Broek served initially in Green Bay, then at Little Chute on the Fox River, areas peripheral to Menominee country by the time he served there. Few Menominees lived around Green Bay by 1832, and he built his mission at Little Chute on land ceded in the 1831 and 1836 treaties. Some Menominees lived in the area and many traveled through it.

Van den Broek apparently moved to the site on the Fox River after Fathers Mazzuchelli and Senderl left the area. In December 1835, he reported arriving at the old Protestant mission house

(probably built with government funds in the agricultural settlement created by the 1831 treaty). Immediately on his arrival,
Menominees living at Butte des Morts (down the Fox River and
west across Lake Winnebago) sent him a woman to do domestic
work. Upon Van den Broek's request, Louis Grignon sent his
daughter Margarith as an interpreter. "[B]eing in the midst of
the savages," Van den Broek lamented in the letter of request to
Grignon, "I can not talk with them at all."[73]

Soon, he reported, as many as forty Menominees came to lodge
with him for a time. He fed them, "and all were entirely satisfied.
Every morning and evening, they sang canticles, and prayed for an
hour with the Rosary, etc." This welcome by the Catholic Menominees pleased Van den Broek. He quickly established a school. He
expressed special satisfaction that, whenever the Congregationalist
minister Cutting Marsh visited, he viewed Van den Broek's crowd
of Menominees with jealousy, as he had hoped to convert some to
the Congregationalist Church.[74]

Even at this time, however, most of the Menominees who lived
in the Lake Winnebago area lived a good distance south and west
of Van den Broek's mission. The following September the tribe
ceded the rest of the land north of Lake Winnebago along the Fox
River. Despite Van den Broek's reported delight at the size of his
flock, he seems to have served only a small number of Catholic
Menominees on a regular basis.

The failure of the U.S. government to control the "chiefs" it
appointed highlights the political sophistication being developed
by the tribe, evident since Sekatsokemau's welcoming of the British.
Oshkosh was not the only Menominee leader the federal agents
denounced, but when the tribe had grievances about unfulfilled
treaties or agreements Oshkosh led the delegation, demanding
redress either from the agent or the territorial governor.[75]

The tribe recognized Oshkosh's leadership, but band leaders
also played important decision-making roles. When any of the
tribe's leaders made decisions without consulting the tribe as a

whole, the younger men and other tribal members demanded accountability. Nonetheless, when the federal government conducted treaty negotiations with the Menominee, as it did in 1831, 1832, 1836, and 1848, it looked to Oshkosh as the Menominee's "Principal Chief." Oshkosh was the first in this new position of authority defined partially by outsiders and partially by the tribe. He did not always succeed in handling or meeting the demands he received from both sides, but his greatest accomplishment was in defining the role as one of active advocacy of tribal rights in the face of unimaginable outside pressure. This skill would be invaluable during the coming months when the United States began the two decade–long attempt to remove the Menominee entirely from their homeland. This attempt would be reinforced by the power of an increasing American presence that coincided with the dissolution of the Menominee tribal economy.

7

A Dissolving
Tribal Economy

A rapid growth in Wisconsin's white population precipitated the 1836 treaty. In 1834 the federal government opened a land office in Green Bay, but Americans were buying land earlier than that from French habitants, some of whom had bought it from the Menominee.[1] By 1836, as Michigan attained statehood and Wisconsin became a separate territory, Governor Henry Dodge of Wisconsin sought to extinguish all Indian title within the territory's lands.

In the summer of 1835 Agent Boyd had anticipated this action, writing to Commissioner of Indian Affairs Elbert Herring that "the great body of the [Menominee] Nation are utterly indisposed to benefit by the expenditure of money in Mills and Farmers in the ground assigned to them for agricultural purposes by the treaty." He believed, therefore, judging "from what has escaped them and their traders lately," that the tribe would be "prepared . . . to sell the residue of their lands." Although Shoneon, Oshkosh, and Aiometah had never expressed such desire, Boyd went on to tell the commissioner what he had already told the secretary of war, "that as an agent for the Government, and a friend to the Menominee, I would advise them to sell the whole of their lands in Ouisconsin territory, and join their red Brethren in the far West."[2]

The Menominee had no such desire. They did offer their houses, built at the agricultural settlement created in the 1831 treaty, for sale to the American speculator Charles Brush, however. Agent Boyd decided that this offered an opportunity to purchase a sizeable quantity of land and broached the subject at the annuity payment on 13 October 1835.[3]

Shoneon, known to the Americans as Silver, did most of the speaking for the Menominee on this occasion, since Kaushkan-naniew had passed away about a year earlier. Oshkosh and Aiometah verified that his statement accurately reflected tribal consensus. He explained that "the reason why we are dissatisfied . . . is because so much [money] is taken to build their houses" at the agricultural settlement. "[W]e have concluded to sell our Great Father another portion of our lands including those houses," he said, adding, "when the Commissioners appointed by our Great Father shall arrive we will point out the Lands we wish to sell."[4]

A note appended to the text of the speeches indicates that at some point a statement was made indicating that the tribe would part with approximately 280,000 acres of land, extending as far north as the mouth of the Wolf River, upstream from the present reservation. No Menominees mentioned this in their speeches, however. Nonetheless, Boyd wrote to Commissioner Herring that the tribe was willing to part with four to five hundred thousand acres, but if the government sent a commissioner a larger amount of land could easily be procured.[5]

In March 1836, Boyd presented Herring with a treaty proposal that spelled out the anticipated costs. In this proposal he assumed the Menominee would not sell all of their land. He estimated that a purchase would cost the United States $330,000, basing the format of the proposed treaty on that of 1831. He ignored the tribe's dissatisfaction with the agricultural settlement plan and proposed instead to expand it, suggesting the creation of mini-agricultural settlements at five separate sites that would be more accessible to all the tribe's bands. Each would have fifty houses, a farmer for ten years, and supplies of corn and cattle for ten years. Besides this, he would include a small annuity of $750 a year to be divided among the entire tribe, which would amount to less than thirty cents per person, and $15,000 of clothing, guns, powder, and tobacco to be divided annually among the tribe, again for ten years.[6]

That summer Governor Dodge, appointed by the War Department as treaty commissioner to purchase Menominee lands, came to Green Bay, where he met with Menominee leaders in council at Cedar Point on the Fox River from 29 August through 3 September 1836. In his opening talk, he proposed both the "purchase [of] the country you now occupy and your removal west of the Mississippi and south of the Missouri rivers." He extolled the virtues of the new country and played his trump hand, the clause in the 1831 treaty allowing the president to purchase Menominee land at federal will.[7] Samuel Stambaugh, the U.S. negotiator in 1831, had inserted that clause to facilitate removal of other eastern Indians into Menominee country.[8] Now the United States wanted the land for the growing white population.

Oshkosh simply greeted Dodge and replied that he would return the next day to discuss the issue. That night the Menominee leaders met. The next day in council Oshkosh told Dodge that this was the first the Menominee knew of the agreement to give up the rest of their land. Aiometah also spoke out. He had become increasingly upset about duplicitous dealings in relation to the treaties. At a council two years earlier he had reacted in astonishment to a discussion of the contents of the treaty by saying, "I don't understand this. When at Washington, the same person put down everything we said. Some of it must have been rubbed out." Now he and other leaders who had participated in the 1831 treaty negotiations in Washington DC said they had been unaware of this stipulation.[9]

Oshkosh said to Dodge, "we always thought that we owned the land that we occupied, but yesterday we heard that our Great Father had a right to take it when he wanted it; we did not so understand the treaty." Aiometah added, "it was understood by us that our land on the east side of Fox river we ceded to our Great Father and no more, nor did we bind ourselves to our Great Father that he should purchase the balance of our land on west side when he should require it." Furthermore, he added, "our Great Father told us at Washington that the balance of our land on the west side of Fox river should . . . be ours as long as we should live."[10]

At this point, Oshkosh broke off the council so he could consult with the rest of the Menominee nation. Later, Oshkosh explained to Dodge why he had to consult with his nation before making decisions: "Our Father [the governor] knows that we are not like him, prepared to give an answer upon business without consulting among ourselves."[11]

When he returned to council on 31 August, Oshkosh offered on behalf of the Menominee to sell over 4 million acres to the United States, one-third to one-half of the tribe's remaining land, for a total consideration of over $770,000. The sale included all of the tribe's northern lands from the Wolf River east to Green Bay, all the way north to the Bay de Noque in Michigan's Upper Peninsula, as well as land east of Lake Poygan from the Wolf to the Fox and a forty-eight-mile-long stretch of valuable land three miles wide on both sides of the Wisconsin River from Point Bas northward (see map 4).[12]

This swath of land along the Wisconsin River was heavily timbered with pine. According to Subagent Ellis the cession was gained "specially to open the country to lumbermen," and according to a later historian, "its acquisition was evidently a clever bit of 'dollar diplomacy.' "[13] Mills were built rapidly; by 1848 there were 24 mills, and by 1857 there were 107 mills operating to feed the Mississippi River lumber trade.[14]

This purchase was much larger than even Boyd had dared hope for after the discussion at the 1835 annuity payout. All the land to which the tribe still held title lay west of the Wolf River. The Menominee had asked for over 2 million dollars as compensation, close to fifty cents per acre; Governor Dodge as treaty commissioner had offered the tribe money, goods, and services totaling $692,110, then added another $80,000.[15] This included $76,000 for the improvements made under the 1831 treaty. Oshkosh requested payment of this money immediately so that the tribe could purchase provisions and other necessaries; instead, the government invested it.

The suddenness and extent of the sale must have shocked the

tribe. This treaty angered many Menominees, especially the northern bands whose lands were sold. Gen. George M. Brooke, the acting Green Bay agent for a few months, suggested immediate removal of the tribe from ceded lands. "To permit them to remain," he wrote to the commissioner of Indian affairs, "would ensure additional trouble and difficulty, when the time arrived for their departure."[16] They did not leave, however, because they were still there in official records in the late 1830s and throughout the 1840s, and several of the bands removed from that area as late as 1852. Indeed, some Menominees never left, and their descendants still live in the Menominee-Marinette area.[17]

In 1838 the leader of the Oconto River band, which had not yet left its land, protested to Governor Dodge that he did not realize the land on the Oconto and Menominee Rivers had been sold in the 1836 treaty. But when Subagent Boyd reminded him that he was there when it occurred, he made no response.[18] Boyd wrote to Governor Dodge, "where the bands living in the vicinity of Green Bay, Oconto, Menominee River &c. will locate themselves it is out of the question to imagine."[19] Census and annuity records from 1842, 1843, 1846, and 1849 indicate villages at the Menominee, Oconto, and Peshtigo Rivers.[20]

Those Menominees who eventually severed their affiliation with the tribe to remain on their ancestral birthright blamed Oshkosh and Carron for the 1836 treaty, which had ceded *their* homelands but not those of Oshkosh or Carron, who lived near Lake Poygan with the southern bands.[21] Bitterness over the loss remained throughout the generations. John Satterlee, a tribal member who in 1933 gathered information from elders whose families broke official ties with the tribe to remain in the Menominee-Marinette area, wrote in his field notes, "But Alas the Ancestors Lost this Place from two other Menomini *Guilty Chieves* of Which Old 'Oscuss' and Chief Carron had Sold that Part or Portion of the Reservation with Menomini River to W. [white] People."[22] Although Oshkosh served as the tribe's principal negotiator, twenty-four Menominees signed the treaty on 3 September, including leaders not only from the southern bands but from the Green Bay, Oconto River, and Menominee River bands, all of whom lived on the ceded lands.[23]

ECONOMIC HARDSHIP

Of the money the Menominee received from the 1836 treaty, the United States set aside $99,710.50 to pay debts owed to traders.[24] Oshkosh had presented the traders' claims totaling $186,421 on 1 September, an amazing increase.[25] As recently as the 1834 annuity payment, traders, together with citizens complaining of depredations, claimed but little more than $5,000 against the Menominee, all of which the tribe's leaders disallowed.[26] But the federal government had begun to allow traders to press claims during treaties in 1825, largely to gain support of the traders for extinguishing Indian title to lands. The policy became fairly regular by 1831. However, the treaty commissioners in several treaties simply halved any claims presented, under the assumption that most were inflated and some untenable.[27] In the 1836 treaty, Governor Dodge proposed cutting all the claims in half, and the final, Senate-approved document halved thirty-two of the claims, allowing the other two in full.[28] The amount allowed totaled nearly 13 percent of the treaty money paid out, or the price for over half a million acres of land. The bulk of the debt money went to old established Green Bay traders.[29]

The traders had accumulated these claims by offering credit to individual Menominees for goods advanced and then collecting on many of these advances at annuity time, to such a degree that in 1834 the tribe requested the next annual payment to be made in goods rather than in money. Oshkosh made the request on behalf of the tribe at the 1834 annuity payment held 25 November. Aiometah supported Oshkosh, telling Agent Boyd, "listen to me. You see that our Great Father has sent us money—and you see how the white people at the Bay take it from us."[30] The federal government, by accepting responsibility to pay the money from tribal funds, made it a tribal rather than an individual obligation. This windfall for the traders came just at the time of the fur trade's decline in the area.

Meanwhile, annuity payments provided traders an additional boon. They could continue offering credit to individual Menominees, knowing that twenty thousand dollars in cash would be distributed among tribal members once a year. The traders attended annuity payments, ready to collect these debts and with goods for sale to get hold of the rest of the money. But the annuity also offered traders and others another way to make money: by providing goods or services. The contracts for providing the goods proved so lucrative that the agents sometimes postponed payments so that their friends could fulfill these contracts.

The 1836 treaty, for example, besides the $20,000 annuity, set aside $500 for farming equipment and cattle and provided for the hiring of two blacksmiths and the annual supply of $3000 of provisions. In addition, the tribe would receive two thousand pounds of tobacco and thirty barrels of salt every year. The annuity was to be provided for twenty years. In 1843 it worked out to $10.35 per share; in 1854 it was $9.75.[31] The $80,000 add-on was paid to the tribe's mixed-blood relatives in exchange for the forty-eight-mile stretch of land along the Wisconsin River. Many of those people were traders as well.

Annuity funds also paid for transportation of the goods to the pay grounds and for transportation and board of the agent, his staff, and guests, as well as military protection. Consideration of all these costs decreased the price the Menominee received for their land even further, while it enriched those fortunate enough to gain the contracts. And whiskey traders plied their goods immediately before and after the agent's departure from the grounds.[32]

An article published in the *Watertown Chronicle* reported that three hundred traders, "black-legs," and spectators attended the 1847 payout. Before the distribution of the cash, they bartered their goods for skins and furs. After the payment, whiskey mixed with Wolf River water sold for ten pounds of pork to the pint, or for $147 a barrel. This mix of whiskey and river water was such that "the Indians . . . got drunk and sober on the same drink," the paper wryly observed. More to the point, the traders got hold of both the money and the goods from the annuity payments.[33]

The money the tribe lost to the traders was part of a larger problem for the Menominee: the sale of a significant portion of their homeland destroyed the tribal economy. As white settlers cleared those lands, traditional Menominee food sources diminished.[34] The money and annuities the tribe received from its land were supposed to help tribal members support themselves by replacing severely diminished resources. The tribe lost important economic resources not only through crooked traders and agents but also through the annuity payment process, and even for the simple reason that federal policy worked slowly. All of this only compounded the problems caused by loss of the land base.

The 1836 treaty called for the annual payment to take place at the lower end of Lake Winneconne, "or at such other place as may be designated by the President of the United States . . . in the month of June or July, or as soon thereafter as the account shall be received."[35] The Menominee therefore expected the payments well in advance of the fall harvest of crops and rice and of the fall hunt. The funds were rarely released before September, however, and the payments were rarely made before October or November, which itself caused serious hardships for the tribe.

Since the bands still lived scattered through a large portion of the territory, to receive annuities they had to gather from distances ranging from the Menominee River to Lake Winnebago and Lake Poygan to the Wolf River. Because the date of the payment was rarely known far in advance, tribal members were left in limbo for nearly half of every year, debating whether to go to winter hunting grounds or to await payment. This caused disruption of both harvests and hunts as they waited with increased impatience.

The loss of productivity was compounded by the harsh weather attendant with the late payments. In 1837, for example, James Madison Boyd, the agent's son and official interpreter, reported that ice had begun to form on the Fox River as officials ascended it on the journey to the pay ground. "In order to get the boats over the rapids at Kaukauna it was necessary for the men to wade in the icey water." They refused to continue once they reached the Grand Chute, just north of Lake Winnebago. So they camped there and sent runners, probably Indian runners paid with a plug of tobacco, to tell the Menominee to come to them.[36] The bands from Green Bay north to the Menominee River, as well as the Little Chute band, having passed this place on their way to the pay grounds, now had to return (see map 5). This incident caused another delay, putting the tribe rather than the federal government through further hardship.

That same year, the federal treasury, in the midst of a national fiscal crisis (the Panic of 1837), ran short of funds. As a result, the War Department decided that part of the annuity money should be paid out in goods rather than in cash. The Menominee charged that they lost forty-five hundred dollars because the traders overpriced the goods and the government failed to provide proper oversight. A federal investigation found that on delivery in New York the goods were all there, but it could not determine if the tribe had been cheated. A common problem in annuity payments was theft of goods in transit. In 1839 Governor Dodge wrote to Commissioner of Indian Affairs Crawford, "a fair remuneration for . . . the over-charge in the goods delivered them [the Menominee] in 1837, in line of the specie payment, would seem just and proper." As late as 1845 the Menominee still sought fair reparations for this payment, which the War Department steadfastly refused to grant.[37]

Although the War Department had instructed the agents to substitute goods for cash only if the tribes agreed, Boyd apparently forced the Menominee to accept goods against their wishes. The Menominee refused in council in the fall of 1837 to accept all of the goods and signed a resolution in February 1838 requesting their payment instead in silver.[38] A year later, an acquaintance of Boyd reported how Boyd explained the matter: "the savages wished to compel their agent to make the distribution of funds on a differ-

Map 5. Wisconsin

ent basis from that for which he had received instructions from Washington." When he "refused their demand and the payment took place according to the agent's ideas," the Menominee were angered. Boyd claimed that most of the Menominees who charged his tent "with the intention of killing him" had been drunk; drunk or not, they were certainly angry. After escaping into the woods, Boyd "was obliged to climb a tree and pass therein the greater part of the night" in the hope of escaping detection.[39]

Little wonder the Menominee were upset, though this was not all they had to be upset about. Perhaps taking after his father, James Madison Boyd too displayed an authoritarian disregard for tribal interests when afforded the opportunity. He reports that he was twenty-one years old at the time of the 1837 annuity, when he mediated in a drunken brawl in which a Menominee man killed two women and injured another, who died later. Boyd grabbed his hickory cane, chased the man down, beat him into submission, and hauled him back to the government campsite, where he tied him up. Here Boyd requested assistance so the man could be guarded long enough to take him to Green Bay to try him for murder. The Menominee wanted him to face tribal justice. Boyd whacked some more Menominees, the friends and family of the women, in his attempt to guard the prisoner, but when no agency officials came to his aid, he finally turned the man over to the tribe. Young Boyd later threw a Potawatomi man in the fire when he came to confront Boyd for taking the captive. His father told James, "you must stop knocking these indians around this way, it wont do, the first thing you know you will get killed yourself." James admitted that he was young and "rather impetuous" at the time.[40] Whether or not this ruffian was the type of frontier character likely to gain a spot on the government's payroll under the spoils system, he served as interpreter, the point man to explain U.S. policy to the Menominee nation. This violent intercession in a domestic Menominee situation far exceeded his official bounds.

The annuities proved costly to the tribe in other ways also.

Most white residents of the area had little contact with Indians; however, annuity payments and council meetings, which brought the tribe together, also attracted white visitors. The agent or sub-agent provided a public table for such visitors at the tribe's expense. As early as the 1831 treaty negotiations, as part of a common practice, all Green Bay citizens were invited to attend.[41] Governor Doty recommended this practice be stopped in 1841, writing to the commissioner of Indian affairs, "If the Sub-Agent resided in the country of the Munnomonees, as is required of him by the Regulations, there would be no occasion or excuse for many of these [financial] charges."[42]

In 1838, Gustave de Neveu, a transplanted Frenchman, attended the annuity payout. According to him, this was the first payment actually made at Lake Winneconne, though it was again made in October. The "larger portion" of the Menominee chiefs were already drunk by the time the payout was to begin, so Sub-agent Boyd postponed the payment for a day while he and fifty soldiers destroyed as much whiskey as possible.

The payment included the delivery of twenty "fat beeves," that is, cattle or oxen. As soon as news came of the animals' arrival, the Menominee gathered their weapons and chased them down, slaughtering and skinning them on the spot and dividing the meat among the tribe. "[T]he distribution was made," de Neveu explains, "with a justice and equity that would have taken much more time among civilized people." No doubt the divisions were made as during a hunt. Two or three of the oxen escaped to Green Bay, some thirty-six miles distant by river travel. So much for using the cattle for farming, but immediate provisions were of primary concern to people whose food gathering had been so greatly disrupted by the land loss and resource encroachment attendant to the American expansion. In addition, community feasting in times of plenty, even be they short lived, remained an important cultural event.[43]

That afternoon the agency officials also delivered flour, salt pork, salt, corn, and tobacco of "detestable quality." The Menominee traded most of the pork and salt to traders "for merchandise." With the salt, only "those who possessed horses" kept their full shares, since salt was apparently difficult to transport.

Alcohol, despite the agents' efforts, remained an important commodity at annuity payments. Order was maintained during the remainder of the 1838 payment until after Boyd and his contingency launched their boats and departed, at which time the whiskey traders' "bateaux shot out from the opposite shore [from land ceded by the Menominee to Americans in 1836] and came to disgorge, in the midst of the camp, their cargoes of poisonous liquids for which the Indians have so ardent a thirst." A drunken orgy followed, during which de Neveu departed.[44]

During annuity times the combination of alcohol readily available on credit with long periods of waiting for the payout created short-term intensive binges of consumption followed by life as usual, except when the binges caused death. Alcohol-related deaths included poisoning, exposure, and occasional murders.[45]

Alcohol was even more destructive as a resource drain. Before the American government stepped in with laws protecting traders, alcohol drained individual rather than tribal resources. As alcohol became an accepted part of the Menominee social system, men often drank away the fruits of their own and their women's labor, encouraged by unscrupulous traders interested in the high profits. Of course, after the federal government made debts a tribal rather than an individual matter, alcohol sold on credit became a cost to the entire tribe.

In 1822, as part of the Indian Trade and Intercourse Acts, Congress passed an Indian Trade Act, outlawing the introduction by traders of "ardent spirits" into Indian country.[46] As late as 1821 whiskey was officially among the rations distributed to Indians from the Green Bay agency. After 1822, Menominees acquired alcohol illegally from traders and not directly from the government. An apparent exception is the 116 barrels of whiskey brought to the 1827 treaty negotiations (see chapter 5). Hypocritically, Colonel McKenney, one of the treaty commissioners, blamed Indians' various problems on whiskey traders, who followed them "from river to river, from wilderness to wilderness, from lake to lake," and he blamed the Christian nation for failing to protect Indians from purveyors of alcohol.[47]

Poor federal administration aided the traders. Federal officials themselves rarely visited Indian country, so before the agent's contingent arrived, no effective barriers to the traders existed. Since the treaty payments were often not made for up to a week after the announced date, the Menominee would arrive at the pay grounds along with the traders and wait for the government's arrival, as in 1838. The later federal officials and soldiers arrived, the better for the traders. Because most of the Menominee lived elsewhere, the time spent at the pay ground was relatively idle.

At the site of the payout, traders accepted Indian-owned goods such as blankets and weapons in hock in exchange for trade goods. The individual could only regain possession of his belongings with cash—which he would receive at the payout. Of course, not all these debts were created at the pay ground. They built up over the course of the year. Many were never repaid, and the traders sought remuneration through a claim in Congress or at treaty time.

MENOMINEE PROTESTS

The Menominee became so disgusted with these late payments that after the 1838 payout their leaders filed a complaint with the Office of Indian Affairs. Less than three days after the payment had been completed, the streams in their country froze, forcing all of the distant bands to travel overland to their winter hunting grounds. Traders took advantage by accepting bulky goods that came in barrels, such as flour, meat, and salt, in trade for alcohol, which could be consumed before leaving, and such necessities that were more easily transported. Since the tribe had missed the fall hunt, many were forced to make the sojourn barefoot (perhaps not having hides from which to make footwear).[48]

Few Menominees owned horses. Most arrived at the pay ground in bark canoes that could not safely navigate ice-filled river waters.

The federal agent, on the other hand, hired sturdy boats or, after the military road was built, hauled goods overland by contract. One year, for instance, 52,304 pounds of goods were transported to the pay ground at a cost of $889.16, or $1.70 per hundredweight. This too was charged to the Menominee.[49]

The late payment in 1838 and loss of the fall hunt caused such a hardship for the tribe that the Menominee chiefs and headmen held a council with Subagent Boyd in February 1839 instructing him to make a formal complaint to Governor Dodge on their behalf. "Our payments have been made so late every year that they do us more harm than good," they said. With the destruction of their canoes by ice and the loss of the fall hunt, "It would be better for us if we had not gone to the Payments." They added that the cost was so great to the Menominee that the federal government ought to reimburse them for the loss of their canoes and their hunt.[50] The problem continued unresolved, however, and some winters later Oshkosh and other Menominee leaders were forced to make the overland trek to Madison to protest directly to Governor Dodge.[51]

These problems were all preliminary to the infamous 1839 payout, after which complaints by the Menominee caused an investigation in which numerous of their charges against Subagent Boyd were proven. As one of the men who helped the Menominee draft the petition of complaint wrote, "If the Menomonies were to refer minutely to every cause of complaint which exists under their Treaty with the Government and the manner in which its provisions are carried out by the Agents of the Government, they would to use their own expression 'almost outnumber the leaves of the forest.[']"[52] Boyd's rebuttal justified rather than denied the charges.

The highlights of the accusations are as follows.[53] First, the Menominee accused Boyd of employing his son James Madison Boyd, who spoke Ojibwe but not Menominee, as official interpreter. Boyd had hired his son for that position in 1834, although no Ojibwes were within the jurisdiction of the Green Bay agency. Young James clearly received the position through patronage.[54]

Aiometah, from a portrait by Samuel Marsden Brookes.
State Historical Society of Wisconsin, NF Iometah.

Grizzley Bear. State Historical Society of Wisconsin (x3) 14573.

Oshkosh, from a portrait by Samuel Marsden Brookes. State
Historical Society of Wisconsin, NF Chief Oshkosh.

Trial of Oshkosh, 1830. Painting by Albert Herter
for the Wisconsin Supreme Court. Photo by James T. Potter AIA.

Souligny. State Historical Society of Wisconsin (x32) 8786.

Menominee men, from a portrait by Samuel Marsden Brookes
(standing: Na-a-Nos-a-ko-sa, Tah-ko;
sitting: Ne-kun-a-quok, His-kan-a-keom, Na-ke-wai-mi).
Courtesy Milwaukee Public Museum.

Menominee women, from a portrait by Samuel Marsden Brookes.
Courtesy Milwaukee Public Museum.

His father defended the hiring by pointing out that few white men spoke Menominee and that the few mixed-blood people who spoke the language were closely allied with the tribe and therefore could not be trusted. He added, "The fact that the Indians have paid their own Interpreters, is a matter of their own choice."[55] The Menominee were forced to hire their own interpreters whenever Agent Boyd held important councils with them or else risked not knowing exactly what they had agreed to. Boyd admitted this charge, and Dodge considered it proven.

Second, the Menominee accused Boyd of using their own cattle as part of the annuity payment—essentially, paying for their land with their own cattle. Dodge found that these charges were not entirely established but that Boyd had provided the cattle for ten cents a pound, when the going rate that October was $5.62½ per hundred pounds—a little more than half of what Boyd charged the tribe.

Third, the Menominee charged that Boyd received the goods and draft for money on 17 September but the annuity was not paid until 24 October. This cost the Menominee four hundred dollars when Boyd sent his son-in-law to Illinois to cash the draft. Governor Dodge reported to the commissioner of Indian affairs that the Menominee had voted in council to postpone the seven thousand dollars involved in the cash portion of the payment until the next year if Boyd would only make the rest of the annuity payment and be done with it. Dodge thought the four hundred dollars should not be charged against the tribe. He made no comment on the time these mishaps cost the Menominee.

Further charges, some proven and others not, involved fraudulent payment of annuities to Boyd's friends and relatives, unauthorized payments of claims, failure to redress past wrongs, and illegal employment of Boyd's relatives to the detriment of the tribe.[56] The charges also included an accusation that $5,000 of the payment was made in five franc pieces and that the government's agents paid part of the annuity by throwing handfuls of money into the air. The five franc pieces all came accidentally in a keg (the silver dollars were delivered in kegs). One deponent said these were paid out at 93¢ each, which was about their actual value; others, including M. E. Merrill from Fort Howard, testified that they were paid out as dollars. If they were paid as dollars, the Menominee were cheated out of approximately $350.[57] As to the money thrown in the air, the Menominee charged that the money was thrown "for the Indians and others to scramble for." Boyd said only one handful, worth about $10, was thus thrown and that Captain Clary had ordered it done to get the attention of the assembled and somewhat unruly crowd.[58]

Dodge reported to the commissioner of Indian affairs that, after a careful examination of the evidence and despite his reluctance to so report on a long-time public servant, Boyd's "conduct has been highly reprehensible, and... he has on frequent occasion acted contrary to" Indian Department regulations. Boyd, while admitting to several of the charges, pleaded innocent, arguing that "my present povity loudly proclaims that I have gained no advantages by peculation from the Office."[59]

Nonetheless, Boyd remained in office, despite further charges, until 1842, when the department finally fired him — not for abusing the federal trust relationship to the tribe but apparently for failing to keep good track of department money.[60] By that time, he had accumulated a string of abuses, many, but not all, occurring at annuity payments. The Menominee never received restitution for his abuses or errors or for those of his employees. Those employees were generally not officially condemned unless they did harm to the U.S. government. The United States simply did not take its treaty-based obligations to the tribe seriously.

8

Intensifying Encroachments

The Indian agents stationed in Menominee country continued to monitor relations between the Menominee and their neighbors, predominately a growing host of white entrepreneurs and settlers, many newly arrived from the east. In addition, agents were charged with fulfilling the federal treaty-based obligations to the tribe. In many cases they failed to do so. In fact, local American citizens were at times more likely to benefit from the treaty promises than were the Menominee.

As early as George Boyd's tenure in the 1830s the Office of Indian Affairs insisted that the Green Bay subagent should reside in Menominee country to be close enough to the tribe to know its needs firsthand. However, neither he nor his successors actually resided in Menominee country. Federal oversight of Menominee affairs was complicated by geography. After the 1836 treaty the Menominee maintained villages on the Menominee, Peshtigo, Oconto, and lower Fox Rivers, all on ceded land; at Lake Poygan, along the Wolf River, near Shawano Lake; and in other locations on the unceded western acreage. Over a dozen bands now made up the tribe, and though the Menominee's white neighbors increasingly surrounded them, the bands still maintained autonomous social, political, and economic arrangements, coming together as a whole only during annuity payments and as large groups during other momentous occasions.

RESOURCE DRAIN

Those Americans who provided goods and services for Menominees as called for in the treaties, both at annuities and on a year-round basis, often maintained cozy relationships with the federal agents. Some would later fall from favor when a new agent took office. Many times these people were simply agents' friends. For example, John DuBay, who had married into the tribe, charged that Subagent David Jones held up the 1844 annuity payment from a Monday until Saturday while awaiting the cattle that one of his friends, Harrison Reed, was to supply at the time of the payout. The new subagent, Albert Ellis, apparently contracted to Reed again in 1845. That year seven of the cattle Reed provided for the Menominee payout reportedly "strayed back" to him; the commissioner of Indian affairs informed Governor Dodge that, if this was true, restitution was to be provided but did not say whether it should be made to the government or to the Menominee.[1]

Others who profited, especially in the years between the 1836 and 1848 treaties, included the blacksmiths, who were supported by the 1836 treaty; the loggers, who increasingly encroached on Menominee land; and the missionaries, who received the treaty-based education funds. All of these people succeeded in their own goals to the detriment of the tribe. Although tribal leaders often protested the abuses, they were rarely remedied and then only after agents visited Menominee country and assessed conditions themselves.

Such a visit happened only twice: Subagents Jones and Ellis both actually visited Menominee country at times other than the annual payout—an occurrence rare enough to deserve mention and significant because they observed firsthand the variety of abuses suffered by the tribe at the hands of Americans who increasingly controlled their resources, both legally and illegally.

Jones toured Menominee country from 28 January to 17 February 1844, with a primary purpose of visiting the two blacksmith shops that the 1836 treaty required "to be located at such places as may be designated by the superintendent or agent."[2] According to Oshkosh, Dodge had promised at the treaty negotiations to locate these blacksmiths on Menominee lands. Agent Boyd had assigned one to Green Bay, the other to the upper Wisconsin River.[3] The Green Bay site, not on tribal land, would have been near the northern bands as well as those that were on the Fox River north of Lake Winnebago in the summer; the Wisconsin River site would have been in the heart of the western bands' country.

In 1841 on a visit to Madison, Oshkosh and others reminded Governor Dodge of his promises and then informed him that these promises were not being kept. Green Bay was a long way for many of the bands to travel, especially in the winter. Boyd had assigned a blacksmith to the upper Wisconsin site, but when Oshkosh sent his son there to have some work done, "the blacksmith could do nothing, as the Agent had not furnished him with iron." As a result, the band had to leave for the sugar camps without supplies.[4]

By 1844 the Green Bay site had been moved to Lake Winneconne. When Jones visited there, he found it well managed by Joseph Jourdain, "an experienced and skillful Smith" who was "Careful of the interest of the Indians and in the economy of his Shop." But at the upper Wisconsin site he found a shop that "was generally rendered of more convenience to the Whites than to the Indians themselves." Jones also learned that the blacksmith had joined together with Amable Grignon to overcharge the United States for the coal used in the shop, so he fired him.[5]

Jones also reported on timber trespass, another problem against which the Menominee had protested for years. He wrote to Governor Doty, "The destruction of [Menominee] timber Land is already very considerable, and becoming more and more immense as the ceded Lands are settled, and the Greater demands for Lumber create new inducements and offer greater rewards for Plunder. . . . It seems to me that every White Man engaged in the Lumbering Business is a trespasser on the Indian Lands." Menominee leaders asked Jones to protect their forests.[6]

Timber trespass was rarely punished, however. The federal policy had become more restrictive regarding mill leases, which only made illegal cutting more common and ensured that the Menominee would gain no profit from their timber. Some Americans attempted to gain timber leases on Menominee lands, sometimes with tribal support, but the Office of Indian Affairs largely stopped this practice by the 1840s. In 1846 Commissioner Medill wrote to Governor Dodge, "I have to remark that such permission has been refused, in every instance for many years." Were such permits to be granted, "in a few years the lands would be stripped of their timber and thereby become valueless."[7]

Medill's observation was apt: the value of Wisconsin timber had grown tremendously in a little over a decade. The market had expanded, and the Menominee land cession fed the Lake Michigan trade, which flowed to the great lumbering center in Chicago. The city of Oshkosh, incorporated in 1846 on ceded land, became a lumber town whose people exploited the Wolf River timber.[8]

In February 1844, immediately following Jones's visit to the Menominee, Oshkosh led a delegation to a council with Governor Doty and strongly protested the trespasses committed by white loggers who cut Menominee pine. "These people, it appears," Governor Doty wrote, "reside on the adjoining lands, and only enter the country to cut the logs and hall them off." He asked the commissioner of Indian affairs "whether proceedings can be instituted against" the trespassers.[9] However, his long-term solution called for the removal of Indians from all lands in Wisconsin to provide American entrepreneurs with access to the valuable oak, pine, and mineral resources.[10] Under the administration of the next subagent, Albert Ellis, a Menominee delegation again visited the governor and charged that eleven of fifteen mills on the Black River and twenty on the Wisconsin River were built on Menominee land.[11] The area surrounding the Black River, which served as a kind of tribal boundary for treaty purposes, had been ceded to the United States by several tribes in 1837.[12] But the Menominee still believed the resources to be theirs.[13]

This drain of Menominee resources was fueled by the missionary efforts as well. This was a double-edged problem for the tribe because not only did the Menominee lose money to missionaries, but the churchmen also tried to change Menominee culture (albeit with little effect) with federal support.

The Protestant mission continued into the early 1840s but succeeded in little more than siphoning off Menominee treaty money. The Catholic priest throughout this time, Theodore Van den Broek, did little better. He lived at the Little Chute site until 1844. Subagent Jones visited his school that same year and reported to the governor that it "has been of little benefit to the Indians — that it has not been kept in the Indian Country, but on lands ceded by the Indians" in the 1836 treaty. For this reason he apparently withheld funding from the school; Van den Broek at this time complained that he had not been paid for two years.[14] After this the priest settled on, or in close proximity to, Menominee land and established a mission at Lake Poygan, where he served until 1846.

In July 1846, after hearing the Menominee protest of wasted education funds, Jones's successor, Subagent Ellis, visited the school. "I found a pretense for a school," Ellis reported to Wisconsin territorial governor Henry Dodge, his immediate supervisor. The school was "of so lame a character, as rather to be injurious than beneficial." The trader's clerk, not the missionary, taught the classes, but he was an incompetent teacher. Only fourteen students attended. Van den Broek had visited the Indians only three times in the ten months since the last annuity payment. He had also committed other frauds: two teachers for whom he had requested funds had worked less than twenty days between them. The trader ran his school at the request of the Menominee, not at that of Van den Broek. Although Van den Broek requested money to pay the trader, none of the money paid to Van den Broek went to the trader, who expected the government to pay him directly. In addition, the school was filthy, with no furniture and but a few spellers for teaching material.[15]

Ellis found other claims by Van den Broek, mostly for money owed him by the tribe, to be unjust. Van den Broek also claimed "that he has reclaimed more than 350 [Menominees] from their wandering habits," but this statement also lacked truth, Ellis wrote. The Menominee in that area were farmers before Van den Broek's arrival. "And the truth is," Ellis added, "that the Indians charge distinctly, that for the last few years in consequence of his neglect of them, they have greatly declined in religious knowledge." Van den Broek failed to cultivate the small Menominee Catholic community that had gained some stability under Father Mazzuchelli. Conditions seemed so bad to Ellis that he fired Van den Broek at the request of the Menominee, and he convinced a reluctant Bishop John Martin Henni to appoint a substitute.[16] According to a biography of Van den Broek's successor, Henni replaced Van den Broek "not on religious grounds, but mainly because he resided at Little Chute, more than 30 miles away."[17] Henni intimated to the archbishop of Vienna that Van den Broek was "too advanced in years to do effective work" and needed to be replaced by "an active and vigorous missionary."[18]

Bishop Henni appointed Florimond J. Bonduel as the new priest to the Menominee in 1846 and also reappointed Rosalie Dousman as a teacher among the Menominee at Lake Poygan. When Bonduel had arrived at Green Bay in 1838, Dousman was teaching Indian and mixed-blood children in Shantytown, which was part of greater Green Bay. Perhaps she continued to teach there, not moving to Indian country until Henni appointed her to serve among the Menominee in 1846. Bonduel founded several missions in the area before being appointed to serve at Lake Poygan in 1846. He founded one, an Indian mission of disputed date, on the Oconto River. Probably this was among the Oconto River band of Menominee, one of the northern bands not identified as Catholic. He also probably founded a mission among Menominees living at Duck Creek, in the vicinity of Green Bay. By 1843 he had been reassigned to Prairie du Chien.[19]

Bonduel said of his 1846 appointment, "the bishop placed me in charge of the Poygan mission, and the government of the United States appointed me superintendent of the English school for the purpose of civilizing the Menominee Indians."[20] Bonduel later claimed to have founded the St. Xavier mission at Lake Poygan, where approximately one-quarter of the Menominee lived, but probably Van den Broek had done some work there previously. In the first year of Bonduel's residency at Lake Poygan, several Menominees moved into log cabins, and they cleared two hundred acres of land for farming, so he felt he had made a success.[21] Yet these were bands that had previously been agricultural, so it is no surprise that they took up farming at Lake Poygan and was not as great a feat as Bonduel believed. However, the Catholic bands again had a priest living among them.

Coupled with a loss of resources, both those of the land and those they received in exchange for the land, the Menominee faced the deeper problem of encroachment onto their territory. In a council meeting in the summer of 1845, blessed by a sharing of the pipe, Oshkosh spoke eloquently of this problem. "He wound up his long harangue," in the words of artist Paul Kane, "by descanting upon the narrow limits in which they were pent up, which did not allow them sufficient hunting grounds without encroaching upon the rights of other tribes. He said that, like the deer chased by the dogs, they would have to take to the water."[22] With tribal land resources increasingly constricted by treaty, old relationships with other tribes in which resources were shared fell by the wayside. These pressures made the tribe increasingly vulnerable.

1848 TREATY

After the negotiation of the 1836 treaty, Governor Dodge wrote to the commissioner of Indian affairs that the Menominee still "owned the most valuable part of the Country on the Fox River," where their farmers and mills were located, "and from which they gained no advantage." The tribe refused to sell all its land, so he had purchased what he could. But he was confident that "When the country is surveyed on the East side of the Fox River, and brought into market, from the fertility of its soil it will sell immediately, and the Menominee will have to sell the balance of their Country, and remove to the Country South of the Missouri River."[23]

Indian removal was a strong tenet of the Democratic Party, and Dodge, a member of the party, continued to urge the purchase of the remainder of Menominee country. In 1838 he asked the Wisconsin territorial legislature to send a memorial to the U.S. Congress, "asking an appropriation to extinguish the title of the Menominee Indians to their Country bordering on both sides of the Fox river from the mouth of the Wolf river to the portage of the Fox and Wisconsin Rivers." The assembly forwarded the memorial to Congress in December 1838, where it was sent to committee.[24] Dodge lost the governorship of Wisconsin Territory to James Duane Doty in 1841, after the Whig Party won the presidency, but he regained the position in 1845, when the Democrats retook the White House. As Wisconsin approached statehood, both men urged the extinguishment of Indian titles to their holdings within the territory.[25]

The United States pursued this policy at all levels, from the subagent to the commissioner of Indian affairs. Subagent Ellis wrote to Governor Dodge in April 1846 that "*buying them out* altogether, East of the Wisconsin River, by the government, and providing for their location elsewhere, would seem to offer the most *effectual* and *satisfactory* mode of removing them quite away from this neighborhood." Several bands living on ceded lands near Lake Winnebago had not left, and settlers complained about it to the governor, but Ellis suggested not forcing the issue with the tribe until a new treaty could be negotiated.[26]

In July 1846, Commissioner of Indian Affairs William Medill wrote to Dodge that Congress had "appropriated two thousand dollars 'to defray the expense of holding a treaty with the Menomonie Indians, for the purchase of their lands north of Fox river.'" Medill asked Dodge to make the preliminary arrangements for the treaty but warned him to be careful in approaching the tribe, making sure that all arrangements should be suitable to the Menominee. The department, Medill wrote, was not sure the

Menominee wanted to sell or, if they did, "where they would prefer to go.... Should you satisfy yourself that the Menomonies may be induced to sell on reasonable terms," he concluded, "you will please give particular consideration to the subject of a suitable future home for them—one with which they would be satisfied, and where they would be comfortable and happy."[27]

In November 1846 Dodge reported to Medill that he had requested Subagent Ellis to sound out the tribe at the annuity payment about its willingness to sell its land. Ellis and Dodge had been corresponding about this for a year already, since Dodge's reappointment to the governorship. In his annual reports through 1847 Dodge continued to urge the purchase of Menominee lands. In a letter to Medill in November 1847, Dodge referred the commissioner to his recent annual report. "The extinguishment of the Indian title to the Menominee Country is a subject of the first importance to the growth and prosperity of Northern Wisconsin," he wrote, stressing that both white Americans and Menominees would be better off if the tribe were moved west.[28]

In the 1847 annual report Dodge argued that, should the Menominee sell only a portion of their home and remain in Wisconsin, they would soon be "surrounded by our advancing settlements." He believed the federal removal policy to be humane because it both saved lives—he did not specify whether Indian or white— and put Indians in a position to raise stock or become agriculturalists. "Should the Menominee Indians be unwilling to remove South of the Missouri River," he wrote, land along the Mississippi or St. Peters Rivers could be purchased for them.[29] He believed the traders to be the greatest obstacle in making a treaty with the Menominee and urged the War Department to work with, rather than against, the traders.

Hoping to speed Menominee acceptance of the removal process, Dodge wrote to Subagent Ellis in October 1847, essentially telling him to bribe the tribe with the interest money from the $76,000 the tribe had been paid in the 1836 treaty for the improvements made under the 1831 treaty. The tribe had been attempting to receive that annual interest directly since 1836, and President James K. Polk had finally agreed to pay it. But, Governor Dodge wrote, the president used erroneous reasoning, so Commissioner of Indian Affairs Medill requested him to reconsider. Dodge wrote to Ellis, "I trust it will be in your power, or that of the Sub-Agent, to Satisfy the Indians that . . . should they treat for a cession of their lands, [the President] shall cause the fund to be promptly applied, in a manner most beneficial to their interests, as originally designed, in the Country to which they may remove."[30] Dodge clearly hoped the promise of the expenditure of this money would help induce the tribe to cede its lands.

In April 1848, as Wisconsin approached nearer to statehood, the U.S. Senate "Resolved, that the President be advised to enter into negotiations with any Indian tribes who may have title to lands within the territory of Wisconsin, for the extinguishment of such title." President Polk referred the task to the secretary of war, who sent Commissioner Medill to negotiate with the Menominee.[31] By the time Medill arrived in Menominee country to make the treaty, the United States was no longer concerned with whether the Menominee wanted to sell or where the people wanted to live. Medill negotiated the treaty as secretly as possible to avoid "the interference of the outsider parties," as one observer put it.[32] "[H]e came quite unexpectedly on the eve of the payment," George Wright wrote to his friends at Ewing, Chute, and Company, a powerful and politically well-connected trading firm based in Fort Wayne, Indiana.[33]

The president authorized Medill to pay the same price as the government had paid for Menominee land in 1836, 18.9¢ an acre, although land values had significantly increased. He told the tribe that it held title to 1.6 million acres; Oshkosh responded that the tribe held close to 8 million. Medill actually believed the tribe held 3,023,800 acres, but as soon as he arrived on the spot he realized the amount was at least 4 million. Previous Indian Department reports put it at about 4 million. In 1853 the Senate Committee on Indian Affairs investigated the issue, revealing that Commissioner

Medill's annual report also stated the figure to be 4 million acres. A General Land Office survey made after the purchase showed the figure to be 5,230,240 acres. The Senate committee admitted that the total acreage of land held by the Menominee at the time of the treaty may have been 7,718,560 acres, including land between the Black and Wisconsin Rivers. Since the United States had previously purchased land along the Wisconsin River from the tribe, the report pointed out, the federal government had already recognized Menominee title to that land.[34]

The Menominee received $350,000 in cash, goods, and debt payments for the land they sold in 1848. The treaty called for the tribe to move onto some six hundred thousand acres of land in the Crow Wing area of Minnesota, which the U.S. government fully expected the Menominee to do. Of the $350,000, the largest portion, $200,000, was to be paid out in ten annuities beginning in 1857, after the 1836 treaty annuity payments ended. An amount of $5,000 would be paid to individual tribal members for "improving" their land, an inducement to agriculture; $11,000 went to supporting a blacksmith shop for twelve years beginning in 1857; $9,000 was set aside to pay for a miller for fifteen years; and $15,000 went to building the mill and establishing a manual labor school, later to become a working farm. The treaty gave $30,000 "To the chiefs" to settle their debts "preparatory to their removal" and gave $40,000 to be divided among people of mixed blood. It also allowed $20,000 in removal expenses and $20,000 subsistence money for the first year after removal. Separately from the land purchase, the government also agreed to pay the expenses of a tribal delegation to explore the new country.[35]

At the authorized rate of 18.9¢ per acre, $350,000 would buy some 1.85 million acres. The United States took all the rest—somewhere between 3.38 million and 5.87 million acres—for nothing. Even Secretary of the Interior Alexander Stuart admitted just three years later that the tribe had been cheated, declaring himself "satisfied that great injustice has been done to the Indians by that treaty."[36]

The 1853 Senate Committee on Indian Affairs figured the loss, conservatively, at $613,515, and the Senate added that price to the Indian appropriation bill that year.[37] The tribe never received the money, and it became a matter of dispute between the tribe, an attorney, and the federal government for the next several years.

The terms of the 1848 treaty surprised even the Oneidas, who had earlier tried to obtain Menominee land at low prices. Two Quaker visitors to the area in 1849 described the Oneida reaction. "They also felt for their brethren, the Menomonies, who, they were sorry to see, had, through ignorance of the value of their lands, lately parted with them, for a very small remuneration. They thought it was remarkable, that the Government, which had expressed such concern that the New York Indians had bought land of the Menomonies, so low, should be unable, when itself became a purchaser, to see its own acts in the same light."[38] The Menominee were defrauded not because of their ignorance of land value, however, but because of Medill's unauthorized negotiation tactics.

A successor of Medill, Luke Lea, believed Medill did not cheat the tribe but merely made "an honest mistake."[39] The Senate committee rejected this argument, saying that had Medill negotiated this treaty with an "enlightened and independent nation" it would be considered one of the greatest diplomatic strokes of all time. The committee added, however, that it did not wish to censure Medill since he had erred in favor of the American nation's pecuniary interests, "an offense, if it be one, with which too few can be charged at this day." The committee merely wished to recompense the tribe.[40] The committee certainly stood correct in judging that Medill had fleeced the Menominee nation, even if it benefited the U.S. Treasury.

The worst aspect of the deal for the Menominee was the loss of all lands in Wisconsin, which they were to exchange for land in Minnesota that they already knew they did not like. Why did the tribe, by now cautious in its dealings with the federal government, agree to such preposterous conditions regarding the land sale, and why did it agree to removal? The answer is clear: federal agents threatened them with military removal. If they did not sign, they would be forced to Minnesota with absolutely no compensation for their land. The government would send the army to remove them westward, as had already happened to the Potawatomis in Wisconsin. The Menominee could not know that no such authority had been granted.

The tribe clearly knew that Medill had come to negotiate to get their land, as the trader Louis B. Porlier also attested.[41] When the council convened, Porlier and the other traders hurried to set up their trading shanties because there would be an annuity payment immediately afterward. He and Augustin Grignon Sr. shared a tent. As the council was about to start, Oshkosh stopped by the tent and asked Grignon to accompany him to the council. Perhaps Grignon would serve as Oshkosh's interpreter, for he spoke Menominee well. As Porlier himself walked across the grounds to the council house, he saw the Menominee leader Shoneon preparing to report to a group of his fellow Menominees, so Porlier stopped to listen. The group asked Shoneon what the American commissioner wanted, to which he replied, "You don't expect he has come to decorate your ears with silver ear-bobs? No, he comes here simply to get the balance of our country!"[42] When Shoneon explained how Medill waxed eloquent on the abundance of food in the Minnesota country, one of his fellows said, "Why don't he go there himself and live in such a fine country, where there is an abundance of everything?" The group told Shoneon he should have immediately refused to discuss the matter. Shoneon said that he had, "but you know how Kechemocoman (or the Great Knife, as they name the American) never gets rebuked at a refusal; but will persist, and try over and over again till he accomplishes his purpose. I left our chief Oshkosh to debate with him, and I will not adhere to any proposition he may make."[43] Shoneon did not sign the 1848 treaty.[44]

Henry S. Baird, the recording secretary for the negotiations, quit on the fourth day of negotiations to return to Green Bay, believing that no treaty would be made. But then Morgan L. Martin became secretary. That night he visited Porlier, urging him to give a message to Grignon.

> Mr. Porlier, I wish you would tell Mr. Grignon that he had better advise the chiefs to make a treaty while they have an opportunity. They ought to make the most advantageous one they can; for if they should persist in refusing to treat, the president can at his pleasure order their removal, without giving them another chance to make a treaty, and then it would be optional with him whether to give them anything or nothing, because it is provided in the existing treaty, that whenever the president should want their lands, they should relinquish their title — they only possessing such lands as hunting grounds. The president has now sent a commissioner to make a treaty, and they ought to embrace the opportunity to make the most favorable one they can; it is a matter of course that the commissioner cannot give beyond his instructions, but he can give to the utmost limit.

Martin then sent Porlier to see Oshkosh and also the leaders of the Shawano band, urging the nation to meet together. The next day, "They accordingly met in council with the commissioner, and in the course of the day the treaty was concluded."[45]

Eyewitnesses report that Oshkosh said to the tribe in council, "My friends we cannot do otherwise, we are forced into it." Several other witnesses testified that they "verily and truly believe that said Indians [Menominee] signed the treaty . . . under the belief that, should they refuse, the government of the United States would violate their repeated pledges of protection, and send troops to force them to leave their homes."[46] The Quaker Alfred Cope reported that when he visited the tribe in 1849 "several very respectable sources" told him and his partner "that the Menominees had been frightened, by the threats of the Commissioner sent to make this treaty, into an apparent acceptance of its terms."[47] Florimond J.

Bonduel, the missionary, reported to acquaintances that Medill threatened to take the medals from any chiefs refusing to sign and to assign new chiefs to serve the tribe.[48] No Menominees wanted to make this treaty ceding the remainder of their homeland, but under the threat that it would be taken from them without recompense should they refuse, they agreed.

9

The Battle for
a Homeland

After the disastrous treaty of 1848 the Menominee fought desperately to remain in Wisconsin. Many of Wisconsin's tribes faced
similar situations as Wisconsin gained statehood and attempted
to drive them from its borders. As Nancy Lurie has observed,
"By 1848, all Indian land in Wisconsin had been ceded by treaty
except for the Oneida Reservation established ten years earlier."
Members of all these tribes, including the Ojibwes, Stockbridge,
and Munsees, intended to remain in Wisconsin.[1]

The Menominee's 1848 treaty stipulated that a Menominee
delegation would view the six hundred thousand acres of land
offered them in the Crow Wing region of Minnesota to decide
whether the tribe wished to remove.[2] Carron, a half-brother of the
late Josette Carron and himself a leader, spoke on behalf of the
tribe at a council meeting in 1849, saying that when they thought
of the prospect of removal "their hearts were in their throats and
choked them, so that they could not speak. They did not want
to go." The Menominee told Alfred Cope and Thomas Wistar
Jr., two Quakers sent to oversee the 1849 payment to mixed-
blood Menominee, that the tribe had occasionally hunted in the
Crow Wing country in Minnesota when their land base was larger,
and they knew they did not like it.[3] The 1848 treaty allowed the
Menominee to stay in Wisconsin for two years, which they hoped
would be long enough to alter federal plans. Nonetheless, the tribe
agreed to send a delegation to visit the Crow Wing country at the
expense of the federal government.

Even before the delegation toured Minnesota, the tribe attempted to reverse the treaty. Oshkosh asked Wistar to take a message to the president. Wistar agreed, despite the vehement opposition of the interpreter, probably William Powell, and Subagent William H. Bruce, the official conduit for tribal communications to Washington. Wistar recognized that he was interfering with Bruce's realm of responsibility, but he knew that the problems could not be remedied with the government official serving as intermediary.[4]

Carron told the Quakers that "all of them [Menominees] looked upon their removal to the Crow-wing river, as an act of destruction and that, if it must be that they were to come to nothing, they would rather it should happen in their old homes, than in a strange land." Tah-ko added, "They were afraid, their Great Father thought no more of them, than of so many cattle, for they had cried to him and he took no notice of their cry."[5] Carron reiterated that the Menominee had already seen the land and knew they did not like it. Bruce told them of improvements such as roads that had been made. "Oshkosh here broke in, with some impatience, saying, there was no use in praising the country; they had seen it."[6]

CROW WING COUNTRY

Subagent Bruce ignored Menominee opposition and ordered the tribe to select nine delegates, one representing each band, to accompany him on the trip to Minnesota. When the leaders told him that they would not decide until all the tribe met together, he insisted that he had to know right away. He needed to make them clothing, he explained, and wanted to be certain the coats would fit. They said he could bring a selection with him when he came to get them at Lake Poygan, if that was what worried him. He said that they would have to select men to fit the coats. They laughed and agreed. "They seemed for a moment, to forget their sorrow, in this small victory."[7]

The tribal delegation made the trip to Minnesota in early summer of 1850, accompanied by Subagent Bruce, Colonel Ebenezer

Childs, William Powell as an interpreter, and several others.[8] Bruce, together with Colonel Childs, "spoke in glowing terms of the clean lakes, abundant fish, [and] swampland for waterfowl, interspersed with large areas of 'rich, black loam,' excellent for farming."[9] He praised the natural riches of the Crow Wing region, but the Menominee who visited the area called the land barren, destitute, and unsuitable for Menominee needs. Some of this land forms the heart of present-day central Minnesota resort country, but for the Menominee it was not home. It held too little game and would have forced the Menominee into conflict with the neighboring Ojibwes and Santees.

Powell described the land as partially well adapted to agriculture and partially marshy and well timbered. The wetlands and waterways provided an abundance of fish and fowl, and the trees grew in as great a variety as those on the land the tribe would abandon. However, even though no one in the delegation mentioned it to him, he believed the Menominee seemed unhappy with the country. "My opinion is that the hunting portion of the tribe will not fare so well after their removal," he wrote in a report to Bruce, "and I think I perceived disappointment in the looks of our delegation, although they forebore to let any expression to that effect escape them," despite his efforts to converse with them on the subject.[10]

Richard Chute, a trader for Ewing, Chute, and Company, which traded in Indian country and profited by collecting claims and by winning removal contracts, wrote more bluntly about the land before the tribe's delegation even visited it. "It is preposterous to suppose that 2500 Indians can live where there is nothing, and never will be anything." He suggested that Commissioner Medill had dealt duplicitously with the tribe, offering them the choice of several tracts of land upon which to settle and then relegating them to the Crow Wing area in the written treaty. "The land assigned by Govt. in Medills treaty, to the Menominees, is the most rascally piece of dirt that ever human beings trod," he wrote to his partner, George Washington Ewing, in March 1850. "It is certain annihilation for them to go there to reside . . . and I have no hesitation in saying that should they go to their Minnesota tract of land, that by that time a more ragged, wretched, miserable, and degraded set of Red men will not exist on this Continent." He also wrote, "The Menominees are much opposed to going to the bleak barren Country assigned them." He said he believed they would prefer going west of the Missouri River.[11] Chute was clearly thinking of ways he could profit from these circumstances, but he does accurately capture the Menominee view of removal.

The Menominee appealed to the Catholic missionary Bonduel for aid, and he in turn contacted Ewing's company. After the 1848 treaty Bonduel supported the tribe's removal to Minnesota, perhaps because it would take the Menominee away from what he considered evil frontier influences. But, possibly at the urging of the Menominee and suspicious that federal agents had coerced the treaty against Menominee wishes, Bonduel withdrew his support for the move west, which would have brought great economic loss to the tribe.[12]

In February 1850, Bonduel wrote a letter to George Washington Ewing stating that the Menominee would permit the Ewing brothers—George Washington and William G.—40 to 50 percent of any of the money they could get from the government if they in turn would help the Menominee to regain a homeland either near the Menominee River or approximately twenty miles east and northeast of Green Bay. "The Indians are willing to do all they can for their friends," Bonduel wrote, "Provided through them they can get for The Tribe The New Home they wish to possess. I hope that you will use your influence at Washington to that effect, Since our Indians act so generously."[13]

Chute probably never even saw the Minnesota land he described, but he hoped to gain the large percentage the tribe had offered if his company could successfully pursue any claims. The Ewings also wanted to profit from both the removal of the Menominee and the treaty-stipulated contracts for provisions, and they desired as well to retain a role in the Menominee trade, no matter where the tribe lived. The Ewings' primary concern here was with their trade, not the tribe. They already had small traders working for them in Menominee country, so no matter where the tribe moved, the Ewings would not suffer. The only question for them seemed to be where they stood to profit most.

For instance, in September 1850, after the tribal delegation had visited and rejected the Crow Wing land, William G. Ewing entered into a contract with P. Choteau Jr. and Co., a large St. Louis trading firm, to trade with the Ho Chunks, the Chippewas, and "prospectively" the Menominee. Should the tribe be moved west, the easiest way to bring trade goods to Menominee country would be up the Mississippi River.[14]

But the Ewings also planned for the possibility that the Menominee might remain in Wisconsin by exerting pressures there as well. As late as 1852, the Ewing company attempted to monopolize the Green Bay fur trade, for example. The Ewing company used a trader in Menominee country, George Cown, who lived at Lake Poygan with the Catholic bands. But the Ewings also had other, more important contacts in Menominee country, including another local trader, George Wright, who formed occasional partnerships with them. The Ewing company rivaled the American Fur Company in Wisconsin, complete with control over traders and Indian agents and influence in Congress. Traders of the companies met at treaty and annuity gatherings and probably competed and cooperated in pressing claims.[15]

However, the decisive factor in the Menominee's decision to remain in Wisconsin was tribal leadership, not the manipulations of traders and others. The Menominee wanted to remain in their ancient homeland and disliked the land in Minnesota. "[I]t did not suit us," Carron later recalled. "[I]t looked like an old burying-ground."[16] The most well-known Menominee response is probably Oshkosh's comment, made to President Fillmore in 1850: "The poorest region in Wisconsin was better than the Crow Wing."[17] Carron said, "Mr. Medill told us we could look at the land destined for our new home, and if we did not like it the government would give us another Section of land in this territory."[18] The Menominee never considered the agreement to look over Minnesota lands as anything more than an opportunity to regroup and reverse the damage done by Medill in 1848. They hoped the two years they were to be allowed to remain in Wisconsin under the terms of the treaty would give them time enough to make such a permanent agreement.

On its return the delegation reported that the land was unsuitable. Then the tribe sent a delegation consisting of Oshkosh, Waukechon, Carron, LaMotte, Souligny, Keshena, Asha'wani'pinas, and Che'quo'tam to Washington. Several non-Indians — including Subagent Bruce, interpreters, traders, and Bonduel — also made the trip.[19] After meeting with President Fillmore, the Menominee obtained permission to remain in Wisconsin for an extra year, and they also hired a lawyer, Richard W. Thompson, whom they promised large amounts of money.

Thompson agreed to work through Congress for two changes: to allow the tribe to remain in Wisconsin and to gain extra compensation for the land sold in 1848. In exchange, Thompson would receive approximately one-third of the claim.[20] Thompson's primary interest was the money; the Menominee's was remaining in Wisconsin. This difference eventually caused a falling out between them.

FINDING A HOME IN WISCONSIN

Thompson claimed responsibility for the Senate investigation, which estimated the tribe had been underpaid by an amount somewhere between $636,515.36 and $1,108,807.84.[21] In addition, the Indian Department agreed that, if the state of Wisconsin allowed it, an arrangement might be made for the tribe to regain some Wisconsin land. Local Americans circulated petitions in the Menominee's favor. The tribe gained several postponements of removal, which finally culminated in the tribe's settlement in its present site along the Wolf River in northeastern Wisconsin.[22]

Meanwhile, some of the local white residents became increasingly hostile toward the Menominee, who now lived on ceded lands. Near Lake Poygan white residents burned several Menominee houses and broke into others to steal clothing and tools while the Menominee were away hunting. They also stole kettles and troughs the Menominee kept in their sugar bush. Members of the tribe swore out affidavits and protested to Subagent Bruce; Bonduel also intervened in their behalf. The Menominee blamed the Irish settlers, some of whom attended Bonduel's church, rather than the Germans or Americans.[23]

During this time, Thompson had allied himself with the Ewing brothers and apparently worked for the appointment of Elias Murray as superintendent of the northern superintendency within the Office of Indian Affairs.[24] When the federal government decided to allow the Menominee to remain in Wisconsin, Murray was assigned to explore the Wolf River site, which he did together with Powell, LaMotte, Waukechon, and Oshkehenaniew. In October, the government granted the tribe permission to move there, although the Menominee still did not own any land in Wisconsin.[25] The move was not yet permanent.

The Ewings and Thompson formed a partnership and together gained the removal contract, for which they were paid $24,900. They subcontracted to George Wright, who removed the southern bands, and to John B. Jacobs, who removed the northern bands. Wright was to receive $8,700 for his share in the work; Jacobs received $800.[26]

Wright had lobbied actively for this role, or alternately for an assignment as the Green Bay subagent, as a reward for his support of Whig politics. He wrote to George Washington Ewing in May 1851 to say that, despite the money he had spent for Whig causes, he had "not yet received the first dollar of Government money." However, he said, "I should like to have some opertunity dureing the Whig Administration to get back some of my Capital invested in the Whig cause.... As regards the removal of the Indians, I should very much like to have an interest in the matter if there is anything to be made at it," he added.[27] Ewing already knew of Wright's interest in this through his partner, Richard Chute.[28]

William G. Ewing Jr. had written to George Washington Ewing in March 1851 that "Our friend Wright will circulate a petition to get a country [for the Menominee] in this State on the head of the Menomonie and Wolf Rivers, or to have the rights to relocate the[m] in Country *West*."[29] Wright's concerns, reflecting those of the Ewings, lay in profit, not in the tribe's welfare.

On 4 October 1852, Superintendent Murray requested that the southern bands gather at Lake Poygan as quickly as possible for their removal to their new homes on the Wolf and Oconto Rivers. "Your worthy friends Col. Thompson and Ewing have the contract for your removal and your subsistence after your arrival here. I shall go with you myself and see that the contract is fulfilled and that you are well provided for."[30] People and goods were to be shipped to the site at the falls of the Wolf River by boat, up the Wolf from Lake Poygan. Meanwhile, Jacobs began the removal of the northern bands. They followed the Oconto River west to join the tribe. As an inducement, the first family to arrive was to be rewarded with five blankets.[31] All 540 female heads of household as well as others, such as 48 chiefs and headmen, received blankets about a week after the removal. These were apparently purchased for $1,470 from Ewing, Chute, and Company with separate tribal monies.[32]

Murray, who was to oversee the removal, reported to Commissioner of Indian Affairs Luke Lea from the falls at Wolf River on 2 November that he was "happy to Certify" that the removal "has been affected in a peaceful, comfortabl, and satisfactory manner" and that the Menominee "have been abundantly supplied with transportation, and good and wholesom provisions."[33]

Thompson boasted that the removal had proceeded smoothly and that he had "subsisted" the entire tribe. The Menominee, he said, were well supplied with corn, flour, and beef, "transported at our expense." In reality, the food was very bad and included rotten meat, and Menominees recall that many tribal members arrived by canoe. In addition, the removal had occurred so late in the fall that the rivers froze before all the goods could be shipped to the

Menominee.[34] On 1 December, Wright wrote to Thompson and Ewing that most of the corn and flour could not be transported to the tribe because of frozen rivers; he had instructed the boatmen to give it to any Indians who made the trip down to collect it. On 15 December, another acquaintance forwarded to George Washington Ewing an abstract of a Menominee council meeting in which the tribe requested more provisions from the government; those on hand were being depleted rapidly. Superintendent Murray wrote a few days later that the Menominee were "going daily to the Forest . . . for Provisions."[35] Many of the federally furnished provisions had spoiled before they arrived. That winter many Menominees died of malnutrition; it was the first of several winters of starvation that, combined with the ravages of disease, reduced the Menominee population from 2,002 at the time of removal to 1,336 by 1870.[36]

An unsigned letter, seemingly from a Menominee to Green Bay Subagent John V. Suydam in the summer of 1853, told of the hardships the tribe suffered. The writer requested permission to gather wild rice, "the only resource left to me to support my family through next winter." He wrote that the provisions distributed at the removal lasted only six months and the three thousand dollars' worth of provisions set aside by the 1836 treaty had all been eaten. "It was well understood last fall or last year," the writer pointed out, "by the Agent of the Government and the Cheifs to affect our removal that we were to be supported the whole year round with provision." The writer lamented, "You are aware I have no doubt of our present situation of starvation we have never been so poor and destitute of provisions as we are this year."[37]

With the loss of the tribal land base and the enforced containment of the bands in a relatively small area that could not support the more than two thousand Menominees moved there, the tribe depended on the federal government for its sustenance. Since Murray had been authorized to make the removal in September, once again, as in all those old annuity payments, the Menominee were forced to wait for the federal government instead of preparing themselves for the winter.[38] Having waited all through the hunting season for the always-imminent removal to take place, and having abandoned the lands on which at least some of the bands grew crops, the Menominee had to rely upon provisions from the Ewing company in its removal partnership with Thompson.

Not only did the company fail to provide the tribe with sustenance, as was agreed upon, but many of the Menominees apparently arrived at their new home destitute after being forced to leave their belongings behind. Carron later said to Thompson, "You brought our people here, and it was our wish. [But] We lost a great many of our little things. You could not bring them, as you transported some of the white people at the same time."[39] These white people are not mentioned by name, but they probably included the missionary Bonduel, the traders, and others fulfilling subcontracts in the removal. In addition to tribal members' losing personal belongings to make room for these non-Indians, these people were transported at the tribe's expense, with money received by the Menominee for their land.

1848 TREATY OBLIGATIONS

Although their removal brought the Menominee to a small homeland that was at least in their old country, it was costly to the tribe in many ways. They had to deal with numerous other problems such as the payment of forty thousand dollars to mixed-blood Menominee and non-Indian people, who were in essence being bought out of the tribe by the government, and the payment of thirty thousand dollars in debt money to the traders.

In the buyout, tribal members of mixed Menominee and white blood accepted a payment to relinquish their affiliation with the tribe. This formally occurred during the summer of 1849 under the oversight of Cope and Wistar, the Quakers commissioned by the federal government to fulfill this obligation. The Menominee leadership was concerned at the time primarily that their money would go to those designated by the tribe, not those designated by the agent. On 18 June, Oshkosh, after conferring with tribal members, pointed out to the Quakers that the tribe had heard that "a great many *foreign* mixed-bloods . . . were on the roll" and that some six hundred people were slated to share in the money. He "feared that men, who had never done any thing for their people, were going to claim an equal share with those who had been helpful to them," which he opposed as "unjust." Tribal leaders were set with the task of preparing a proper list; when they accepted or rejected names for that list they did so with unanimous consent.[40]

The final list contained some five hundred names. The commissioners proposed that each person on the list should receive fifty dollars, with the remainder of the money going to fifty people designated by tribal leaders as "their particular friends," who would receive approximately three hundred additional dollars apiece. LaMotte, speaking for the tribal leaders, "declared . . . that this was the very thing they had desired," because "There were some persons who had been their very good friends, whom they had desired to consider in this distribution, as it would be the last opportunity they would ever have of rewarding them for the good they had done."[41]

Although the federal government considered this a buyout of the people of mixed blood, the tribe did not see it the same way. The Menominee were rewarding their friends, not selling out tribal members. Most of the people on the list probably did not live with any of the bands except perhaps as merchants. Cope in his journal wrote, "They were very little like Indians."[42]

Individuals, on the other hand, viewed the situation differently, and their reasons for accepting the payment varied. Some did so with the belief that this was their only chance to avoid forced removal to Minnesota. A number of these people remained in the Menominee, Michigan, and Marinette, Wisconsin, areas.[43] Others accepted the payment because they felt they were, or wanted to be, more American than Menominee. Still others, including Menominee women married to white men and their children, accepted without having a choice in the matter. Many of these women and children later tried to gain reinstatement to the tribal rolls, charging coercion by the white husband and father who merely wanted the family's money.[44]

Another payment of the 1848 treaty—thirty thousand dollars to the traders—caused immense conflict from the beginning. The problems began with a fight over who should receive the money. The treaty called for the thirty thousand dollars to go "To the chiefs . . . to enable them to arrange and settle the affairs of the tribe preparatory to their removal," but Subagent Bruce paid out the claims without the consent of the entire tribe.[45] The Menominee discussed this in their meetings with the acting commissioner of Indian affairs in Washington in 1850. Waukechon said that the Menominee thought they were to receive the money to pay their debts but that Subagent Bruce had taken the money and "distributed it among the claimants as he pleased." Shaw-ne-ke-ness-ish agreed "that he had *never heard* of this claim being paid *until* he reached Washington."[46] Trader George Cown received a large portion of the claim, but all of that went directly to his suppliers, the Ewings, and his attorney, Richard Thompson. Bonduel, interestingly, supported Cown's claim "with some warmth," according to Commissioner of Indian Affairs Manypenny, as a proper debt of the Christian bands. The issue was abruptly dropped in this meeting, however, when Carron pointed out that the Menominee were interested first in regaining land in Wisconsin and that the tribe would deal with its other concerns later.[47]

Cown claimed $12,000, receiving $3,657 from Subagent Bruce at the 1849 annuity pay ground and another $4,171.50—half his remaining claim—from the U.S. Treasury in 1850.[48] Bruce, who died before the investigation of these transactions, said that Cown's $12,000 claim was certified by the Christian bands at the urging of Bonduel. Bruce claimed that Bonduel and Cown held a feast for Oshkosh and others, with no interpreter present, and induced the tribal delegates present to sign the agreement. "Although the Indians have heard nothing," wrote Commissioner of Indian Affairs Manypenny, "they confidently touch the quill, for there sits their father in God to protect them, and he knows what the whispers mean if they do not." The claim was amended to request $12,800, which included $800 for Bonduel.[49]

According to Bonduel, many of the other claimants paid by Bruce were whiskey traders, among whom were the Grignons.[50] The $30,000 payment left not only the Menominee but also the traders dissatisfied. Again the Ewings went to work. They collected powers of attorney from all traders who maintained claims against the tribe, in order to consolidate them into one large claim, which was a regular practice of the firm. They used printed powers of attorney forms, with blanks to fill in for the person signing over the claim, the tribe against which the claim was made, and the percentage of fee to be received by the Ewing company. In most cases, Ewing, Chute, and Company was to receive 50 percent.[51]

Between February and April, the company collected at least thirty-four of these powers of attorney, one of the largest being Augustin Grignon's claim of seven thousand dollars. Even more important to the Ewings was Grignon's support in the process. He only permitted them a one-third share, although they no doubt requested 50 percent. Subagent Bruce, who was desperately short of money, also had collected powers of attorney, but the Ewings bought him out by loaning him over one thousand dollars. In return Bruce certified their powers of attorney, although only at one-third of each claim.[52] Thompson initially joined the Ewings in the pursuit of these claims but later attempted to disassociate himself from them when the claimants' methods were investigated.[53] In any case this conniving was all for naught since the claims had already been paid, however unsatisfactorily. Repugnant as these machinations may have been to the Menominee, their primary concern remained gaining title to some land in Wisconsin. Next to this concern, the other treaty stipulations, whose ramifications would spill over for decades, paled in significance as far as tribal members and leaders were concerned. The Menominee grimly understood they would need to exert all of their strength to simply maintain a small portion of their original homeland.

10

Reclaiming a Piece
of the Homeland

The move to the Wolf River was not the end of the Menominee battle for a homeland but only the beginning. Despite the escape clause the Menominee had inserted into the treaty, the federal government decided it would permit the Menominee to remain in Wisconsin only if the state approved of it. According to attorney Richard Thompson, he retained respected Wisconsin citizens to lobby the state legislature for this. The missionary Florimond Bonduel traveled on foot to Madison in the winter of 1852–53 for that same purpose. He claimed to have bribed several officials to support the Menominee, as someone else, possibly the ex-subagent David Jones, bribed other officials to vote against the tribe. Thompson claimed he paid for this effort, but he did not know that Bonduel was there too.[1] On 14 February, the state legislature passed a joint resolution granting the tribe permission to remain on land set aside for the Menominee by the federal government.[2] This resolution paved the way for negotiation of the 1854 treaty. The northern superintendent of the Office of Indian Affairs would oversee the negotiations.

From 1851 to 1857 the northern superintendency served as go-between for the Green Bay agency and the commissioner of Indian affairs.[3] The first superintendent, Elias Murray, who served from 1851 to 1853, seems to have been a typical political appointee of the time — someone who received the job as a political favor and used it to dispense such favor. His friendship with members of the Ewing brothers' trading company, whose agents may have had a hand in his appointment, helped that company profit from the tribe's removal to the Wolf River in October and November of 1852; in turn the Ewings tried to use their political connections in Washington to protect his appointment.[4]

Despite assurances from the Ewings' business associate and friend George Wright that their friend Murray would not be replaced by a new administration, George W. Manypenny, when he became commissioner of Indian affairs in 1853, appointed Francis (Franz) Huebschmann to replace him.[5] Huebschmann more than any other man shaped federal policy as it applied to the development of the U.S.-Menominee relationship throughout the rest of the nineteenth century.

Huebschmann negotiated the final two treaties between the United States and the Menominee in 1854 and 1856 and oversaw the beginnings of reservation political life. The issues and concerns of the federal government and its policies toward the tribe as Huebschmann defined them remained much the same until the passage of the 1908 logging act and even later. Huebschmann believed the Menominee to be "uncivilized or wild Indians" on the verge of becoming civilized. "[P]erhaps the history of the civilization of Indian tribes will not show an instance where more has been accomplished in so short a time," he reported to Manypenny in an annual report.[6]

His basis for this belief was firmly rooted in his paternalistic view of the tribe, which manifested itself in his negotiations of the 1854 treaty and his views of the beginning of reservation life. He believed that two key factors would lead the Menominee on the road to prosperity: education for the children and agricultural self-sufficiency. These two factors, following Jeffersonian reasoning, would make the Menominee self-reliant individualists, disciplined by the opportunity to make a living while working the land for themselves. This was the policy for all Indians and, the Menominee timber resource notwithstanding, the United States focused its efforts on making Menominees into individual farmers.

1854 TREATY

In December 1853, a year after the tribe had been removed to the falls of the Wolf River, and nearly eleven months after the state of Wisconsin passed a joint resolution inviting the tribe to remain in the state, Huebschmann wrote to Commissioner Manypenny summarizing the government's philosophy regarding its new wardship duties. Reporting on a council he had held with the tribe at the October annuity payment, Huebschmann mentioned the Menominee's enthusiastic approval of farming. "The views of the Indians as to the necessity of becoming agriculturalists and educating their rising generation, as expressed by them in council, was very satisfying," he wrote. But in the next sentences he betrayed the methods he had used to convince the tribe to express such views: their remaining in Wisconsin hinged upon it. "I explained to them that before the question, if they would remain at their present location, would be settled, a new treaty would have to be made and approved, that the State of Wisconsin had only given her consent to their remaining expecting, that they would become civilized and agriculturalists, and that the General Government would not leave them there, unless it believed in the sincerity of their efforts to improve their condition." Even Shoneniew, the tribe's "most constant" opponent to schools and agriculture, "made a fine speach on behalf of the Pagan Bands, giving a solemn pledge, that they will turn their attention to agriculture and send their children to school like the Catholic Bands."[7] This statement is not surprising, given that their opportunity to remain on their homelands was at stake.

In May 1854, Huebschmann secretly negotiated a federal treaty with the Menominee, without inviting Keshena's band, which lived at nearby Lake Shawano, because he feared traders would hear of the proceedings and demand shares of the money.[8] The 1854 treaty granted the Menominee twelve townships in northern Wisconsin, ten of which make up the present Menominee reservation. Huebschmann claimed that "but few treaties have heretofore been concluded . . . with as full an understanding on the part of the Indians of the subject before them." Huebschmann viewed the exclusion of Keshena as unimportant because he believed he knew better than Keshena what was best for the Menominee.[9]

The tribe received $242,686 (in fifteen annuity payments beginning in 1867) to pay for the difference in value of the land in Minnesota, to which they had relinquished their rights. They renounced their claims to the money owed them from previous fraudulent dealings by the government, between $613,515.36 and $1,108,807.84 from 1848 alone. Huebschmann had negotiated a payment of $150,000, but the Senate added $92,686.[10] According to Huebschmann the tribe's leaders were willing to sign the treaty because of his promise of "large amounts of means to be immediately expended for their improvements."[11] Since many Menominee faced starvation, he may have been right. Moreover, as in 1848, the Menominee were again threatened with removal to Minnesota if they did not sign the treaty. Huebschmann denied that threat but observed: "If the late sub-agent, Mr. Suydam, to obtain their consent to the amendment of the senate, giving them $92,000 additional pay, did use the threat of the removal to the Mississippi, I should be sorry for him . . . for I am positive I could have obtained that consent without any such threat."[12]

Huebschmann apparently did not view as a threat his 1853 statement that the government predicated the tribe's remaining in Wisconsin on its acceptance of agriculture. He probably saw it as providing proper guidance; he simply wanted to eliminate tribal ways. Oshkosh refused to sign the 1854 treaty, which did not bother Huebschmann. "And as to the Head Chief Oshkosh," he wrote to Manypenny, "if he had been really opposed to the Treaty, I have no idea that Sho-ne-niew and the other pagan chiefs would have signed it."[13] The Senate refused to ratify the treaty without Oshkosh's or Keshena's approval, however, so in August Huebschmann sent Manypenny a supplemental agreement signed by them.[14] No records can be found to show why Oshkosh changed his mind.

Huebschmann worked hard in this treaty to meet the needs of Wisconsin's nascent lumber industry. The 1848 treaty had opened millions more acres of Menominee land to the timber industry, but even the small reservation that the tribe eventually gained was contested and remapped by politicians and timber interests. The 1853 resolution passed by the state legislature would have permitted the tribe to live on fifteen townships of land surrounding the Wolf and Oconto Rivers. The 1854 treaty moved the boundaries of Menominee land west of the area granted by the state, centering the tribal lands on the Wolf River and its tributaries (see map 6).

The nine eastern townships proposed by the state legislature were lopped off of the reservation, and six townships were added on the west because "Most of the valuable pine lands are in the east along the two branches of the Oconto," Huebschmann wrote to the commissioner's office in 1854. In 1857 he stated: "In giving the Menomonee Reservation a new shape by the treaty of 1854 we opened to the public nine townships containing some of the best pine lands existing."[15]

The Menominee lost all but a tiny slice of the land on the Oconto River, which flows directly into Green Bay and whose timber was thus easily accessible to the Chicago market. Yet the new reservation still held valuable timber that could be banked on the Wolf River or its tributaries. Huebschmann commented in 1854 that the area between the Wolf and Oconto contained valuable pinelands. Timber trespass and depredations continued to be a problem for the Menominee, who were unable to gain control over the use of their timber resource for some seventeen years.[16]

The tribe was satisfied with the land being offered, but the Menominee wanted better recompense for their 1848 cession.[17] However, threatened with removal, they were quick to accept the terms, despite a large financial loss and the suffering it entailed, in exchange for the twelve townships of Wisconsin land. During these years the Menominee were fighting for survival, had to form new communities and villages under the bleakest of conditions,

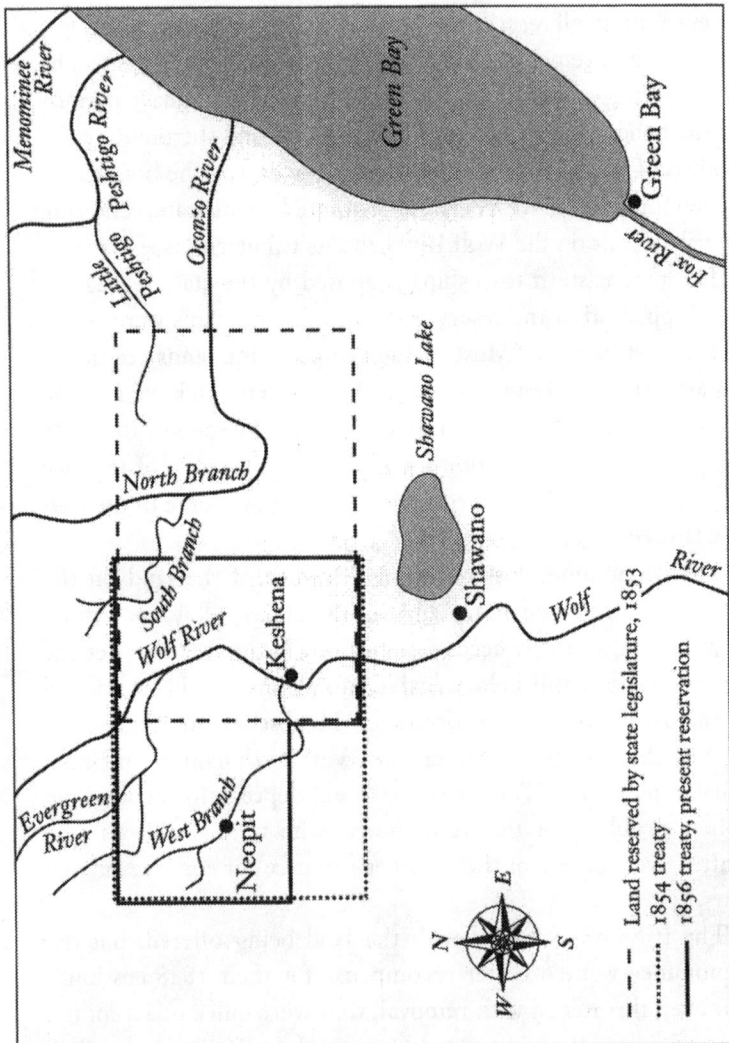

Map 6. Menominee Reservation

Green Bay

Menominee River

Little Peshtigo River

Peshtigo River

Oconto River

North Branch

South Branch

Wolf River

Keshena

Evergreen River

West Branch

Neopit

Shawano Lake

Shawano

Wolf

River

Fox River

Green Bay

- - - Land reserved by state legislature, 1853
.... 1854 treaty
——— 1856 treaty, present reservation

N
E
W
S

experienced for the first time the full weight of federal political domination, and lacked the further energy necessary to fight for resources that would become valuable in the future. The continued threats of forced and uncompensated removal overrode any concerns that were not related to their remaining in Wisconsin.

The Menominee faced two overriding problems at the time and funneled all their governmental efforts into solving them. The 1854 treaty accomplished the first problem: they wanted to remain in Wisconsin and retain a part of their homeland, which they had ceded in the 1848 treaty but had never given up or left. The treaty stipulations were to solve the second problem: starvation and want, caused by bunching all the bands into a small area and the loss of lands from which Menominees could make a living. Those two factors made the Menominee easy victims of Huebschmann's efforts to negotiate the treaties, which stipulated that the Menominee learn farming and building skills with the assistance of white farmers, carpenters, and teachers.[18]

Huebschmann clearly recognized the Menominee's dilemma. In the autumn of 1853 he wrote to Manypenny that without government help the tribe would face starvation. The Menominee had left their stock behind when they removed from their village sites to the Wolf River area. When spring arrived, after a terribly harsh winter, they were unable to break ground. The new land, though containing an important source of sturgeon for some bands, did not contain enough fish, game, and rice to support the entire tribe. This remained a constant problem, which the application of federal policy exacerbated.[19]

Superintendent Huebschmann, however, enthusiastically envisioned that the Menominee would rapidly cast off tribal ways in exchange for American "civilization."[20] He wrote his superiors in the fall of 1854 that "The leading idea is, that as much as practicable all the work to be done for the Menominees is to be done by them, and the whites are to be emploied only to Superintend the work and to teach them how to work, so as to enable them in time to be their own mechanics and their own farmers." At first a carpenter and a farmer would have to be employed, but Menominees would do most of the work. For communal work they would be paid. If they brought lumber to the mill it would be milled for their use. He believed that within two years most Menominees would live in houses they had built and the rest of the tribe would soon follow their example.[21] Poor farmland, however, caused the tribe's members to live near starvation in the early reservation years.[22]

Immediately after the signing of the treaty, the Menominee, Thompson, and the Ewings all raised cries against it. On 3 July 1854, Menominee chiefs and headmen sent a petition to the Senate, no doubt with the aid of traders, quite possibly the Grignons since it was signed at Butte des Morts. They requested the $613,515 that the 1853 Senate report had determined to be their due. They said they "reject the aforesaid treaty that we may have Opertunity for a fair open Treaty where we may recive from our white Brothers even handed Justice." They "most respectfully" informed the Senate "that we ware haistely called togeather on the 12th of May 1854 by our Superintendent F. Huebschmann Equ. without the least knowledg of what we ware called togeather for untill we met in council on the 11th one day preciding the sighning of the treaty of the 12th of May." In this hastily arranged meeting they were "called upon to sign away interests the most sacred, the inheritance of our children, and our pledged faith to our Friends who were Employed by us to look after our intrests."[23] According to the government, however, the protest came too late. The Menominee continued to expose these illegal treaties and as late as the 1870s refused to accept what they considered to be insufficient annuity money.[24]

Non-Indians protested too. Wisconsin senators Henry Dodge and J. P. Walker apparently received a letter in November 1854 signed by Wisconsin citizens who wished Congress to pay them for their claims against the Menominee for debts made after the 1836 treaty and prior to 1 September 1852. The letter stated that the tribe had petitioned the president and the Congress and had requested the help of the senators in achieving an early payment.[25]

The Ewings apparently blamed the tribe for being injudicious.

Angry notes, written in pencil, probably in late 1854 and possibly by one of the Ewings, appear to be for a talk to be made to the tribe. These notes bitterly blamed the tribe's leaders for signing the crooked treaty, when the Menominee had already entrusted their well-being to their American allies. The writer disregarded that the Menominee desired above all to regain title to some land in Wisconsin but saw his own hopes to collect money from tribal or individual debts vanish.

> [T]hey were and their friends such *old* fools as to agree to give up a Million of Dollars for a mere nothing, why did they not all *say* as I hear Oshkosh did say — we will not interfere with that buisiness it is in the hands of our friends. that is what they should have said and not Listened to the old Low dog that was sent there *secretly* to *swindle* them a *second* time.
>
> If Oshkosh who is the principal Chief is not satisfied with this *second swindle* and did not sign it he and his people would send on a remonstrance, against it, at once. Let it be sent to the Hon. J. P. Walker, the US. Senator from Wisconsin the senate would not ratify such disonest [illegible] if they knew it.
>
> The Indians are d'd. fools, to *place* a matter in the hands of an *ally* and then go throw it all away at the suggestions of a *second Medille*. Tell them, I say so. I have worked three years for them for nothing, so has Col. Thompson.[26]

In September 1855 the tribe met in council to consider the claims of Thompson and the Ewings but rejected them. A U.S. official named Clark oversaw the proceedings. Shoneon reported that on the night of 7 September, during an adjournment in the council proceedings, George Washington Ewing tried to bribe him with a hundred dollars. According to Huebschmann, Rosalie Dousman, the schoolteacher, also refused a bribe. The trader George Cown apparently threatened the Menominee that the government could still remove them as well as the remains of their dead to Minnesota if they did not cooperate. Carron believed that Thompson had encouraged Cown to make this threat and, despite Thompson's protests, joked about it in open council.

> Mr. Clark has been sent here to hear our sentiments, and I am expressing my views. As I have heard you would take my bones away to the Mississippi after I am dead, I want to tell you what you had better do. [Here Mr. Thompson interrupted by denying that he made any such remark.] I am perfectly astonished, if it is true what I have heard; and I am astonished at you. If it is not true, it has to come out here. [Here he turned to J. Cown, with whom Thompson boarded, and who had reported the remark as Thompson's.] I laughed when I heard it. I recommend you will not drop my bones. I want them together, if they are here or on the Mississippi. Put them in a strong bag, and keep a strong watch, so the dogs do not run away with some of my bones. Not only this has been used to frighten our chiefs. If you should want to get the removal of myself and the others, I think you could not get it if you said you wanted to remove my bones. You may get my good bones, but you cannot get my soul; that will go where all the good spirits go. You are welcome to my bones.[27]

Thompson, therefore, had to pursue his claim through the Senate.

ESTABLISHING A RESERVATION

Several months later, on 11 February 1856, the Menominee signed their last treaty with the U.S. government, this time ceding one-sixth of their reservation to some of the same eastern tribes who had purchased their land in the 1820s, the Stockbridge and Munsees. American settlers had pressured the Stockbridge and Munsees to leave their lands near Lake Winnebago. Carron and other Menominee leaders spoke in council on 9 February to the effect that they had been neighbors with these tribes for some thirty years, that the Great Spirit had made both tribes, and that they felt they could live as neighbors.[28] Huebschmann wrote to Commissioner Manypenny, "The Menominees evinced a liberal spirit towards the Indians proposed to be located in their neighborhood, a sense of gratitude to the government for the measures taken for their welfare, and a firm resolution to avail themselves of the facilities offered them to improve."[29]

The 1856 Menominee treaty established the current boundaries of the reservation with ten townships consisting of some 234,000 acres. The treaty, also negotiated by Huebschmann, was signed by, among others, Oshkosh, Keshena, LaMotte, Carron, Waukechon, and Shoneon. The United States agreed to pay sixty cents an acre for Menominee land, the money to be applied to the tribe's "improvement."[30]

Thompson wrote one last letter to Oshkosh, in May 1856, acknowledging a letter in which Oshkosh had wished Thompson well in collecting from the Senate, which he eventually succeeded in doing. Thompson replied, "If I shall not be paid it will be very hard after all that I have done for you. If you had sent word to your Great Father that you wanted me paid, it would have been done long ago. But as they would not let you do that, I have not been paid and have been put to a great deal of trouble. But I do not know how to mend it now—as you have already hurt an old friend who served you. Even Carron who was the first to employ me, was the first to try to hurt me."[31]

Although some Menominees never left their homelands, much of the tribe did settle on the reservation, both before and after the completion of the 1854 treaty, moving into various settlements at first based on band affiliation. The area had long been used by several bands of Menominee, especially the Keshena Falls and Wolf River sites. Weshonaquet Mosehart, a tribal member, later recalled, "After I grew up to manhood I came upon the present Reservation. My people were accustomed to roam all over the present Reservation every spring when the sturgeon came up the Wolf River as far as Keshena Falls. It was the custom of all the

Indians from the various bands that were scattered far and near to gather together at the Keshena Falls to catch the fish and would camp there for months for the purpose of catching the sturgeon." He added that women picked cranberries, reed bull rushes, and sweet flags in the area to weave for the mats used to build wigwams.[32]

The Christian bands that had lived in the Lake Poygan area moved to the east bank of the Wolf River near Keshena Falls at the pay ground, near the place where the agency town of Keshena would eventually be established. These bands include those led by Aiometah, Carron, LaMotte, Oshkenaniew, Watasau, and Akinepoway, who later moved north and founded the current community of West Branch, in 1871.[33]

Father Bonduel accompanied the tribe to the falls of the Wolf River, where he founded St. Michael the Archangel mission on 6 November 1852, almost immediately upon arrival. The schoolhouse he and Dousman used there was a decrepit shanty on the pay ground, with half-inch cracks between the boards that had been covered over with clapboards.[34]

As his predecessors had done, Bonduel claimed extravagant success in converting Menominees to Catholicism. He said that in his twenty years of service he saved from the devil more than seven thousand Indians in the Upper Great Lakes. Specifically regarding the Menominee, in an 1855 lecture to the Paris Council, "he told the members that it was the forces of grace which had triumphed among the Indians, and especially since it was only a few years earlier that these people were 'committed to magic and to all the superstitions of paganism and even to the influences of the demons [but were] now, for the most part, models of virtue and Christian piety worthy to be emulated.'" This claim amounts to exaggeration, since less than half of the tribe's members at the time were Christian and several bands' leaders "would continue to resist both the culture and the religion of the Christians until the day they died."[35]

Bonduel described a return visit he made soon after the creation of the reservation and after Father Skolla had taken over the mission. He attended the Corpus Christi celebration, saying the Menominee welcomed him affectionately. At the time, he said, the Catholic Menominees numbered between twelve and fifteen hundred.[36] Perhaps he based his numbers on the hundreds of people who helped celebrate Corpus Christi, many of whom were Catholic but many of whom were probably not. The pageantry surrounding this event, which brought visiting church officials to the reservation and included a grand parade, would have attracted many members of the tribe.[37] Although Bonduel's figures were exaggerated, Catholicism had become an important aspect of tribal culture by the early reservation years.[38]

Father Bonduel soon left the reservation in anger at not being compensated in treaty money for losses incurred during the removal. In March 1854, Bonduel's superior, Bishop Henni, recalled him to Milwaukee, effectively ending his service among the Menominee just two months before the tribe signed the treaty gaining for them a permanent home in Wisconsin.[39]

In his anger Bonduel ordered the mission cross that had been placed on a hill above the settlement removed by two Christian Menominees, who refused to do so on the grounds of impropriety. "The Father thereupon chopped down the cross himself saying that these Indians were not worth having the mission cross," according to oral history collected from John Warrington by a church historian in the late 1880s, who added that the Pope ordered Bonduel to wear a crucifix for five years as atonement.[40]

The non-Christian bands settled together in two general divisions based on the distinction between the Bear and Thunder clans. Bear clan leaders including Oshkosh, Souligny, Chickeney, and Shawano settled on the west side of the river near Keshena Falls. Thunder clan leaders settled with their bands on Wayka Creek, led by Wayka (Poegonah), Keso, and Niaqtawapomi. Northern bands from the Green Bay area settled away from this area, including at South Branch on the Little Oconto River.[41]

With the departure of Father Bonduel, few non-Indians remained living in Menominee country. The agents assigned to oversee the federal obligations to the tribe in the early treaty years did not reside on the reservation; only the schoolteacher and a few traders did. The Menominee land base was now small, and until the 1870s loggers considered the tribe's forest relatively insignificant. Farmers and a string of missionaries would come to work among the Menominee in the early reservation years, but the primary immediate tribal concern, now that a land base had been permanently secured, would be survival.

The tribe's economy had been destroyed by the rapid advance of the white population into Menominee country. Hunting, fishing in the small lakes and on the Wolf River, where sturgeon spawned each spring, and gathering, especially of wild rice and maple sugar, even when these activities were carried on off of the reservation, could provide only a nominal supplement to individual diets on this much-reduced land base. The reservation land was largely unsuitable for the farming practiced in 1850s Wisconsin. Rations promised in the treaties in exchange for the land sales were often inedible or late. Most Menominees were forced to live on the sharp edge between survival and starvation. In the first two decades of reservation life the tribal population would drop by some 30 percent.[42]

Nonetheless, despite the catastrophic circumstances of the previous four decades, the Menominee had been able to accomplish a remarkable achievement: securing a land base in a part of their ancient homeland on which future generations could begin to create a stable base not only for physical survival but for relatively autonomous rule and cultural maintenance. Such accomplishments, however, would take nearly all of the tribe's energy for a period lasting well over a century.

11

Siege And Survival

The European expansion remade the Western Hemisphere, bringing new people, reshaping the landscape, and changing the people who were already there. This, however, was not a history of Western civilization triumphing over barbarism, nor even a history of Western imperialism destroying native cultures, though the latter sometimes happened. It was instead the story of a massive invasion by technologically superior peoples who carried diseases to which they were largely inured and the varied responses of myriad societies to secure survival. What is remarkable, given the tremendous destruction wrought time and again, sometimes over a period of centuries, is the survival of so many Indian nations, tribes, bands, and peoples and their retention of separate cultural and political identities within the boundaries of conquering societies. Ultimately, survival may not be possible without an economic separateness or basis as well, yet thus far survival has occurred without this base for many tribal nations.

Survival is not enough to give meaning to a person's life or a people's world, however. It is merely the foundation for the opportunity to define a culture, to shape a future. The Menominee, whose territory and life ways came under siege nearly four centuries ago, managed to survive by keeping the vision of a distant future containing a Menominee tribal culture ever at the forefront and by shaping that future in tribally defined ways.

Menominee survival had long depended on their adaptability to their changing woodland environment. The European era, how-

202 ▼ *Siege and Survival*

ever, dramatically challenged Menominee survival in new ways. The siege on Menominee culture built slowly, reaching a crescendo during the American treaty period. It occurred on a variety of levels that individually, for the most part, may seem innocuous but in concert with each other came to be overwhelming. They fended off the worst threats posed by the Mesquakies and French, adapting to the French presence in their country despite the traumatic losses it brought with it. They accommodated the British and later tried to accommodate the eastern tribes that desired Menominee land. Each new incursion, however, brought new challenges that in the long run began to constrict Menominee options. Tribal independence was weakened as the Menominee became involved in a world-economy, even if tribal culture consistently adapted.[1]

The American assaults proved most destructive. The massive upheavals of the seventeenth and eighteenth centuries in Menominee country paled in comparison with those that began in the early nineteenth century. For the Menominee, as for other tribes in the Great Lakes region, the balance of power tipped to the Euro-Americans in the years between the French-British Seven Years' War and the British-American War of 1812.[2] As a result, Menominee governmental independence seriously eroded in the early American period.

Menominee tribal survival into the reservation period was based on two principal factors: perceptive, stalwart, farseeing leadership and maintenance of core cultural values. Sekatsokemau and Oshkosh, though from different eras, both reflect the strength of Menominee leadership. The established practice of *apēkon ahkīhih*, used so adeptly by Sekatsokemau, lost its reliability with the advent of eastern tribes into Menominee territory in the 1820s. When the Menominee refused to accept duplicitous dealings, and the U.S. government decided it needed to appoint Menominee leaders to deal directly with federal agents, Oshkosh shaped his position to be one of strong advocacy for a Menominee-defined tribal future. One of the favorite ruses of colonialist powers — creation of a "collaborative elite" to do the government's bidding — was thus foiled.[3] Although these government-appointed positions were new in the structure of Menominee leadership, the Menominee had long used orators as mouthpieces to foreign powers, so it was not entirely unprecedented.

Although Oshkosh's and other leaders' appointments represent a first step in the Menominee government's loss of control, band leaders continued to exert authority within the internal governing system. Indeed, they continued to play key roles in tribal decision making. And even more importantly, despite the increasing American power, Menominee leaders succeeded in shaping the tribe's future to a larger degree than the Americans wanted.

The second factor, maintenance of core cultural values, helped the Menominee to both maintain their identity and survive. Although conditions forced material changes, including shrinkage of the tribe's land base and exploitation of its resources, and changes in the structure of its government, key values remained unchanged and continued to shape the way the tribe responded to outside threats. In the political and economic realms these values determined interactions with outside society, internal governance, and the use of resources. They defined how leaders needed to act, and Menominee leaders needed to act on behalf of all their people, keeping especially the needs of future generations in mind. Oshkosh reflected this value when, speaking in council on 12 May 1856, he said, "I wish to pursue a course which will be the best for our children who will follow us."[4]

Leaders needed the support of their whole group when dealing with outsiders and seldom successfully made decisions without consulting with the entire band or tribe. They needed to keep the health of the community as the highest priority, even though Americans have always insisted that individual rights receive primacy. They needed to remember that tribal resources, tribally controlled, remain an important base of the tribe's identity. And they needed to be able to provide for their people, especially those unable to provide for themselves. These values remained consistent over the entire period of contact. From the so-called sturgeon war to the quick and equitable division of the "beeves" hunted down and slaughtered at the 1838 annuity payment, the Menominee rewarded generosity and sharing of resources and decried as non-Menominee the failure to do so.

Economics lay at the base of European and American incursions into Menominee country and life, beginning with the Euro-American fur trade and continuing with the American desire for Menominee land and timber. These three resources provided the focal point for the Euro-American invasion described in this work and provided the basis for Euro-American political involvement as well. Two changes stand out as leading causes of the decimation of tribal political power: the fur trade and treaties. The fur trade not only drew the Menominee into the world economic market system but also established a system of credit that would impact the Menominee for generations. The French credit system, sheared of the tribal generosity that had initially shaped it in Menominee country, remained only as the vicious shell of profit-oriented trade in the American years.

Federal collusion with traders established a series of controls that changed the debt relationship from one of individual concern to a basis in which, for the first time, tribal resources were at stake. This had a crippling effect on the tribal economy in its own right and also as the United States enlisted the help of traders and others in stripping the tribe of its lands. It was the treaties themselves that swept away the Menominee land base and with it the resources necessary for survival. This swift change forced the Menominee into a state of economic dependence that translated into a loss of political independence as well.

But the treaties were important for reasons beyond the loss of land. They stipulated not only compensation for the land, which was often meager and unjust, but also the retention of rights, sometimes on lands ceded but most often on lands retained. Menominee responses to the treaties provide more insights than the documentation itself.[5] Throughout the decades a pattern emerged, showing an increasingly more sophisticated understanding of the results and meanings of treaty negotiations. The Menominee not only knew what they had agreed to but acted on that knowledge.

That Menominee leaders signed the 1854 treaty relinquishing rights from 1848, for example, tells us little more than that their primary goal was to remain in Wisconsin. The Menominee in fact challenged the federal government to recognize that the agreement as understood by the United States differed greatly from the tribe's understanding of it. The Menominee had no intention of selling what they referred to as "the inheritance of our children." That tribal leaders refused to accept the validity of the 1854 treaty from the time of its inception is evidence that they believed the words as written did not reflect what they had agreed to. The tribe would accept coercion when reason dictated that no other viable option existed and would fight successfully against any outside definition of the Menominee future whenever possible.

Powerful forces pressured Menominee decision makers, whose concerns with physical survival in these times of increasing economic destruction and social upheaval had to be balanced with retention of homelands. Settlement on the reservation ended the treaty-making period, in which the Menominee sold between 8 and 12 million acres, or possibly more, of valuable land to the United States. The costs of the battle for land were excessive for the Menominee: the government paid a pittance for the coveted land, treaty negotiations were at best dishonest, and much of the money never reached the tribe but instead enriched traders, suppliers, missionaries, and federal officials. Thus the Menominee lost most of their land as well as the money they were to receive for it.

Other costs cannot be figured on a ledger: the people who died or became ill during removal; the bands that were forced to leave their ancient homelands to share a small part of their old hunting grounds with all the other bands; or the disassociation of certain people in the 1849 mixed-blood payment. Most important, the Menominee lost their ability to sustain themselves. The loss of economic independence made them further dependent on governmental annuities and rations. They traded wild game and fish for rancid pork, and wild rice for flour, and became enmeshed in a cycle of dietary problems undermining their health. At the same time, the federal wardship that was forced on the Menominee deepened governmental paternalism.

Yet unlike many other tribes, the Menominee still owned a rich resource, their forest. This resource, together with the waters in their reservation — especially the Wolf River — is as significant for maintaining cultural definition of the people as it is for providing an economic foundation.[6] Many outsiders would covet the Menominee forest as earlier they had coveted Menominee land. The forest would eventually give the Menominee the base from which to rebuild a tribal economy in a tribally defined way, although that process too would involve long and costly battles.

Appendix

Table A1. Menominee population estimates and figures, 1683–1855

1683	Disease takes numerous Menominee lives
1718	80–100 warriors (French count)
1721	200 men (British count)
1736	160 warriors (French count)
1757	1,100 (ca. 300 of these die of smallpox)
1763	110 Meynomeny men (British count)
	110 Folsavoins men (British count)
1818	730 (Green Bay agency)
	270 (Illinois River)
1819	500 warriors (Green Bay)
	490 total (Prairie du Chien)
	Number for Chicago combined with other tribes
1820	3,900 (Morse's estimate)
1824	272 Menominee and Chippewa warriors
	40 Menominee and Winnebago warriors
	140 Menominee warriors
1834	Approximately one-fourth of tribe dies of smallpox
1842	2,464 first tribal roll
1843	2,512 annuity shares
1852	2,002 removed to falls of Wolf River
1855	1,930

Sources: Annual Reports of the Commissioner of Indian Affairs; Letters Received, M234-327; Bloom, Territorial Papers of the United States, vol. 27; Collections of the State Historical Society of Wisconsin, vol. 20; Green Bay and Prairie du Chien Papers SHSW Archives; Morse, A Report to the Secretary of War; O'Callaghan, ed., Documents, vol. 7; Ourada, The Menominee Indians; Rosholt and Gehl, Florimond J. Bonduel; Tanner, Atlas of Great Lakes Indian History.

Table A2. Agents among the Menominee, 1671–1857

Known French Indian agents

1665–1690s	Nicolas Perrot
1754–ca. 1760	Charles de Langlade

British Indian agents

1761–ca. 1780	Charles de Langlade
1813–15	Col. Robert Dickson

Agents at Green Bay agency (1815–37)
and Green Bay subagency (1837–55)

1815–16	Charles Jouett, appointed 20 June 1815
1816–20	John Bowyer, appointed 15 March 1816
1821–22	John Biddle, appointed 10 March 1821
1822	Capt. William Whistler (acting)
1822–29	Henry Brevoort, appointed 30 July 1822
1830–32	Samuel C. Stambaugh, appointed (notified) 12 June 1830; appointment lapsed March 1831; served until replaced
1832–36	George Boyd, transferred from Mackinac 18 April 1832
1837	Bvt. Brig. Gen. George M. Brooke (acting), appointed 1 January 1837
1837–42	George Boyd, appointed 31 March 1837
1842–43	George W. Lawe, appointed 24 May 1842
1843–45	David Jones, appointed (notified) 17 November 1843
1845–49	Albert G. Ellis, appointed 21 August 1845
1849–51	William H. Bruce, appointed 2 April 1849
1851–53	George Lawe, appointed 28 March 1851
1853–54/55	John V. Suydam, appointed 11 May 1853
1855	Ephraim Shaler, appointed 21 February 1855
1855–57	Benjamin Hunkins, appointed 8 May 1855

Agents at Prairie du Chien

1802–8	John Campbell
1808–27	Nicholas Boilvin

Agent at Chicago

1816–	Charles Jouett

Agents at Michilimackinac

1815–18	William Henry Puthuff
1818–32	George Boyd
1832–36	Henry Rowe Schoolcraft

Table A3. Federal superintendents overseeing Green Bay agency, 1815–1857

Michigan superintendency, 1815–36

1813–31	Lewis Cass (governor)
1831–34	George B. Porter (governor)
1834–35	Stevens T. Mason (acting, after Porter's death)
1835–36	John S. Horner (acting)
1836–41	Henry R. Schoolcraft (Mackinac agent)

Wisconsin superintendency, 1836–48

1836–41	Henry Dodge
1841–44	James Duane Doty
1844–45	Nathanial P. Tallmadge
1845–48	Henry Dodge
1848–51	Green Bay agent reported directly to Washington

Northern superintendency, 1851–57

1851–53	Elias Murray, appointed 12 March 1851
1853–57	Francis Huebschmann, appointed 18 April 1853

Table A4. Known interpreters among the Menominee, 1671–1857

1671, 1701	Nicolas Perrot
1761–63	Charles Gautier
1763	Thomas Carty
1805–6	Pierre Rousseau, for Zebulon Pike
1817	J. B. LaBord
1818–34	Richard Prickett
1834–39	James Madison Boyd
1857–ca. 1866	William Powell; served off and on for twelve years, 1830–57
1850s–1899	Joseph Gauthier; Satterlee said he served forty-two years; Powell replaced him for several years

Table A5. Missionaries and priests among the Menominee, 1669–1857

Catholic Missions

1669–70	Fr. Claude Jean Allouéz, 1669 at Green Bay; 1670 at Oconto River
1671–84	Fr. Claude André, Menominee River
1707	Jesuits abandoned Green Bay
1830–35	Rev. Samuel Mazzuchelli, O.P.
1830	Rev. Frederic Rézé
1832–34	Rev. Samuel/Simon(?) Senderl, Redemptorist Father Another Redemptorist Father
1832–46	Theodore van den Broek, O.S.D. (Dominican), 1832–38 at Green Bay; 1838–44 at Little Chute; 1844–46 at Lake Poygan
1846–52	Florimond J. Bonduel, Lake Poygan; later moved to reservation
1853–57	Fr. Otto Skolla, O.S.F.

Episcopal Mission

1830–34	Rev. Fish Cadle, Green Bay
1834–38	Rev. D. E. Brown, Green Bay
1836–37	Rev. Henry Gregory
1838	Green Bay Episcopal mission closed

Notes

INTRODUCTION

1. The word *Americans*, when it stands alone, is used throughout this work to mean people of the United States.

2. According to the Menominee Historic Preservation Department, the plural of Menominee is Menominee when referring to the tribe and is Menominees when referring to individuals. This is based on the translation of the tribe's name from the Menominee language.

3. Although Menominee history was not maintained in written form by tribal members until recently, mnemonic engravings on boards and barks were at least occasionally used for recording. See Kasprycki, "Sirens, Tapirs, and Egyptian Totems."

4. White, *The Middle Ground*.

5. Calloway, *New Worlds for All*, xiv.

6. Österhammel, *Colonialism*, 27.

7. The term *mixed blood* here means more than a biological mixture of blood; it also implies a cultural mix. Some people of mixed blood became part of the tribe, while others became part of white society. The people referred to here maintained allegiance to both societies to some degree, hence their being referred to as standing between cultures and races.

1. THE MENOMINEE WORLD BEFORE INVASION

1. Since Menominee history and literacy were largely oral based previous to the coming of Europeans, this chapter is based largely on ethnographic information, including tribal language and oral narrative, much of which was recorded after the period it is intended to portray.

2. The ethnologist Edwin James wrote this term as Kiash Machatiwuk. See Kasprycki, "'A Lover of All Knowledge,'" 2.

3. One of the tribe's historians believes the origin story should not be taken literally to mean that a bear, an eagle, and the other animals became human. She suggests that perhaps the first great Menominee leaders came from these clans. Interviews with Menominee people. As noted in the bibliography, the present author offered anonymity to interviewees he himself deposed.

4. Menominee Indian Tribe of Wisconsin, *Menominee Tribal History Guide*, 15–18; Hoffman, *The Menomini Indians*, 39–42; interview with Marvin Steven Askenette, Menominee Historic Preservation Department; interview with Earl Wescott Sr., Menominee Historic Preservation Department. The interviews conducted by the Menominee Historic Preservation Department are identified as such, and those citations include the names of interviewees.

5. Ritzenthaler, *Prehistoric Indians of Wisconsin*, 29; McKern, "The First Settlers in Wisconsin," 169; Cleland, "Indians in a Changing Environment," 85; interviews with Menominee people; Mason, "The Historic Period in Wisconsin Archaeology," 381; Overstreet, "Overview of Theoretical Frameworks." Ronald J. Mason, "Archaeoethnicity and the Elusive Menominees," raises the question of Menominee longevity in their homeland.

6. Interviews with Menominee people.

7. McKern, "The First Settlers in Wisconsin," 161–69; Edmunds and Peyser, *The Fox Wars*, 9–11; Kellogg, *French Régime*, 70–72.

8. Hurley, *An Analysis of Effigy Mound Complexes*, 1–4, 169; Birmingham and Eisenberg, *Indian Mounds of Wisconsin*, 101–16, 138–41, 165–72; interviews with Menominee people. Recent excavations for the new community of Middle Village have uncovered arrowheads and copper points left behind in the aftermath of a big battle, which may lend credence to the Menominee version of this history.

9. Spindler and Spindler, *Dreamers with Power*, 44.

10. Slotkin, *The Menomini Pow Wow*, 25.

11. Story taken from Skinner, *Medicine Ceremony of the Menomini*, 24–83.

12. Spindler and Spindler, *Dreamers with Power*, 46–49.

13. See Skinner and Satterlee, *Folklore of the Menomini Indians*; Skinner, *Material Culture*; Hoffman, *The Menomini Indians*; Bloomfield, *Menomini Texts*; Densmore, *Menominee Music*; Spindler, "Menominee," 710–12, 714–17; and Keesing, *The Menomini Indians*, 44–50.

14. Bieder, *Native American Communities in Wisconsin*, 29.

15. The language of the society's "well-being" as among the primary purposes of a leader's activity is from the late Robert V. Dumont Jr., cofounder of NAES College.

16. Hoffman, *The Menomini Indians*; 40–41; Skinner, *Material Culture*, 379–82.

17. See map entitled "Forest Communities and Subsistence Patterns" in Cleland, "Indians in a Changing Environment," 88.

18. Kay, "The Land of La Baye," 42.

19. Jenks, *Wild Rice Gatherers*, 1089. Jenks translated it as "wild rice gathering moon."

20. Satterlee, "Menomini Legend very true," in State Historical Society of Wisconsin, Green Bay Area Records Center (SHSW-GBARC).

21. Letter from Father Louis André, "De la Mission de la Folle-Avoine Près de la Baie des Puants," Thwaites, ed., *The Jesuit Relations*, vol. 58, 272–81.

22. A. E. Jenks to W. J. McGee, 23 October 1899, in Jenks, Letters Received 1888–1906, Smithsonian Institution, National Anthropological Archives (SI-NAA).

23. Quimby, *Indian Life in the Upper Great Lakes*, 143.

24. Keesing, *The Menomini Indians*, 20.

25. Jenks, *Wild Rice Gatherers*, 1092–93. In his text Jenks mistakenly refers to Weskineu as Wishki'no, which is the Menominee word for bird. He is also incorrect in saying that Māqnabus created the bear, probably misinterpreting what Menominees told him. Interviews with Menominee people.

26. Kay, "The Land of La Baye," 33.

27. Jenks, *Wild Rice Gatherers*, 1083, 1047, 1036, 1113.

28. Dablon, "Part Third. Relation of the Missions to the Outouacs

[Ottawa] during the years 1670 and 1671," in Thwaites, ed., *The Jesuit Relations*, vol. 55, 101–3, 183–85.

29. Quoted from Thwaites, *Historic Waterways*, in Jenks, *Wild Rice Gatherers*, 1033.

30. "Of the first Voyage made by Father Marquette toward new Mexico, and How the idea thereof was conceived," 87–163. Report written by Marquette, 1674, in Thwaites, ed., *The Jesuit Relations*, vol. 59, 95.

31. Kay, "The Land of La Baye," 33, 113; Mason, *Introduction to Wisconsin Indians*, 102.

32. Hoffman, *The Menomini Indians*, 291; Trowbridge, "Excerpts," SI-NAA; Child, "A New Seasonal Round."

33. Skinner, *Material Culture*, 199.

34. Hoffman, *The Menomini Indians*, 39–44.

35. Skinner, *Social Life and Ceremonial Bundles*, 8.

36. Bloomfield, *Menomini Texts*, 70–73. The story does not specify what type of kettle this was.

37. Trowbridge, "Excerpts,"SI-NAA; Hoffman, *The Menomini Indians*, 217–18; Skinner and Satterlee, *Folklore of the Menomini Indians*, 445–46; Brown, "Battle of the Pierced Forehead," 34–38; interviews with Menominee people. Trowbridge dates the incident "fifteen or twenty years before the arrival of french troops in the country." The only disagreement regarding this battle is Ourada, *The Menominee Indians*, 11, and Krog, "The Menominee," 27–28, Menominee Tribal Archives. These authors call this a war between the Chippewa and the Menominee. Krog begins the story "according to legend" and credits Father Jean Claude Allouez with details, unfortunately without citation, while Ourada also cites no sources for her interpretation.

38. "Monument", Menominee Historic Preservation Department.

39. McDonough and Grignon, "Menominee Indian Tribe of Wisconsin."

40. Kay, "The Land of La Baye," 102–4; Cleland, "Indians in a Changing Environment," 87.

41. This is amply documented during the American years. According to Bieder, "Maple sap . . . was not that important as a dietary supplement until after the Menominee acquired metal pots from the French, in which

they could boil down the sap into sugar." *Native American Communities in Wisconsin*, 29.

42. Whether these men served as wives in economic, social, or sexual roles, or some combination thereof, cannot be interpolated from the evidence. Like many aspects of Menominee culture, definition of gender was more complex than in Western culture, which has a penchant toward dichotomy. The historic complexity of gender among the Menominee is minimally documented; clearly, however, people of both genders lived a cross variety of social and economic roles.

43. Trowbridge, "Excerpts," SI-NAA.

44. Trowbridge, "Excerpts," SI-NAA.

45. A few were witches as well. Spindler, *Menomini Women and Culture Change*, 16–19.

46. Trowbridge, "Excerpts," SI-NAA.

47. Bloomfield, *Menomini Texts*, 6–9.

48. Skinner, *Material Culture*, 154–56.

49. Skinner, *Material Culture*, 143–45. The prayers were also held to ensure good weather, since the Thunderers control storms. Interviews with Menominee people.

50. Skinner, *Material Culture*, 143–45.

51. Kaushkananiew, 23 October 1832, *Documents Relating to the Negotiation of Ratified and Unratified Treaties*, reel 2, frame 622.

52. Trowbridge, "Excerpts," SI-NAA; Four Legs, 8 August 1827, *Documents Relating to the Negotiation of Ratified and Unratified Treaties*, reel 2, frame 17.

53. Interview with Alex Askenette, Menominee Historic Preservation Department.

54. Kane, *The Wanderings of an Artist*, 22–23.

55. Prucha confirms this in part in *American Indian Treaties*, when he says, "the written document, for the Indians, was of less importance than the exchange of speeches at the council," 431.

56. Interviews with Menominee people.

57. Trowbridge, "Excerpts," SI-NAA.

58. Trowbridge, "Excerpts," SI-NAA.

59. Hoffman, *The Menomini Indians*, 44.

60. Interviews with Menominee people.

61. Parker, *The Journals of Jonathan Carver*, 76. The part of the sentence beginning "whose" is marked by the editor as being from "Version II."

62. Hoffman, *The Menomini Indians*, 40–46; Skinner, *Material Culture*, 52; interviews with Menominee people; Keesing, *The Menomini Indians*, 35–37; Keesing, "Leaders of the Menomini Tribe," in State Historical Society of Wisconsin Archives (SHSW Archives).

63. Hoffman, *The Menomini Indians*, 40–41, 126–27; Skinner, *Material Culture*, 52.

64. Interviews with Menominee people.

65. Skinner, *Material Culture*, 51.

66. Menominee governmental leaders before the twentieth century were male.

67. Trowbridge, "Excerpts," SI-NAA.

2. MENOMINEE COUNTRY BECOMES A TRADING FRONTIER

1. The account is based on oral history. Trowbridge, "Excerpts."

2. Mason, *Introduction to Wisconsin Indians*, 252.

3. Skinner, *Material Culture*, 369–72; La Potherie, *History of the Savage Peoples*, in Blair, *The Indian Tribes*, vol. 1, 291, 294, 301; interviews with Menominee people; Kasprycki, "'A Lover of All Knowledge,'" 2.

4. Edmunds and Peyser, *The Fox Wars*, 9–10, 214, see also 224–26 n. 13.

5. Tanner, *The Settling of North America*, 28–29.

6. Jennings, "American Frontiers," 354, 363–64. See also Martin, Quimby, and Collier, *Indians before Columbus*, 40–46.

7. Sagard-Theodat, *Histoire du Canada*, 194.

8. Skinner, "The Sinews of Empire," 31–34; Clifton, *The Prairie People*, 10; Heidenreich, "Huron," 383–85.

9. Skinner, "The Sinews of Empire," 32; Mason, *Introduction to Wisconsin Indians*, 250–52.

10. Tanner, *Atlas of Great Lakes Indian History*, 36–37; White, *The Middle Ground*, 14; Kellogg, *French Régime*, 99–100.

11. Edmunds, *The Potawatomis*, 3–5. On the Iroquois-Huron battle for control of the trade in the 1640s, see Hunt, *The Wars of the Iroquois*, chaps. 4–7, and Kellogg, *French Régime*, 92–93. See also Eccles, *The Canadian Frontier*, and Skinner, "The Sinews of Empire."

12. Charlevoix, *History and General Description of New France*, vol. 5, 142.

13. La Potherie, *History of the Savage Peoples*, in Blair *The Indian Tribes*, vol. 1, 293.

14. La Potherie, *History of the Savage Peoples*, in Blair, *The Indian Tribes*, vol. 1, 293–300; Hunt, *The Wars of the Iroquois*, 119; Kellogg, *French Régime*, 100; Edmunds and Peyser, *The Fox Wars*, 225 n. 13.

15. Hunt, *The Wars of the Iroquois*, 155. "M. Du Chesneau's Memoir on the Western Indians, &c.," 13th 9ber 1681, in O'Callaghan, ed., *Documents*, vol. 9, 161, describes the Ottawa middleman role and the failure of other western tribes to trade directly with Montreal.

16. "M. Du Chesneau's Memoir on the Western Indians, &c.," 13th 9ber 1681, in O'Callaghan, ed., *Documents*, vol. 9, 161.

17. La Potherie, *History of the Savage Peoples*, in Blair, *The Indian Tribes*, vol. 1, 173–75.

18. Miquelon, *New France*, 150.

19. Harris and Warkentin, *Canada before Confederation*, 57–59; Miquelon, *New France*, 145–64; Eccles, *The Canadian Frontier*, 109–14, 128; Kellogg, *French Régime*, 203–5, 219; Kellogg, *British Régime*, 203; La Potherie, *History of the Savage Peoples*, in Blair, *The Indian Tribes*, vol. 1, 228–30 n. 164.

20. La Potherie, excerpt from *Histoire de l'Am'rique Septentrionale*, *Collections of the State Historical Society of Wisconsin* (hereafter *Collections* SHSW), vol. 16, 101 (Keesing, *The Menomini Indians*, 58, incorrectly cites this as vol. 7); Father Thierry Beschefer, Superior of the missions of the Society of JESUS in Canada, to the Reverend Father Provincial of the Province of France, Quebec, 21 October 1683, in Thwaites, ed., *The Jesuit Relations*, vol. 62, 203–5.

21. Bieder, *Native American Communities in Wisconsin*, 59, 61.

22. Radisson, "Excerpts," 78. The Namekagon Lake site is located a little over ten miles north of the present Lac Court Oreilles Ojibwe Reservation.

23. *Castor gras* is discussed in Miquelon, *New France*, 56.

24. Radisson, "Excerpts," 75–77. A fascinating analysis of gender roles as divined from artifacts in conjunction with ethnohistorical sources, in relation to a Wahpeton Dakota village, is Spector, *What This Awl Means*.

25. For example, see Perrot's description of trade in an early visit to the Miami Indians. La Potherie, *History of the Savage Peoples*, in Blair, *The Indian Tribes*, vol. 1, 330–32.

26. Miquelon, *New France*, 150; Anderson, "The Flow of European Trade Goods," 107–9. Figures regarding proportion of items traded are not available for the seventeenth century.

27. Kellogg, *French Régime*, x–xi; Thwaites, ed., *The Jesuit Relations*.

28. Grant, *Moon of Wintertime*, 22–25.

29. Reese, *Dictionary of Philosophy and Religion*, 268; Grant, *Moon of Wintertime*, 4–5, 11.

30. Grant, *Moon of Wintertime*, 23–52.

31. The Noquets, so-called by the French, were a tribe or band located north of the Menominee on Lake Michigan, at the site of the present Bay de Noc. Tanner, *Atlas of Great Lakes Indian History*, 62, says they were "an early community of Ojibwa"; Kellogg, *French Régime*, 71, says they later "probably coalesc[ed] with the Menominee."

32. Thwaites, ed., *The Jesuit Relations*, vol. 44, 247; Kellogg, *French Régime*, 140–41, 161.

33. Thwaites places the site approximately equidistant between the Menominee and Fox Rivers, or about eight leagues from the Menominee River. *The Jesuit Relations*, vol. 54, 305–6 n. 6. This site is easily found today since it is marked by a Wisconsin state historical marker. Cited in Kellogg, *French Régime*, 152.

34. Thwaites, ed., *The Jesuit Relations*, vol. 54, 234–35. Allouéz knew Algonquin, to which Menominee is related.

35. For descriptions of the ceremony from the perspectives of a government official (St. Lusson), a trader (Perrot), and a Jesuit missionary (Dablon), see Saint-Lusson's Procès-Verbal, 14 June 1671, *Collections*

SHSW, vol. 11, 26–29; Perrot, *Memoir on the Manners*, in Blair, *The Indian Tribes*, vol. 1, 220–25; La Potherie, *History of the Savage Peoples*, in Blair, *The Indian Tribes*, 346–48; and Claude Dablon, in Thwaites, ed., *The Jesuit Relations*, vol. 55, 104–15. See also Kellogg, *French Régime*, 179–92, 241–42; Margry, *Mémoires et Documents*, vol. 1, 81; and Turner, *The Character and Influence*, 36.

36. Thwaites, ed., *The Jesuit Relations*, vol. 55, 109–15.

37. La Potherie, *History of the Savage Peoples*, in Blair, *The Indian Tribes*, vol. 1, 347.

38. Kellogg, *French Régime* 180, 186.

39. J. Tailhan, introduction to Perrot, *Memoir on the Manners*, in Blair, *The Indian Tribes*, vol. 1, 26–27. Although the Ojibwes and Ho Chunks are not mentioned by Tailhan, Perrot dealt with them also.

40. This incorrect observation laid the basis for later historical misrepresentation of Menominee numbers. Menominee village population ranged from forty to two hundred throughout most of the times in which colonial estimates were made. A conservative guess would place the population between five hundred and fourteen hundred during the seventeenth century (see appendix, table 1).

41. La Potherie, *History of the Savage Peoples*, in Blair, *The Indian Tribes*, vol. 1, 303–4.

42. Smith, *The History of Wisconsin*, 24–25, has it the other way around, with the French taking control and the Potawatomis attempting to displace them. La Potherie, excerpt from *Histoire de l'Am'rique Septentrionale*, *Collections SHSW*, vol. 16, 38–39, however, indicates the Potawatomis as the trading force to be reckoned with in the La Baye region.

43. La Potherie, *History of the Savage Peoples*, in Blair, *The Indian Tribes*, vol. 1, 310–13; Clifton, *The Prairie People*, 62–63.

44. Clifton, *The Prairie People*, 62–63.

45. Turner, *The Character and Influence*, 32.

46. La Potherie, *History of the Savage Peoples*, in Blair, *The Indian Tribes*, vol. 1, 188.

47. Kellogg, *French Régime*, 129.

48. Smith, *The History of Wisconsin*, 23, 25; Eccles, *The Canadian Frontier*, 145.

49. Letter from Louis André, in Thwaites, ed., *The Jesuit Relations*, vol. 58, 272–81. Sections of this text appear in Beck, "Return to *Namä'o Uskíwämît.*"

50. This is Reuben Thwaites's translation of André's interpretation of what he may have heard directly or through an interpreter. Extract from a letter of Father Louis André written from the Bay de Puants, 20 April 1676, in Thwaites, ed., *The Jesuit Relations*, vol. 60, 200–203.

51. Grant, *Moon of Wintertime*, 35.

52. Kellogg, *French Régime*, 155.

53. Extract from a letter of Father Louis André, 20 April 1676, in Thwaites, ed., *The Jesuit Relations*, vol. 60, 200–203.

54. Father Beschefer to the Reverend Father Provincial, 21 October 1683, in Thwaites, ed., *The Jesuit Relations*, vol. 62, 203–5.

55. At any rate, this is Perrot's opinion. La Potherie, *History of the Savage Peoples*, in Blair, *The Indian Tribes*, vol. 1, 354.

56. Father Beschefer to the Reverend Father Provincial, 21 October 1683, in Thwaites, ed., *The Jesuit Relations*, vol. 62, 205.

57. See Kellogg, *French Régime*, 173–76, for a discussion of the causes of this abandonment.

58. Menominee oral history says the Jesuits purposefully left such bands out of their reports; interviews with Menominee people.

59. O'Callaghan, ed., *Documents*, vol. 9, 619–26.

60. Kay, "The Land of La Baye," 85.

3. SOVEREIGN ALLIANCES

1. Kellogg, *French Régime*, 386–87; Eccles, *The Canadian Frontier*, 109.

2. As with missionary efforts, the French military efforts have received more than their due share of coverage in written Indian history of the period. Most French in the *pays d'en haut* did not put their thoughts to writing and rarely discussed the Menominee. Ourada, *The Menominee Indians*, 13–41, devotes a single chapter, "French Relations," to Menominee history during the French period and concentrates entirely on Menominee-French relations, in much of which she describes military exploits. She describes the French battles, often enumerating how many or which

Menominees joined them. It is not Menominee history so much as how and where the Menominee fit into French colonial/imperial history.

3. Interviews with Menominee people; Trowbridge, "Excerpts," si-naa.

4. "Narrative of the most remarkable occurrence in Canada. 1694, 1695." In O'Callaghan, ed., *Documents*, vol. 9, 620–26. The narrative identifies that leader as Kioulouskau, but the Menominee Historic Preservation Department cannot identify that as a Menominee name.

5. Both Nicholas Perrot and a Jesuit missionary, Father Anjelran, served as translators.

6. Charlevoix, *History and General Description of New France*, vol. 5, 142–52; "Ratification of the Peace between the French and the Indians," in O'Callaghan, ed., *Documents*, vol. 9, 722–25.

7. Charlevoix, *History and General Description of New France*, vol. 5, 142.

8. Edmunds and Peyser, *The Fox Wars*, 9–10, 46–48, 60–61.

9. Historians call this the French and Fox War or the Fox War; in Menominee history, it is recalled as the war with the Sac and Fox. Interviews with Menominee people.

10. Kellogg, *French Régime*, chap. 13, 268–89.

11. King Louis XV wrote Governor Vaudreuil on 14 May 1728, "His majesty is persuaded of the necessity of destroying that nation [Mesquakie], as it cannot be kept quiet, and as it will cause, so long as it exists, both trouble and disorder in the upper country." He continued, warning that "Possibly even the other nations, who have been apparently animated against the Foxes, will be touched at their destruction, and become more insolent should we not succeed." Quoted by Lyman C. Draper in "Renewal of the Fox War," *Collections* shsw, vol. 5, 86. In 1728 the Mesquakies escaped de Lignery's attack, but the expedition cut their abundant cornfields and burned their villages, prompting de Lignery to write to Governor Beauharnois, "This, Monsieur, terminated our Expedition which will be no less advantageous to the glory of the King and the welfare of both Colonies [New France and Louisiana], inasmuch as one-half those people [the enemy] will die of hunger." Lignery's Report in Lignery to Governor Beauharnois, 30 August 1728, *Collections* shsw, vol. 17, 31–35. The French meant to eliminate the Mesquakies not just as a political power but as a people.

12. Kellogg, *French Régime*, 291; Lignery's Report of the Expedition in a letter from Lignery to Governor Beauharnois, 30 August 1728, *Collections SHSW*, vol. 17, 31–35.

13. Messrs. De Beauharnois and De Argemait to the French Minister of War, 1 September 1728, *Collections SHSW*, vol. 5, 93.

14. *Collections SHSW*, vol. 5, 89; *Collections SHSW*, vol. 10, 50.

15. *Collections SHSW*, vol. 17, 31–32.

16. Extract of Marin to Beauharnois, 11 May 1730, dated in the Country of the Folles-Avoines, *Collections SHSW*, vol. 17, 88–100.

17. Wm. J. Snelling, "La Butte des Morts—The Hillock of the Dead," *Collections SHSW*, vol. 5, 95–103.

18. Edmunds and Peyser, *The Fox Wars*, 189–90; Kellogg, *French Régime*, 338–39; Beauharnois's annual report for 1737, *Collections SHSW*, vol. 17, 263.

19. Thwaites, "Preface," xii; Eccles, *The Canadian Frontier*, 145–48; Kellogg, *French Régime*, 273, 275–76, 313, 328.

20. Eccles, *The Canadian Frontier*, 147–48.

21. Thwaites wrote this in 1906. "Preface," xii.

22. Charlevoix, "Excerpt from Charlevoix's *Journal historique*," 411. For discussion of early Menominee demography, see Beck, "Proof of the Existence."

23. Kay, "The Land of La Baye," 157–60, 170.

24. Keesing, *The Menomini Indians*, 76–77.

25. Anderson, "The Flow of European Trade Goods," 101–9.

26. Hoffman, *The Menomini Indians*, 214–16; interviews with Menominee people.

27. Bruce Herman Grant, in a doctoral dissertation written for the Department of Anthropology of the Catholic University of America, asserts on weak evidence that the Menominee embraced French brandy as a method to enhance dreaming and replaced significant aspects of social culture, including warfare, with alcoholism. "Spirituality and Sobriety," 40–43. This is hotly disputed by tribal historians. Interviews with Menominee people.

28. Eccles, *The Canadian Frontier*, 57.

29. Eccles, *The Canadian Frontier*, 57.

30. See Unrau, *White Man's Wicked Water*.

31. Eccles, *The Canadian Frontier*, 146. Although each *engagé* was limited to four pots of brandy, the post itself could be stocked with thirty to forty casks, each holding sixteen pots. "Agreement regarding the exploitation of the post at La Baie des Puants," *Collections* SHSW, vol. 17, 451–55; and Partnership to Exploit La Baye, *Collections* SHSW, vol. 18, 7–10. See also Kellogg, *French Régime*, 378–79.

32. In 1727 the French government legalized the use of brandy in the trade to counteract the increasingly powerful English trade. One contemporary observer, a Sulpician missionary, recognized that most Indians did not drink. Miquelon, *New France*, 151–52.

33. Extract of Beauharnois and Monsieur Duprey to the French Minister, 25 September 1727, *Collections* SHSW, vol. 17, 15–17.

34. For discussion of licensing see Miquelon, *New France*, 159–61.

35. Kellogg, *French Régime*, 366–73.

36. Kellogg, *French Régime*, 374. The economic advantages for the post commandants included a large income from the fur trade. This was a common practice for eighteenth-century European imperial governments with overseas empires. In Mexico, for example, "the political officials' handbook of 1777 openly declared the *corregimiento* [an area of governance] of Chalco to be worth thirty times the *corregidor's* salary." Gibson, *The Aztecs under Spanish Rule*, 409.

37. For comparison of value of goods traded at these different locations see Turner, *The Character and Influence*, 46; and Smith, *The History of Wisconsin*, 47.

38. This policy is described in detail in relation to tobacco in Price, *France and the Chesapeake*.

39. See Jacobs, *Wilderness Politics and Indian Gifts*, for a general discussion of gift giving.

40. Beauharnois to the French Minister, 5 September 1742, *Collections* SHSW, vol. 17, 409–12. See also speeches of western Indians and Governor Beauharnois to each other, in document dated 8 July 1742, *Collections* SHSW, vol. 17, 380–409.

41. Letter from Beauharnois to the French Minister, 5 September 1742, *Collections* SHSW, vol. 17, 409.

42. Kellogg, *French Régime*, 230–31; Smith, *The History of Wisconsin*, 38.

43. "Return of Western Tribes who traded at Oswego, 1749," in O'Callaghan, ed., *Documents*, vol. 6, 538.

44. Extract from Beauharnois to the French Minister, 13 October 1743, *Collections* SHSW, vol. 17, 439–40.

45. Kellogg, *French Régime*, 374–75.

46. Beauharnois and Intendant Gilles Hocquart to French Minister, 22 September 1746, *Collections* SHSW, vol. 17, 450–51.

47. Kellogg, *French Régime*, 376; Raney, "The Grignon Family in Wisconsin to About 1760," SHSW Archives.

48. The best sources available for understanding these partnerships are the 1747 lease of the post at La Baye and the contract between the lessees and traders for that same three-year lease. These two documents outline costs and responsibilities of the traders. "Agreement regarding the exploitation of the post at La Baie des Puants," *Collections* SHSW, vol. 17, 451–55; and Partnership to Exploit La Baye, *Collections* SHSW, vol. 18, 7–10. See also Kellogg, *French Régime*, 378–79.

49. Kellogg, *French Régime*, outlines the methods of the French trading system, 367–71.

50. Eccles, "A Belated Review of Harold Adams Innis's *The Fur Trade in Canada*," in *Essays on New France*, 62–63; Miquelon, *Dugard*, 69–78; Miquelon, *New France*, 157–58.

51. *Collections* SHSW, vol. 18, 17 n; Kellogg, *French Régime*, 381–83; Beauharnois to the French Minister, 5 September 1742, *Collections* SHSW, vol. 17, 410.

52. Peterson, "Ethnogenesis," 51.

53. See Mazzuchelli, *The Memoirs*, 95, for example. Mazzuchelli worked in Menominee country in the 1830s.

54. Biddle, "Recollections of Green Bay in 1816–17," 58–61.

55. *Collections* SHSW, vol. 18, 196, 211, 213; Ourada, *The Menominee Indians*, 39–40.

56. Journal of Occurrences in Canada, 1757, 1758, in O'Callaghan, ed., *Documents*, vol. 10, 840. Copy also in *Collections* SHSW, vol. 18, 203.

57. Extract from Pouchot's *Memoir* in *Collections* SHSW, vol. 18, 211.

58. Kellogg, *French Régime*, 434.

59. "Lieut. James Gorrell's Journal," 27.

60. Parker, *The Journals of Jonathan Carver*. Carver indicates that several Menominees who fought with the French in 1757 bore the scars of smallpox, 75–77.

61. Or it may have been that two reports listed the tribe under different names, which the British Indian Department failed to recognize. Wm. Johnson, "Enumeration of Indians Within the Northern Department," 18 November 1763, in O'Callaghan, ed., *Documents*, vol. 7, pp. 582–84; "Lieut. James Gorrell's Journal," 30–32.

62. "Lieut. James Gorrell's Journal," 32.

63. "Lieut. James Gorrell's Journal," 24–30.

64. Hoffman, *The Menomini Indians*, 41–45, 50–51; interviews with Menominee people. Frederick Haldimand, governor of Quebec, issued a certificate of appreciation to Chawanon in 1778, thanking the grand chief of the Folles Avoines for his fidelity to the Crown. The State Historical Society of Wisconsin holds that document in its archives. A transcription and photocopy of it are in *Collections* SHSW, vol. 18, 369–71. It also appears in Hoffman, *The Menomini Indians*, after p. 46.

65. Hoffman says Carron was half-Abenaki; Augustin Grignon says he was half-Menominee. The Thomas Carron who moved to the area in the 1740s married a Menominee woman. The difference of opinion seems to be whether he or his son became Sekatsokemau's public speaker. Hoffman, *The Menomini Indians*, 45, 50–51; Grignon, "Seventy-Two Years' Recollections of Wisconsin," 226; Keesing, "Leaders of the Menomini Tribe," SHSW Archives.

66. Interviews with Menominee people.

67. "Lieut. James Gorrell's Journal," 30.

68. Kellogg, *British Régime*, 20–21.

69. Kellogg, *British Régime*, x, 8.

70. Smith, *The History of Wisconsin*, 93.

71. Eccles, *The Canadian Frontier*, 186–87.

72. "Lieut. James Gorrell's Journal," 39.

73. Kellogg, *British Régime*, 37.

74. Kellogg, *British Régime*, 37–39.

75. Johnson to Cadwallader Colden, 23 August 1764, in *The Papers of Sir William Johnson*, vol. 4, 511–12.

76. "A Conference with Foreign Nations," *The Papers of Sir William Johnson*, vol. 4, 478, also in vol. 11, 273; "Nations at Indian Congress at Niagara," *The Papers of Sir William Johnson*, vol. 11, 276; "An Indian Congress," *The Papers of Sir William Johnson*, vol. 11, 274.

77. The six chiefs are listed as Grand Pee, Monsieur Carot, Chicconaway, Succamoy or Musketo, Wabashago or White Crab, and Wenosachey or Bever. "An Indian Congress," 15 July 1764, *The Papers of Sir William Johnson*, vol. 11, 274.

78. "An Indian Congress," 15 July 1764, *The Papers of Sir William Johnson*, vol. 11, 274–76.

79. "A meeting with the Menominees," 17 July 1764, *The Papers of Sir William Johnson*, vol. 4, 487–88.

80. "An Indian Congress," 17 July–4 August 1764, *The Papers of Sir William Johnson*, vol. 11, 278–81.

81. Johnson to Colden, 23 August 1764, *The Papers of Sir William Johnson*, vol. 4, 513; "Equivalents to Govern Indian Trade," 18 July 1764, *The Papers of Sir William Johnson*, vol. 4, 489–90; "Equivalents in Barter," *The Papers of Sir William Johnson*, vol. 4, 490–91.

82. "Answer to the Meynomeneys of La Baye," 21 July 1764, *The Papers of Sir William Johnson*, vol. 11, 288–89.

83. "A Certificate to a Menominee," 1 August 1764, *The Papers of Sir William Johnson*, vol. 4, 499. The documents identify the Menominee leaders as Ogemawnee. Kellogg says this is the Old King, in *British Régime*, 34. The Old King is Sekatsokemau.

84. Ourada, *The Menominee Indians*, 45–46.

85. William Howard to Johnson, 24 June 1765, in *The Papers of Sir William Johnson*, vol. 11, 809. Ourada mistakenly identifies this source as vol. 14.

86. Kellogg, *British Régime*, 37–39.

87. Calloway, *Crown and Calumet*, 52; Bradley, *Sir Guy Carleton*, appendix W, 325, note by A. L. Burt from 1926 edition.

88. Calloway, *Crown and Calumet*, 250–53; Powell, "William Powell's Recollections," 164.

89. Kellogg, *British Régime*, 47–48, 103.

90. Kellogg, *British Régime*, 47–48, 103–4, 241; Smith, *The History of Wisconsin*, 61–62,63 n. 8, 68, 71–72, 75–76.

91. Zebulon Pike, 13 March 1806, in Coues, ed., *The Expeditions of Zebulon Montgomery Pike*, vol. 1, 183.

92. Coues, ed., *The Expeditions of Zebulon Montgomery Pike*, vol. 1, 183; Ourada, *The Menominee Indians*, 47–51.

93. Ourada, *The Menominee Indians*, 47–51.

94. Kellogg, *British Régime*, 147–57.

95. *Collections* SHSW, vol. 18, 370.

96. Ourada, *The Menominee Indians*, 49–51.

4 · DIMINISHING FUR TRADE

1. Keesing, "Leaders of the Menomini Tribe," 6, SHSW Archives. Although Keesing incorrectly asserted that the tribe consisted of only a single band up to this point, he is probably correct that the number of bands grew during this time period.

2. The Red Cedar River is located in what is now far western Wisconsin.

3. Perrault, "Narrative," 547–53.

4. Kellogg, *British Régime*, 216–17, 326–27; Bemis, *Jay's Treaty*, 109–11, including map between 110–11. For discussion of American rejection of the idea of a neutral barrier state, see also Calloway, *Crown and Calumet*, 241; and Kellogg, *British Régime*, 327.

5. See, for example, De Peyster to General Haldimand, 8 June 1780, *Collections* SHSW, vol. 12, 49–51.

6. Johnson's full title was superintendent general and inspector general of Indian affairs. He took over the post in 1782. Calloway, *Crown and Calumet*, 53.

7. "Ainsée's Expedition," *Collections* SHSW, vol. 12, 84–91. Text also appears in *Michigan Pioneer and Historical Collections*, vol. 11, pp. 501–6 under the title "From Mr. Ainssè. Unaddressed."

8. Perrault, "Narrative," 543.

9. The ceremony at Michilimackinac is briefly described in Smith, *The History of Wisconsin*, 74–75.

10. Extracts from Mr. Deases [*sic*] Journal for the Year 1787, *Michigan Pioneer and Historical Collections*, vol. 11, 499–500.

11. Arbre Croche is in what is now Michigan's Lower Peninsula. "Indian Council" contains proceedings of the meeting on 11 July, in *Michigan Pioneer and Historical Collections*, vol. 11, 490–93. There is no text of the actual treaty, only a mention that it was read.

12. Council with Ottawa at Arbor Croche, 3 August 1787, *Michigan Pioneer and Historical Collections*, vol. 11, 494.

13. Calloway, *Crown and Calumet*, 5, 223–39.

14. Smith, *The History of Wisconsin*, 76–77.

15. Forsyth Richardson & Co. to Jacques Porlier, 8 June 1810; "Statement of Peltries on Mr. Jac Porlier Sold by the Undersigned [Berthelot] to Mons. Pothier," 11 July 1814; and "Mka August 3 Southwest Company Dr for the Peltries of the invoice of Merchandize 1816," *Collections* SHSW, vol. 19, 338, 357, 429.

16. In 1806 Augustin Grignon and Jacob Franks sent 120 kegs, or ten thousand pounds, of deer tallow to Mackinac. Grignon, "Seventy-Two Years' Recollections of Wisconsin," 255. Menominees also produced abundant maple sugar, but no export market existed since Mackinac area tribes manufactured it there in large quantities.

17. Coues, ed., *The Expeditions of Zebulon Montgomery Pike*, vol. 1, 180, 190.

18. This practice still exists today, as Louis Hawpetoss (Cawtackasic) pointed out in a public ceremony welcoming the sturgeon back to Keshena Falls on 17 April 1993. During a giveaway he presented a representative of the Wisconsin Department of Natural Resources with a blanket but reminded the audience that both sides would again be bargaining hard for their own needs afterward.

19. Pike to Wilkinson, 18 April 1806, in Coues, ed., *The Expeditions of Zebulon Montgomery Pike*, vol. 1, 91, 263–64; Kellogg, *British Régime*, 258. Regarding this expedition, Calloway, *Crown and Calumet*, 134, reminds the reader that "Indian friendship was bought with goods and guns, not with flags and speeches." He might have added that Indian friendships with the British were products of Indian diplomacy as well as British diplomacy.

20. Pike says Santees, Ojibwes, and "Fols Avoins" wintered as far north as Mille Lacs. Coues, ed., *The Expeditions of Zebulon Montgomery Pike*, vol. 1, 309, 312–14. He also discusses a Fols Avoin Sauteaux, or Wild Rice Ojibwa, band but does not seem to confuse them with the Menominee, and it is clear from specific references to Tomau and Shawanoe that these bands of the tribe wintered far to the north and west of what is often considered Menominee territory.

21. Tanner, *Atlas of Great Lakes Indian History*, map 20, 98–99.

22. Interviews with Menominee people. Louis B. Porlier, in "Capture of Mackinac," quotes a Menominee speaking of Americans and referring to them by the Menominee word Kechemocoman, which means "Great Knife." *Collections* SHSW, vol. 8, 228. By contrast, a translation of a Menominee term for the French is "Men with hair on their faces," and another is "Men with hats." Interviews with Menominee people. See also Trowbridge, "Excerpts," SI-NAA.

23. The appointment of Robert Dickson was effective 14 January 1813. Calloway, *Crown and Calumet*, 280 n. 13.

24. Kellogg, *British Régime*, 284–85, 296–97, 299–303.

25. Kellogg, *British Régime*, 328.

26. Sims, "Algonkian-British Relations," 47. See Keesing, *The Menomini Indians*, 92.

27. For a description of events leading up to Tomau's death, see Biddle, "Recollections of Green Bay in 1816–17," 56–57.

28. See Recommendations by Cass on Indian Posts, attached to Cass to Dallas, 20 July 1815, in Carter, ed., *Territorial Papers of the United States*, vol. 10, 576.

29. Cass to Dallas, 20 June 1815, *Collections* SHSW, vol. 19, 378.

30. Report to the President of the United States by A. J. Dallas, Department of War, 19 June 1815, approved by James Monroe, 20 June 1815; and Dallas to Jouett, 20 June 1815, both in *Collections* SHSW, vol. 19, 380–81.

31. Skinner, *Material Culture*, 379–82; Census in Letter to Major Brevoort, 21 August 1824, Not signed, Folder 1821–1823, RG 75, No. 59, Green Bay [Factory] Accounts 1815–1823, NARS, Washington DC; Mazzuchelli, *The Memoirs*, 63.

32. See 1819 Indian Census in *Collections* SHSW, vol. 20, 50.

33. "1821: Census of Tribesmen," *Collections* SHSW, vol. 20, 237–38. The Chicago report that year failed to enumerate Indians by tribe.

34. The Prairie du Chien agent reported to the territorial governor of Illinois, while those at the Chicago and Green Bay agencies reported to the territorial governor of Michigan. The Milwaukee River divided the Chicago and Green Bay jurisdictions. The Green Bay agency, established in 1815, oversaw Menominee affairs until 1909. Oneida, Stockbridge, and Munsee Indians also eventually came under the jurisdiction of this agency, as did some Ho Chunks before that tribe was officially removed from Wisconsin, but the agency's major jurisdictional function became the oversight of Menominee and New York Indian affairs.

35. Menominees had lived in the Michilimackinac area since at least the time when du Lhut prosecuted one of them for murder in 1683. In 1838 the Green Bay subagent apparently exiled two bands of Menominee from the tribe for continuing to visit the British at Drummond Island and wrote to the acting governor that at least one of these bands had moved within the jurisdiction of the Mackinac agency. George Boyd to Acting Governor Slaughter, 28 June 1838, in Bloom, ed., *Territorial Papers of the United States*, vol. 27, 1025. As the bands moved from one area to another, their jurisdictions within the U.S. system changed.

36. Smith, *The History of Wisconsin*, 91.

37. Humins, "George Boyd," 73–74.

38. Lockwood, "Early Times and Events in Wisconsin," 131.

39. Matthew Irwin to the Secretary of War, 7 November 1816; James Thomas to Irwin, 8 August 1816; and James W. Biddle to Irwin, 20 August 1816, in Carter, ed., *Territorial Papers of the United States*, vol. 17, 422–25.

40. See, for example, a note from Green Bay Indian agent John Bowyer to trader Louis Grignon, allowing him permission to trade six gallons of whiskey to Indians for sturgeon, 23 July 1817, *Collections* SHSW, vol. 19, 468.

41. Terrell, *Furs by Astor*, 249–53.

42. Kay, "John Lawe, Green Bay Trader," 14.

43. Terrell, *Furs by Astor*, 249–53.

44. Pierre Rocheblave to Jacques Porlier and Rocheblave to Louis Grignon, both 20 June 1816, *Collections* SHSW, vol. 19, 415–16, 416–17; Haeger, "A Time of Change," 288, 290–91, 293, 298; Smith, *History of Wisconsin*, 112; Kay, "John Lawe, Green Bay Trader," 15; Lavender, *The Fist in the Wilderness*, 321. For a discussion of these traders' attempts to gain U.S. citizenship, see Smith, *History of Wisconsin*, 108.

45. Kay, "John Lawe, Green Bay Trader," 20.

46. Letter from J. Lawe to Wm. Belcher, 22 October 1821, *Collections* SHSW, vol. 20, 221.

47. Kay, "John Lawe, Green Bay Trader," 15–16; Lavender, *The Fist in the Wilderness*, 285, 321.

48. Letter from Jacob Franks to John Lawe, 11 March 1818, and Letter from L. Grignon to J. Porlier & Lawe & Co., 3 September 1823, *Collections* SHSW, vol. 20, 35–36, and 307–8. See also Kay, "The Land of La Baye," 272.

49. The eight sites were listed as Bay de Noquet, Munoaminee River, Kaukaulin, Winnebaagoa Lake, Butte des Morts, Portage of the Ouisconsin, Upper Ouisconsin, and Millwaukee. See "List of places to be licensed for the Indian trade, within the Superintendency of Lewis Cass, Governor of the Territory of Michigan," in RG 44, Box 232, Folder 4, State Archives of Michigan.

50. Lockwood, "Early Times and Events in Wisconsin," 131.

51. Kay, "John Lawe, Green Bay Trader," 15.

52. Keesing, "Leaders of the Menomini Tribe," 5–7, SHSW Archives. Keesing based his observations on interviews with elders and a study of Hoffman. Carron, in *Documents Relating to the Negotiation of Ratified and Unratified Treaties*, reel 2, frame 452.

53. "Treaty of Ghent, 1814," Article 9.

54. The treaties are in Kappler, *Indian Treaties*, 110–24, 126–33, 138–40. This is also discussed in Calloway, *Crown and Calumet*, 241.

55. Bowyer to Cass, 22 July 1817, *Collections* SHSW, vol. 19, 467.

56. Keesing, "Leaders of the Menomini Tribe" (SHSW Archives) claims that Wéka was a Thunder clan leader. Clan identity is inherited through the father. Interviews with Menominee people.

57. Calhoun to Bowyer, 16 May 1818, and Bowyer to Calhoun, 20 October 1818, both in Carter, ed., *The Territorial Papers of the United States*, vol. 17, 590, 608–9.

58. Bowyer to Calhoun, 10 June 1819, in Carter, ed., *Territorial Papers of the United States*, vol. 10, 834–35.

59. Calhoun to Bowyer, 24 August 1819, in Carter, ed., *Territorial Papers of the United States*, vol. 10, 852.

60. Morse, *A Report to the Secretary of War*, 15; Wrone, "The Menominee Perspective on the Oneida Treaties," 5.

61. Cass to David A. Ogden and Cass to Eleazer Williams, both 11 December 1820, in Jennings, ed., *Iroquois Indians, a documentary history*, reel 46.

62. Cass to Calhoun, 11 November 1820, in Carter, ed., *Territorial Papers of the United States*, vol. 11, 69–70.

63. Calhoun's instructions called for cession of "a tract of twenty or thirty miles square." This can be interpreted either as twenty to thirty square miles, or twenty to thirty miles by twenty to thirty miles. If Bowyer interpreted it the latter way, his proposed purchase would not amount to nearly so large an overpurchase as Governor Cass thought it to be. Calhoun to Bowyer, 16 May 1818, in Carter, ed., *Territorial Papers of the United States*, vol. 17, 590.

64. Quoted in abstract of letter from Bowyer to Calhoun, 30 June 1820, in Hemphill, ed., *The Papers of John C. Calhoun*, vol. 5, 232.

65. This per-person figure is based on Bowyer's estimate of the tribe's population. Morse estimated the Menominee population at 3,900: 600 warriors, 900 women, and 2,400 children. Letter to Calhoun, 22 June 1820, in Hemphill, ed., *The Papers of John C. Calhoun*, vol. 5, 210. Given these numbers, the payment would amount to just over twenty cents per Menominee.

66. The translation should probably read "three important leaders." See Morse, *A Report to the Secretary of War*, appendix, 53–54. Bieder mistakenly refers to this as "the 1816 treaty," *Native American Communities in Wisconsin*, 143–44.

67. Morse, *A Report to the Secretary of War*, 15.

68. Cass to Calhoun, 11 November 1820, in Carter, ed., *Territorial Papers of the United States*, vol. 11, 70.

69. Morse to Calhoun, 15 August 1820, in Hemphill, ed., *The Papers of John C. Calhoun*, vol. 5, 332.

70. Horsman, "The Origins of Oneida Removal," 203–5.

71. Horsman, "The Origins of Oneida Removal," 208–15.

72. Wrone, "The Menominee Perspective on the Oneida Treaties," 5.

73. Abstract of Calhoun to Cass, 4 April 1821; Calhoun to Cornelius Beard, John Anthony Brandt, and one other Oneida Indian, 14 April 1821; and Calhoun to Rev. Eleazer Williams, 4 June 1821, all in Hemphill, ed., *The Papers of John C. Calhoun*, vol. 6, 13, 49, 169.

74. Wrone, "The Menominee Perspective on the Oneida Treaties," 5–6.

75. Trowbridge, "Journal of a Tour to Green Bay," in Jennings, ed., *Iroquois Indians, a documentary history*, reel 46.

76. Cass to Biddle, 29 June 1821, in Carter, ed., *Territorial Papers of the United States*, vol. 11, 129.

77. Copies of the treaty are in *Documents Relating to the Negotiation of Ratified and Unratified Treaties*, reel 8, frames 1–2 and 5–8; *Collections* SHSW, vol. 20, 284.

78. Stambaugh to Secretary of War, 4 August 1831, *Documents Relating to the Negotiation of Ratified and Unratified Treaties*, reel 2, frames 384–86.

79. Trowbridge to Cass, 7 September 1821, *Documents Relating to the Negotiation of Ratified and Unratified Treaties*, reel 8, frames 12–18.

80. Stambaugh to Eaton, August 4, 1831, *Documents Relating to the Negotiation of Ratified and Unratified Treaties*, reel 2, frame 389, provided a historical synopsis of the advent of the New York Indians into Menominee territory.

81. Speeches of 7 August 1827, in "Journal of a Treaty Made and concluded at Butte des Morts," *Documents Relating to the Negotiation of Ratified and Unratified Treaties*, reel 2, frame 15.

82. Cope, "Visit to the Menomonies," 23 (5): 33.

83. Trowbridge, "Journal of a Tour to Green Bay," in Jennings, ed., *Iroquois Indians, a documentary history*, reel 46.

84. "Journal of a Treaty Made and concluded at Butte des Morts," *Documents Relating to the Negotiation of Ratified and Unratified Treaties*, reel 2, frames 9–10. Stambaugh to Eaton, *Documents Relating to the Negotiation Ratified and Unratified of Treaties*, reel 2, frame 365, also discusses this treaty. Weekay and Makometa, known to Americans as Bear's Fat or Bear's Grease, were also two of the six Menominees who signed the 1821 treaty negotiated by a delegation of New York Indians. See copies of the treaty of 18 August 1821 between the Menominee, Winnebagos, and New York Indians, in *Documents Relating to the Negotiation of Ratified and Unratified Treaties*, reel 8, frames 1–2 and 5–8. Neither of these two men was among the ten Menominees who signed the treaty of 23 September 1822. A copy of the 1822 treaty is with 1831 treaty documents in Jennings, ed., *Iroquois Indians, a documentary history*, reel 47.

85. Speeches of 7 August 1827, in "Journal of a Treaty Made and concluded at Butte des Morts," *Documents Relating to the Negotiation of Ratified and Unratified Treaties*, reel 2, frame 12–14.

86. Abstract of letters from Cass to Calhoun, 22 October 1821; Calhoun to Cass, 22 November 1821; and Calhoun to Solomon U. Hendrick, 22 November 1821, all in Hemphill, ed., *The Papers of John C. Calhoun*, vol. 6, 452, 522, 524; Stambaugh to Eaton, 4 August 1831, *Documents Relating to the Negotiation of Ratified and Unratified Treaties*, reel 2, frame 363.

87. Calhoun to Hendrick, 13 February 1822 in Hemphill, ed., *The Papers of John C. Calhoun*, vol. 6, 695–96; Calhoun to Joseph Parrish, Sub-Agent of the Six Nations, 15 April 1822, in Hemphill, ed., *The Papers of John C. Calhoun*, Volume 7, 43–44.

88. For copies of this treaty, see Jennings, ed. *Iroquois Indians, a documentary history*, reel 46.

89. Stambaugh to Eaton, 4 August 1831, *Documents Relating to the Negotiation of Ratified and Unratified Treaties*, reel 2, frame 376.

90. Stambaugh to Eaton, 4 August 1831, *Documents Relating to the Negotiation of Ratified and Unratified Treaties*, reel 2, frame 365.

91. Stambaugh to Eaton, 4 August 1831, *Documents Relating to the Negotiation of Ratified and Unratified Treaties*, reel 2, frame 396.

92. Stambaugh to Eaton, 4 August 1831, *Documents Relating to the Negotiation of Ratified and Unratified Treaties*, reel 2, frame 364. Extract

of letter from E. Williams to T. L. Ogden, 15 May 1823, and extract of letter from Calhoun to Chiefs and Head Men of the Onondaga, Seneca, Tuscarora, Oneida, and Stockbridge, 27 October 1823, in Hemphill, ed., *The Papers of John C. Calhoun*, vol. 8, 229, 330.

5. MENOMINEE RESOURCES

1. The name Wabonockies comes from Wabanaki, the name by which the Abenaki tribes of the east coast identified themselves. These people are Algonquian speakers. See Snow, "Eastern Abenaki," 137, and Day, "Western Abenaki," 148. The Menominee may have picked this term up from traders or from their own travels eastward.

2. Wrone, "The Menominee Perspective on the Oneida Treaties," 1.

3. See sworn statements of Paul Grignon, Lewis Rouse, and Pierre Grignon, 16 and 17 June 1824, *Documents Relating to the Negotiation of Ratified and Unratified Treaties*, reel 2, frames 424–26.

4. The other Menominee signers of this petition are listed as Kits kau no num, Pe way tinet, Say kee tuk, Amable Corron, and Muk kay tay' wet. Petition of 16 June 1824, *Documents Relating to the Negotiation of Ratified and Unratified Treaties*, reel 2, frames 422–23. See also abstract of letter from Chiefs of the Menominees to James Monroe, 16 June 1824, in Hemphill, ed., *The Papers of John C. Calhoun*, vol. 9, 161.

5. "Memorial to Congress from inhabitants of Green Bay a l'honorable Chambre du Senat des Etats Unis de l'Amérique," 4 February 1823, in its original French and a contemporary translation, in Carter, ed., *Territorial Papers of the United States*, vol. 11, 335–39.

6. The description of this meeting is from Petition from Green Bay residents to the President of the United States, 21 Sept. 1824, *Documents Relating to the Negotiation of Ratified and Unratified Treaties*, reel 2, frames 426–428. Some of the French Canadians who signed this petition had also signed the 1823 petition to Congress.

7. Treaty with the Sioux, etc., 1825, and Treaty with the Chippewa, etc., 1827, in Kappler, *Indian Treaties*, 250–55, 281.

8. Stambaugh to Eaton, 4 August 1831, *Documents Relating to the Negotiation of Ratified and Unratified Treaties*, reel 2, frames 366–67.

9. Journal of Treaty at Butte des Morts, *Documents Relating to the Negotiation of Ratified and Unratified Treaties*, reel 2, frames 5–6.

10. Four Legs, 8 August 1827, in Journal of Treaty at Butte des Morts, *Documents Relating to the Negotiation of Ratified and Unratified Treaties*, reel 2, frame 17.

11. Treaty with the Chippewa, etc., 1827, Article 1, in Kappler, *Indian Treaties*, 281.

12. Statements of the first and second chiefs of the Menominees (appointed that day) to the commissioners, 7 August 1827, in Governor Cass's speech of 6 August 1827, in Journal of Treaty at Butte des Morts, *Documents Relating to the Negotiation of Ratified and Unratified Treaties*, reel 2, frame 11.

13. Speech of Four Legs, 7 August 1827, in Journal of Treaty at Butte des Morts, *Documents Relating to the Negotiation of Ratified and Unratified Treaties*, reel 2, frame 15.

14. Treaty with the Chippewa, etc., 1827, Article 2, in Kappler, *Indian Treaties*, 281–82.

15. Treaty with the Chippewa, etc., 1827, Article 2, Article 3, in Kappler, *Indian Treaties*, 282.

16. Cass and McKenney to Barbour, 11 August 1827, *Documents Relating to the Negotiation of Ratified and Unratified Treaties*, reel 2, frame 44.

17. Cass and McKenney to Barbour, 11 August 1827, *Documents Relating to the Negotiation of Ratified and Unratified Treaties*, reel 2, frames 42–43.

18. Cass and McKenney to Barbour, 11 August 1827, *Documents Relating to the Negotiation of Ratified and Unratified Treaties*, reel 2, frames 44–47; Treaty with the Chippewa, etc., 1827, Articles 4 and 5, in Kappler, *Indian Treaties*, 282. On the whiskey, see Viola, *Thomas L. McKenney*, 136.

19. Stambaugh to Eaton, 4 August 1831, *Documents Relating to the Negotiation of Ratified and Unratified Treaties*, reel 2, frame 399.

20. Journal of Treaty at Butte des Morts *Documents Relating to the Negotiation of Ratified and Unratified Treaties*, reel 2, frames 7–9; Keesing, "Leaders of the Menomini Tribe," 5–7, SHSW Archives; interviews with Menominee people.

21. Speech by Governor Cass, 6 August 1827, *Documents Relating to the Negotiation of Ratified and Unratified Treaties*, reel 2, frames 5–7.

22. Speech of Colonel McKenney to the Menominee, 7 August 1827, *Documents Relating to the Negotiation of Ratified and Unratified Treaties*, reel 2, frame 8.

23. Childs, "Recollections of Wisconsin Since 1820," 168; Ellis, "Some Account of the Advent of the New York Indians into Wisconsin," 415–49; Grignon, "Seventy-Two Years' Recollections of Wisconsin." Oshkosh's name, written there as Oskashe, along with Josette Carron's, both make their first appearance on the Butte des Morts treaty in 1827. "Treaty with the Chippewa, Etc., 1827," in Kappler, *Indian Treaties*, 282.

24. Interviews with Menominee people; Keesing, "Leaders of the Menomini Tribe," 16, SHSW Archives.

25. Morse, *A Report to the Secretary of War*, appendix, 54–55.

26. Our best insight into the complex geography of the Menominee nation in this time period can be gained through ethnological and oral history sources combined with a view of the fur trade and federal agency jurisdictions. Skinner, *Material Culture*, 379–82; Beck, "The Historical Limits of Menominee Country"; interviews with Menominee people.

27. Interviews with Menominee people. Agent Boyd recognized this in admitting that the tribe hired its own interpreters, Boyd to Crawford, 5 February 1840, in Bloom, ed., *Territorial Papers of the United States*, vol. 28, 134–35.

28. Lawe's son David ran a post at Shawano Lake in 1835.

29. Kay, "John Lawe, Green Bay Trader," 15, 18.

30. Kay, "John Lawe, Green Bay Trader," 19.

31. Terrell, *Furs by Astor*, 399; Thomas Forsyth to William Clark, in "1824: Sauk and Fox Traders," *Collections* SHSW, vol. 20, 364; Smith, *The History of Wisconsin*, 113.

32. Kay, "John Lawe, Green Bay Trader," 13–19; Smith *The History of Wisconsin*, 114; Haeger, "A Time of Change," 298; H. B. McGulpin to Judge John Lawe, 18 May 1825, *Collections* SHSW, vol. 20, 375–76.

33. This was the same fee earned by federal treaty negotiators for their services.

34. See "M'Call's Journal of a Visit to Wisconsin in 1830," esp. 180–98.

35. Ourada, *The Menominee Indians*, 87.

36. Treaties with the Menominee, 1831, in Kappler, *Indian Treaties*, 281–83 and 319–25.

37. Treaty with the Menominee, 1831, in Kappler, *Indian Treaties*, 321–22.

38. Treaty with the Menominee, 1831, Article 4, in Kappler, *Indian Treaties*, 321–22.

39. Keesing, *The Menomini Indians*, 131.

40. Stambaugh to Secretary of War, 8 November 1831, *Collections* SHSW, vol. 15, 433–34.

41. Ourada, *The Menominee Indians*, 89–90.

42. Cass to William B. Lewis, 30 November 1830, in Carter, ed., *Territorial Papers of the United States*, vol. 12, 215–16, also 215 n. 11.

43. Secretary of War to Stambaugh, 23 April 1831, in Carter, ed., *Territorial Papers of the United States*, vol. 12, 279–81.

44. Elbert Herring to Governor Porter, 10 April 1832, in Carter, ed., *Territorial Papers of the United States*, vol. 12, 464.

45. Stambaugh to Secretary of War, 10 June 1832, in Carter, ed., *Territorial Papers of the United States*, vol. 12, 485–87.

46. Ourada, *The Menominee Indians*, 92–93.

47. First quotation is from Preamble to Treaty with the Menominee, 1832, in Kappler, *Indian Treaties*, 379. Second quotation is from Keesing, *The Menomini Indians*, 133. See also Ourada, *The Menominee Indians*, 94.

48. Stambaugh to His Excellency G. B. [letter torn, probably Porter], Detroit, 15 November 1831, Records of Executive Office, 1810–1910, RG 44, Box 14, Folder 8, G II Correspondence, State Archives of Michigan.

49. Stambaugh to Secretary of War, 8 November 1831, *Collections* SHSW, vol. 15, 407–8; Boyd to Commissioner of Indian Affairs Elbert Herring, 23 February 1835, in *Letters Received*, M234, reel 316 (hereafter M234–316), frame 204. For the treaty addendum see appendix, Treaty with the Menominee, 1832, in Kappler, *Indian Treaties*, 381–82.

50. Grizzley [*sic*] Bear [Kaushkannaniew] to Governor Porter, 23 October 1832, in "Journal," *Documents Relating to the Negotiation of Treaties*, reel 2.

51. Grizzley Bear to Governor Porter, 23 October 1832, in "Journal," *Documents Relating to the Negotiation of Treaties*, reel 2.

52. Grizzley Bear to Governor Porter, 23 October 1832, in "Journal," *Documents Relating to the Negotiation of Treaties*, reel 2.

53. Treaty with the Menominee, 1831, Article 6, in Kappler, *Indian Treaties*, 322.

54. Grizzley Bear to Governor Porter, 23 October 1832, in "Journal," *Documents Relating to the Negotiation of Treaties*, reel 2.

55. Penaitenaw to Governor Porter, 23 October 1832, in "Journal," *Documents Relating to the Negotiation of Treaties*, reel 2.

56. Grizzley Bear to Governor Porter, 23 October 1832, in "Journal," *Documents Relating to the Negotiation of Treaties*, reel 2.

57. Grizzley Bear to Governor Porter, 26 October 1832, in "Journal," *Documents Relating to the Negotiation of Treaties*, reel 2.

58. Porter to Cass, 24 January 1833, *Documents Relating to the Negotiation of Treaties*, reel 2.

59. "Journal," *Documents Relating to the Negotiation of Treaties*, reel 2.

60. Grizzley Bear to Governor Porter, 23 October 1832, in "Journal," *Documents Relating to the Negotiation of Treaties*, reel 2. Brackets in original.

61. "Treaty with the Menominee, 1832," in Kappler, *Indian Treaties*, 377–82.

6. "CIVILIZING" INFLUENCES

1. Smith, *The History of Wisconsin*, 162.

2. Kellogg, "Old Fort Howard," 136.

3. Tenney, "A Case of *Lex Talionis*," in SHSW Archives; Ourada, *The Menominee Indians*, 85, and Keesing, *The Menomini Indians*, 123, both mention the case but not within the context of tribal law or sovereignty. A painting of the trial is at the Wisconsin Supreme Court; it was used on a poster for a conference at the University of Wisconsin-Stevens Point entitled "Forum on Sovereignty: Divergent Jurisdictions" and is reproduced in this book.

4. Cronon, *Nature's Metropolis*, chap. 4, 148–206, discusses the role of lumber in the development of Chicago.

5. Fries, *Empire in Pine*, 6; Hurst, *Law and Economic Growth*, 2; Martin, *The Physical Geography of Wisconsin*, map, p. 16.

6. Fries, *Empire in Pine*, 6; Cronon, *Nature's Metropolis*, 152–53.

7. See, for example, Lockwood, "Early Times and Events in Wisconsin," 132–33.

8. Childs, "Recollections of Wisconsin Since 1820," 169, locates the site "twenty six miles below Fort Howard, on the west side of the Bay." Since the Fox River flowed north, "below" at times meant north; if the site was on the Green Bay, it could hardly have meant south. "A Mill Site on the West Shore of Green Bay," contract between John P. Arndt and the United States, signed by Oaskash alias the Claw, Ok-ko-me-me-chaw alias Great Wave, and Sthai-ke-tok Alias Scare All, and Hy. B. Brevoort, Indian Agent, 25 August 1826, *Collections* SHSW, vol. 15, 16–17, locates the site "adjacent to a creek or stream of water usually called *Paussacue*, situated about twenty miles from Fort Howard and on the west side of Green Bay." The creek below the Oconto River, some twenty to twenty-five miles north of the site of Fort Howard, is Pensaukee River.

9. "A Saw Mill Site at Wisconsin River Rapids," contract signed by Daniel Whitney and Acting Indian Agent S. C. Stambaugh, 24 April 1832, based on agreement with Menominees, 16 August 1831; "A Mill Site at Little Chute," signed by A. G. Ellis before Justice of the Peace Alexander J. Irwin, 11 July 1832, based on agreement with Menominees, 22 April 1831; "A Mill Site on Doty's Island," signed by James Duane Doty and G. Boyd, U. S. Ind. Agt., 19 July 1832, based on agreement with Menominees, 15 August 1831, all in *Collections* SHSW, vol. 15, 9–15. The Whitney contract is also mentioned in Lockwood, "Early Times and Events in Wisconsin," 141, and his mill site location is discussed in de la Ronde, "Personal Narrative," *Collections* SHSW, vol. 7, 358.

10. "A Mill Site on the Waubunkeesippe River, a draft," agreement signed 7 August 1835 by Oshkush, Yah-Mith-Taw (Aiometah), Sou non nee, Peag tham, Toh ne quay, Ne caum nan qu om, Amable, Keecaum Mekishin, Paish-can wet, Mow way say, and Oge Man shay, *Collections* SHSW, vol. 15, 18–19.

11. Commissioner Whitcomb to Secretary of Treasury, 27 April 1837, in Bloom, ed., *Territorial Papers of the United States*, vol. 27, 768–69.

12. Humins, "George Boyd," 266–67.

13. Tanner, "Sketch of George and James M. Boyd," 266.

14. Schoolcraft to Crawford, 24 December 1840, in Bloom, ed. *Territorial Papers of the United States*, vol. 28, 312 n.

15. Stambaugh to Secretary of War, 8 November 1831, *Collections* SHSW, vol. 15, 433–34.

16. See Petition to Congress by Henry Baird and others, October 1837, in Bloom, ed., *Territorial Papers of the United States*, vol. 27, 868–70.

17. See correspondence regarding the Dickinson contract in *Letters Received*, M234–316, frames 58–60 and 83–86, and correspondence regarding Whitney's contract, frames 200–209 and 245–48; Treaty with the Menominee, 1831, in Kappler, *Indian Treaties*, 321.

18. Treaty with the Menominee, 1831, in Kappler, *Indian Treaties*, 321.

19. Grizzly Bear and Porter speaking 23 October 1832, in "Journal," *Documents Relating to the Negotiation of Ratified and Unratified Treaties*, reel 2.

20. Kemper, "Journal," 443.

21. Boyd to Herring, 25 September 1834, *Letters Received*, M234–316, frame 64.

22. Kemper, "Journal," 443.

23. Report of Francis Huebschmann, Superintendent, Northern Superintendency, 1 October 1855, in *Annual Report of the Commissioner of Indian Affairs*, 1855, 41.

24. Lieutenant Clary to Major Gould, 31 August 1837, in Bloom, ed., *Territorial Papers of the United States*, vol. 27, 865–66.

25. Boyd, in a letter to Herring, 13 April 1835, mentions that the northern bands, comprising at least half the tribe, refused to move to the agricultural settlement. *Letters Received*, M234–316, frame 224.

26. Boyd to Herring, 18 October 1835, *Letters Received*, M234–316, frame 284.

27. Colonel Stambaugh's speech, "Journal of the Proceedings at a Council held at Green Bay, by Col. Stambaugh," 18 July 1831, *Documents Relating to the Negotiation of Ratified and Unratified Treaties*, reel 2, frame 446. Grizzly Bear and Porter, speaking 23 October 1832, in "Journal," *Documents Relating to the Negotiation of Ratified and Unratified Treaties*, reel

2. Boyd to Herring, 3 November 1835, *Letters Received*, M234–316, frame 295, includes a statement of funds on hand that shows four thousand dollars available to build the gristmills and sawmills. Boyd to Cass, 25 August 1834, mentions Oshkosh's protestations, *Letters Received*, M234–316, frame 57; Porter to Herring, 8 January 1834, discusses potential benefits of the mills to the Stockbridge, Munsees, and Brothertons, *Letters Received*, M234–316, frame 146.

28. Commissioner of Indian Affairs Crawford to Joseph G. Knapp, 8 March 1839, in Bloom, ed. *Territorial Papers of the United States*, vol. 27, 1210.

29. Oshkosh and Josette Carron were not the only Menominee leaders appointed chiefs by the U.S. government. According to Agent Boyd, Aiometah, another son of Old Carron, who died in 1831, "was made a chief *at my instigation*, by Governor Porter, in 1832." Boyd to Commissioner of Indian Affairs Casey A. Harris, 10 March 1838, in Bloom, ed., *The Territorial Papers of the United States*, vol. 27, 941.

30. Major John Biddle to Cass, 24 October 1821, extracted in Cass to Calhoun, 6 January 1822, in Carter, ed., *Territorial Papers of the United States*, vol. 11, 217; Mazzuchelli, *The Memoirs*, 95.

31. Moranian, "Ethnocide in the Schoolhouse," 243; organizational papers published in "Documents Relating to the Episcopal Church," 451–55.

32. See "Documents Relating to the Episcopal Church," 455–57; "Cutting Marsh's Report to the Scottish Society, 1831," in "Documents Relating to the Stockbridge Mission, 1825–48," *Collections* SHSW, vol. 15, 59; editor [Reuben Gold Thwaites], *Collections* SHSW, vol. 14, 411–12 n. 2; Peterson, "Ethnogenesis," 51.

33. Mazzuchelli, *The Memoirs*, 109.

34. "Full blood" apparently meant those living with the tribe as Menominees and accepted as such by the tribe.

35. See Letters of R. F. Cadle in "Documents Relating to the Episcopal Church," *Collections* SHSW, vol. 15, 455–57.

36. Treaty with the Chippewa, Etc., 1827, in Kappler, *Indian Treaties*, 282; Cadle to Boyd, 27 May 1833, and Cadle to Boyd, 14 July 1833, and Letter from W. Ward for E. Herring, Commissioner of Indian Affairs,

28 July 1834, in "Documents Relating to the Episcopal Church," 473–75, 487.

37. Draft, Henry S. Baird to Reverend Cadle, n.d., in response to letter of 27 April 1833, in "Documents Relating to the Episcopal Church," 469.

38. "Journal of the proceedings of a Council held at Green Bay, by Col. Stambaugh, U. S. agent, with the Menominie Indians," 18 July 1831, *Documents Relating to the Negotiation of Ratified and Unratified Treaties*, reel 2, frame 443.

39. Shannon, foreword to Mazzuchelli, *The Memoirs*, vi–vii.

40. Mazzuchelli, *The Memoirs*, 110–11.

41. Mazzuchelli, *The Memoirs*, 40–48.

42. Mazzuchelli, *The Memoirs*, 47, 50, 96.

43. [Mazzuchelli], *Indian Almanac*.

44. Mazzuchelli, *The Memoirs*, 62, 44–45; "Subscription for a R. C. Ind'n. free school," *Collections SHSW*, vol. 14, 176–77.

45. Mazzuchelli, *The Memoirs*, 94–95. Mazzuchelli, 108, also said that over one thousand Christian Indians attended the Green Bay mission in the spring of 1834 but did not enumerate them by tribe. Most were probably Menominee.

46. Mazzuchelli, *The Memoirs*, 101–3.

47. Mazzuchelli, *The Memoirs*, 101–3.

48. Mazzuchelli, *The Memoirs*, 102.

49. Mazzuchelli, *The Memoirs*, 102–4.

50. Mazzuchelli, *The Memoirs*, 102–4.

51. Tanner, *Atlas of Great Lakes Indian History*, 173–74; Keesing, *The Menomini Indians*, 136–37.

52. Subagent Albert G. Ellis, in a report to Governor Dodge, 19 February 1847, stated that approximately two hundred Menominee "were known as the Catholic band." This was some thirteen years after Mazzuchelli left, at a time when an incompetent priest served among the Menominee, but Ellis does not imply that the number had dropped significantly. Bloom, ed., *Territorial Papers of the United States*, vol. 28, 1049.

53. Boyd to Harris, 10 March 1838, in Bloom, ed., *Territorial Papers of the United States*, vol. 27, 941.

54. Boyd to Cass, 25 August 1834, *Letters Received*, M234–316, frame 55. The words "request" and "unworthily" are inferred from nearly illegible text.

55. Boyd to Herring, 25 September 1834, *Letters Received*, M234–316, frame 65.

56. Mazzuchelli, *The Memoirs*, 108–9. He entitled chapter 26 "The Anglican Mission at Green Bay Receives the Annual Sum of Twenty-One Hundred Dollars, in Justice Due to the Catholic Mission."

57. "A Rejected Bill," *Collections* SHSW, vol. 14, 191–92.

58. Boyd to Cass, 25 August 1834, *Letters Received*, M234–316, frame 59.

59. Kemper, "Journal," 414. Brackets in text.

60. Cadle to Boyd, 18 June 1833, in "Documents Relating to the Episcopal Church," 473.

61. Boyd to Herring, 9 February 1835, *Letters Received*, M234–316, frame 198.

62. See Rev. Cadle to Boyd, 23 February 1835, and Boyd to Commissioner of Indian Affairs Elbert Herring, 23 February 1835, *Letters Received*, M234–316, frames 213, 204.

63. Kemper, "Journal," 419–22, 425.

64. "Documents Relating to the Episcopal Church," 485–86; Kemper, "Journal," 414–15.

65. He complained bitterly that he had to board his family "in an Indian hut." See 672 n and Gregory to Commissioner of Indian Affairs Harris, 1 May 1837, 774–75, both in Bloom, ed., *Territorial Papers of the United States*, vol. 27.

66. Harris to Gregory, 22 November 1836, in Bloom, ed., *Territorial Papers of the United States*, vol. 27, 672.

67. Gregory to Harris, 1 May 1837, is his letter of resignation, in Bloom, ed., *Territorial Papers of the United States*, vol. 27, 774–75.

68. Boyd to Harris, 10 March 1838, and Harris to Boyd, 27 April 1838, in Bloom, ed., *Territorial Papers of the United States*, vol. 27, 940, 992.

69. Solomon Davis to Boyd, 16 September 1841, in "Documents Relating to the Episcopal Church," 514.

70. Kemper, "Journal," 425.

71. David E. Brown to Boyd, 1 October 1836, *Letters Received*, M234–316, frame 402.

72. Solomon Davis to Boyd, 16 September 1841, *Collections* SHSW, vol. 14, 513.

73. Van den Broek to Louis Grignon, 24 December 1835, translated from the French, *Collections* SHSW, vol. 14, 196–98.

74. Van den Broek to Louis Grignon, 24 December 1835, and Van den Broek to Miss Elizabeth Grignon, 27 December 1835, both translated from the French, *Collections* SHSW, vol. 14, 196–98.

75. See, for instance, Oshkosh's speech to Agent Boyd at Green Bay, 19 February 1839, and Oshkosh's discussion with Governor Henry Dodge on 17 February 1841 in Madison, both in "Indian Talks and Communications, 1836–1845," *Records of the Wisconsin Superintendency of Indian Affairs*, reel 3.

7. A DISSOLVING TRIBAL ECONOMY

1. Turner, *The Character and Influence*, 29; Smith, *The History of Wisconsin*, 166. For an example of a previous land sale, see the Menominee 1794 land cession to Jacob Franks, *Collections* SHSW, vol. 15, 3–4.

2. Boyd to Herring, 21 August 1835, *Letters Received*, M234–316, frame 259.

3. The reports of what was actually said differed widely, although no Menominee interpretation of the meeting was recorded. See Boyd to Herring, and accompanying Menominee speeches, 18 October and 13 October 1835, *Letters Received*, M234–316, frames 288–92.

4. Speech of Silver, 13 October 1835, at annuity, *Letters Received*, M234–316, frame 291.

5. Description on paper dated 13 October 1835 follows I ya ma taw's speech, *Letters Received*, M234–316, frame 292; Boyd to Herring, 18 October 1835, *Letters Received*, M234–316, frame 289.

6. Boyd to Herring, 18 March 1836, *Letters Received*, M234–316, frames 385–86.

7. "A Journal of the proceedings of a treaty held by Hon. Henry Dodge, Governor of Wisconsin Territory . . . at Cedar Point . . . August 29, 1836," *Documents Relating to the Negotiation of Ratified and Unratified*

Treaties, (hereafter "Journal of a treaty held by Dodge"), reel 3, frames 410–13.

8. Stambaugh to Secretary of War, 8 November 1831, *Collections* SHSW, vol. 15, 435.

9. "Journal of a treaty held by Dodge," frames 410–415; Aiometah, 25 June 1833, "Journal of a Council held at Green Bay," *Michigan Pioneer and Historical Collections*, vol. 37, 269.

10. Oshkosh and I-Yam-a-taw, 30 August 1836, "Journal of a treaty held by Dodge," frames 413–15.

11. "Journal of a treaty held by Dodge," frames 413–16, 418.

12. "Journal of a treaty held by Dodge," frames 416–31.

13. Treaty with the Menominee, 1836, in Kappler, *Indian Treaties*, 464; Gen. A. G. Ellis, "The 'Upper Wisconsin' Country," *Collections* SHSW, vol. 3, 438.

14. Raney, "Pine Lumbering in Wisconsin," 76.

15. Kellogg, "The Menominee Treaty at the Cedars, 1836," 133; *Documents Relating to the Negotiation of Ratified and Unratified Treaties*, reel 3, frames 423–24.

16. Gen. Brooke to Commissioner Harris, 2 March 1837, in Bloom, ed., *Territorial Papers of the United States*, vol. 27, 743. Ourada incorrectly states that in the spring following the treaty signing, the northern bands left their villages on the Menominee and Oconto Rivers, in *The Menominee Indians*, 98.

17. Krog, "The Menominee," 30, Menominee Tribal Archives; interviews with Menominee People.

18. Dodge to Harris, 8 September 1838, Letters Sent to Washington Officials 1836–1848, in *Records of the Wisconsin Superintendency of Indian Affairs*, reel 4.

19. Boyd to Dodge, 1 February 1838, in Reports of Agents 1836–1848, in *Records of the Wisconsin Superintendency of Indian Affairs*, reel 3.

20. Green Bay and Prairie du Chien Papers, vol. 74, doc. 106, and vol. 75, 17–29; "Division aus Bands du Sauvages 1846," Green Bay and Prairie du Chien Papers, vol. 75, doc. 43; Letter to Col. Francis Lee, 4 December 1849, Henry S. Baird Papers, Box 2, Folder 1, all in SHSW Archives.

21. Carron, in this case, is referring to Glode, a half-brother of Josette Carron.

22. Satterlee, "Menomini Legend very true, SHSW-GBARC."

23. Names of signatories are listed in Treaty with the Menominee, 1836, in Kappler, *Indian Treaties*, 465. Documents of the 1842 census and 1843 annuity payment, in Green Bay and Prairie du Chien Papers, SHSW Archives, identify several band leaders, and Letter to Col. Francis Lee, 4 December 1849, Henry S. Baird Papers, SHSW Archives, specifies locations of the bands, listing principal leaders of each. Comparing the documents for the northern bands, we find the following: (1) Menominee River: Pay-maw-ba-may signed the 1836 treaty, and Pay maw bo me is listed in the 1842 census. Chee-chee-go-waw-way signed in 1836, Chi-chi-gwon-oh-way is listed in the 1849 letter. (2) Oconto River: Shee-pan-aga signed in 1836, and She paw na go is listed in the 1842 census. Chin-nay-paw-mawly signed in 1836, and Che-naw-bo-may is listed in the 1843 annuity account. This latter may be two different people. (3) Peshtigo River: Apparently, none of those signing the treaty is listed as leaders on any of the other three documents. (4) Green Bay: Maw-baw-so signed in 1836, Mau bau go is listed on 1842 census, and Maw burn zho is listed in 1843 annuity account. In almost all cases where federal employees wrote Menominee names, they spelled them differently.

24. Treaty with the Menominee, 1836, in Kappler, *Indian Treaties*, 466.

25. "Journal of a treaty held by Dodge," frames 418–422.

26. Boyd to Herring, 5 December 1834, *Letters Received*, M234–316, frame 178.

27. Clayton, "The Impact of Traders' Claims," 301–9.

28. Treaty with the Menominee, 1836, in Kappler, *Indian Treaties*, 466; "Journal of a treaty held by Dodge," frames 418–22.

29. Treaty with the Menominee, 1836, in Kappler, *Indian Treaties*, 465–66; "Journal of a treaty held by Dodge," frames 418–22; Kellogg, "The Menominee Treaty at the Cedars, 1836," 132.

30. Speeches made by Oshkosh and I. aw-ma-taw or Fish Spawn, 25 November 1834, attached to Boyd to Herring, 5 December 1834, *Letters Received*, M234–316, frame 181.

31. Documents 17–29, Green Bay and Prairie du Chien Papers, vol. 75, SHSW Archives; Document 121, *Annual Report of the Commissioner of Indian*

Affairs, 1855, 254; "Journal of a treaty held by Dodge," frames 418–29; and Treaty with the Menominee, 1836, in Kappler, *Indian Treaties*, 463–66.

32. Doty to Crawford, 29 November 1841, *Records of the Wisconsin Superintendency of Indian Affairs*, reel 4; reprinted in Bloom, ed., *Territorial Papers of the United States*, vol. 28, 363–65; de Neveu, "The Menominee Indian Payment in 1838," 153–64.

33. Keesing, *The Menomini Indians*, 138.

34. Kay, "The Land of La Baye," 294.

35. Articles 3 and 4, Treaty with the Menominee, 1836, in Kappler, *Indian Treaties*, 464–65.

36. Boyd, "Menominee Indian Payment in 1837," in Tanner Papers, SHSW Archives.

37. Commissioner of Indian Affairs Harris to Major John Garland, 23 June 1837, in Bloom, ed., *Territorial Papers of the United States*, vol. 27, 805–7; Dodge to Crawford, 27 March 1839, *Records of the Wisconsin Superintendency of Indian Affairs*, reel 4; Crawford to Indian Superintendents, 25 July 1843, in Bloom, ed., *Territorial Papers of the United States*, vol. 28, 573–74. Commissioner Medill to Dodge, 10 January 1846, in Bloom, ed., *Territorial Papers of the United States*, vol. 28, 910–12.

38. See Garland to Harris, 9 September 1837, in Bloom, ed., *Territorial Papers of the United States*, vol. 27, 847, also 963 n.

39. de Neveu, "The Menominee Indian Payment in 1838," 157.

40. Boyd, "Menominee Indian Payment in 1837," 4–8, in Tanner Papers, SHSW Archives.

41. *Collections SHSW*, vol. 14, 468–69.

42. Doty to Crawford, 29 November 1841, *Records of the Wisconsin Superintendency of Indian Affairs*, reel 4, reprinted in Bloom, ed., *Territorial Papers of the United States*, vol. 28, 363–65.

43. de Neveu, "The Menominee Indian Payment in 1838," 153–64.

44. de Neveu, "The Menominee Indian Payment in 1838," 153–64.

45. In 1862, for example, Agent Moses M. Davis reported that Indians who were burned or frozen while intoxicated accounted for "many" deaths. *Report of the Commissioner of Indian Affairs*, 1862, 332.

46. Act for Regulating the Indian Trade, 6 May 1822, reprinted in part in Prucha, ed., *Documents of United States Indian Policy*, 34–35.

47. McKenney, *Memoirs*, 92–93; "Abstract of Provisions issued to the Indians of this Agency for the third quarter of the year 1821," John Biddle, Indian Agent, 1 October 1821, Records of Executive Office, 1810–1910, RG44, Box 247, Folder 1, State Archives of Michigan.

48. Letter to Secretary of War J. R. Poinsett, written for the Chiefs and Headmen of the Menominee tribe of Indians, first by Ben C. Eastman, and then by Morgan L. Martin, 1 November 1839, Green Bay and Prairie du Chien Papers, vol. 74, doc. 66 and 67, SHSW Archives; Receipt of money paid to Alexander Irwin by George Boyd, doc. 64 of the same volume.

49. October 1839 receipt, Green Bay and Prairie du Chien Papers, vol. 74, doc. 64, SHSW Archives.

50. Letter regarding council of Menominee chiefs and headmen, sent to Governor Dodge, 19 February 1839, *Records of the Wisconsin Superintendency of Indian Affairs*, reel 3.

51. Report of talk between Oshkosh and Governor Dodge, 17 February 1841, *Records of the Wisconsin Superintendency of Indian Affairs*, reel 3.

52. Eastman to Poinsett, 1 November 1839, Green Bay and Prairie du Chien Papers, vol. 74, doc. 66, SHSW Archives.

53. The Menominee's charges in 1839, Boyd's responses, and Governor Dodge's decisions based on his investigation can all be traced through three letters: Martin to Poinsett, 1 November 1839, Green Bay and Prairie du Chien Papers, vol. 74, doc. 67, SHSW Archives; Boyd to Crawford, 5 February 1840, in Bloom, ed., *Territorial Papers of the United States*, vol. 28, 131–39; and Dodge to Crawford, 9 May 1840, *Records of the Wisconsin Superintendency of Indian Affairs*, reel 4.

54. Boyd to Crawford, 5 February 1840, in Bloom, ed., *Territorial Papers of the United States*, vol. 28, 131–39.

55. Boyd to Crawford, 5 February 1840, in Bloom, ed., *Territorial Papers of the United States*, vol. 28, 134–35.

56. Martin to Poinsett, 1 November 1839, Green Bay and Prairie du Chien Papers, vol. 74, doc. 67, SHSW Archives; Boyd to Crawford, 5 February 1840, in Bloom, ed., *Territorial Papers of the United States*, vol. 28, 131–39; and Dodge to Crawford, 9 May 1840, *Records of the Wisconsin Superintendency of Indian Affairs*, reel 4.

57. Martin to Poinsett, 1 November 1839, Green Bay and Prairie du Chien Papers, vol. 74, doc. 67, SHSW Archives; Boyd to Crawford, 5 February 1840, in Bloom, ed., *Territorial Papers of the United States*, vol. 28, 131–139; Report from M. E. Merrill to Henry Dodge, 8 January 1840, *Records of the Wisconsin Superintendency of Indian Affairs*, reel 3; unsigned draft of letter to Dodge, 24 December 1839, Green Bay and Prairie du Chien Papers, vol. 74, doc. 69, SHSW Archives.

58. Martin to Poinsett, 1 November 1839, Green Bay and Prairie du Chien Papers, vol. 74, doc. 67, SHSW Archives; Boyd to Crawford, 5 February 1840, in Bloom, ed., *Territorial Papers of the United States*, vol. 28, 131–39; unsigned draft of letter to Dodge, 24 December 1839, Green Bay and Prairie du Chien Papers, vol. 74, doc. 69, SHSW Archives.

59. Dodge to Crawford, 9 May 1840, *Records of the Wisconsin Superintendency of Indian Affairs*, reel 4; Boyd to Crawford, 5 February 1840, in Bloom, ed., *Territorial Papers of the United States*, vol. 28, 131–39.

60. Crawford to Boyd, 2 February 1842, in Bloom, ed., *Territorial Papers of the United States*, vol. 28, 396.

8. INTENSIFYING ENCROACHMENTS

1. Krug, *DuBay*, 37–41, Medill to Dodge, 10 January 1846, in Bloom, ed., *Territorial Papers of the United States*, vol. 28, 910–12.

2. Article 2, Treaty with the Menominee, 1836, in Kappler, *Indian Treaties*, 464.

3. Report of talk between Oshkosh and Dodge, 17 February 1841, *Records of the Wisconsin Superintendency of Indian Affairs*, reel 3.

4. Report of talk between Oshkosh and Dodge, 17 February 1841, *Records of the Wisconsin Superintendency of Indian Affairs*, reel 3.

5. Jones to Doty, 24 February 1844, in Bloom, ed., *Territorial Papers of the United States*, vol. 28, 666.

6. Jones to Doty, 24 February 1844, in Bloom, ed., *Territorial Papers of the United States*, vol. 28, 666–67.

7. Boyd to Commissioner of Indian Affairs Harris, 2 October 1837, and Boyd to Harris, 4 December 1837, in Bloom, ed., *Territorial Papers of the United States*, vol. 27, 858, (858 n), 878; Medill to Dodge, 10 January 1846, in Bloom, ed., *Territorial Papers of the United States*, vol. 28, 911.

8. Hurst, *Law and Economic Growth*, 5; Fries, *Empire in Pine*, 4–5; Cronon, *Nature's Metropolis*, 27–29, 148–206; Clifton, *The Prairie People*, 228–45.

9. Report of Talk between Oshkosh and Dodge, 17 February 1841, *Records of the Wisconsin Superintendency of Indian Affairs*, reel 3; Doty to Commissioner of Indian Affairs T. H. Crawford, 16 February 1844, in Bloom, ed., *Territorial Papers of the United States*, vol. 28, 644.

10. Doty urged that all nonagricultural Indians be removed from Wisconsin in a message to the legislative assembly, 10 December 1841, in Bloom, ed., *Territorial Papers of the United States*, vol. 27, 312–13.

11. Both these rivers flow into the Mississippi. See Speech of an Indian, in "Speeches of Oshkosh, Man-ba-za, Little Wave," File: 1836, SHSW Archives. The date is incorrect; these documents were written during the time that Albert G. Ellis was subagent at Green Bay, between 1845 and 1849.

12. Treaty with the Chippewa, 1837; Treaty with the Sioux, 1837; Treaty with the Winnebago, 1837, in Kappler, *Indian Treaties*, 491–93, 493–94, 498–500; Royce, *Indian Land Cessions*, 766–69 and map 64.

13. "Report of Senate Committee on Indian Affairs," 14 February 1853, U.S. Congress. Senate. Ex. Doc. No. 72 (hereafter Ex. Doc. No. 72, Senate), 36–39.

14. These are the governor's words. Governor Nathanial P. Tallmadge to Commissioner of Indian Affairs T. H. Crawford, 25 October 1844, in Bloom, ed., *Territorial Papers of the United States*, vol. 28, 737.

15. Ellis to Dodge, 19 February 1847, in Bloom, ed., *Territorial Papers of the United States*, vol. 28, 1044–46.

16. Ellis to Dodge, 19 February 1847, in Bloom, ed., *Territorial Papers of the United States*, vol. 28, 1046–50, also 1046 n.

17. Rosholt and Gehl, *Florimond J. Bonduel*, 75.

18. Henni to the Most Reverend Archbishop of Vienna, 18 December 1845, in "Letters of Bishop John Martin Henni," 73–74.

19. Bloom, ed., *Territorial Papers of the United States*, vol. 28, 1046 n; Rosholt and Gehl, *Florimond J. Bonduel*, 40, 44, 56–57, 59. Rosholt and Gehl, 57, say a Menominee band lived at Duck Creek, known primarily as an Oneida settlement, "as late as 1844."

20. Rosholt and Gehl, *Florimond J. Bonduel*, 75.

21. Rosholt and Gehl, *Florimond J. Bonduel*, 6–79, 158.

22. Kane, *The Wanderings of an Artist*, 22–23.

23. Dodge to Harris, 29 October 1836, *Records of the Wisconsin Superintendency of Indian Affairs*, reel 4.

24. Message of Governor Dodge to the Legislative Assembly, 27 November 1838, in Bloom, ed., *Territorial Papers of the United States*, vol. 27, 176, also 176 n.

25. For example, see Message from Governor Dodge to the Legislature, 11 June 1838; Message from Governor Dodge to the Legislature, 27 November 1838; and Message from Governor Doty to the Legislature, 10 December 1841, in Bloom, *Territorial Papers of the United States*, vol. 28, 156–58, 165–77, 299–314.

26. Ellis to Dodge, 16 April 1846, in Bloom, ed., *Territorial Papers of the United States*, vol. 28, 954–55.

27. Medill to Dodge, 30 July 1846, in File: 1846, SHSW Archives.

28. Dodge to Medill, 23 November 1846; Dodge to Medill, 9 November 1847, *Records of the Wisconsin Superintendency of Indian Affairs*, reel 4; Ellis to Dodge, 16 April 1846, in Bloom, ed., *Territorial Papers of the United States*, vol. 28, 954–55.

29. Annual Report in Dodge to Medill, October 1847, *Records of the Wisconsin Superintendency of Indian Affairs*, reel 3.

30. Dodge to Ellis, 18 October 1847, in Green Bay and Prairie du Chien Papers, vol. 75, doc. 48, SHSW Archives.

31. *Documents Relating to the Negotiation of Ratified and Unratified Treaties*, reel 4.

32. Handwritten copy of memorial from Wisconsin legislature to U.S. Senate requesting that Menominee title to their land be extinguished, ca. 1847 or 1848, Green Bay and Prairie du Chien Papers, vol. 75, doc. 50–52, SHSW Archives.

33. G. F. Wright to Mssrs. Ewing, Chute, and Co, 23 October 1848, in George W. Ewing Collection, Indiana Division, Indiana State Library (Ewing Collection, ISL).

34. "Report of Senate Committee on Indian Affairs," 14 February 1853, Ex. Doc. No. 72, Senate, 36–39.

35. Treaty with the Menominee, 1848, Articles 3, 4, and 6, in Kappler, *Indian Treaties*, 572–73.

36. Alexander H. H. Stuart, "Opinion of the Secretary of the Interior," 25 April 1851, in Ex. Doc. No. 72, Senate, 22. Actually, in 1848, at the time of the treaty, the War Department oversaw Indian affairs for the U.S. government; in 1849 this duty was transferred to the newly created Department of the Interior. In admitting this injustice, Stuart did not admit any fault of his department.

37. Report of Senate Committee on Indian Affairs, 14 February 1853, in Ex. Doc. No. 72, Senate, 40–45.

38. Cope, "Visit to the Menominies," 23 (24): 193.

39. Lea to Stuart, 23 April 1851, in Ex. Doc. No. 72, Senate, 26–36.

40. Report of Senate Committee on Indian Affairs, 14 February 1853, in Ex. Doc. No. 72, Senate, 43–44.

41. Porlier's description is in "Capture of Mackinac," 227–31.

42. Earbobs were a rather common trade item.

43. Porlier, "Capture of Mackinac," 227–28 (parentheses in original).

44. Sho-nee-nieu signed the treaty, but this is probably not Shoneon. Other signers included Shaw-waw-on and Sho-na-new Jr. "Treaty with the Menominee, 1848," in Kappler, *Indian Treaties*, 574.

45. Porlier, "Capture of Mackinac," 230–31.

46. Testimony of Walter H. Besley and John H. Kitson, reported in Lea to Stuart, 23 April 1851, in Ex. Doc. No. 72, Senate, 32.

47. Cope, "Visit to the Menominies," 23 (17): 130.

48. Rosholt and Gehl, *Florimond J. Bonduel*, 89.

9. THE BATTLE FOR A HOMELAND

1. Lurie, *Wisconsin Indians*, 21.

2. Treaty with the Menominee, 1848, Articles 3 and 6, in Kappler, *Indian Treaties*, 573–73.

3. Cope, "Visit to the Menomonies," 23 (17): 130. The 1849 payment was authorized by the 1848 treaty.

4. Cope, "Visit to the Menomonies," 23 (15): 113–14.

5. Cope, "Visit to the Menomonies," 23 (18): 137.

6. Cope, "Visit to the Menomonies," 23 (17): 130.

7. Cope, "Visit to the Menomonies," 23 (17): 130.

8. Bruce to Capt. Maloney, 27 May 1850, and Powell to Bruce, 1 August 1850, both in Henry S. Baird Papers, SHSW Archives, Box 2, Folder 2; Ourada, *The Menominee Indians*, 115–16.

9. Ourada, *The Menominee Indians*, 116.

10. Powell to Bruce, 1 August 1850, Henry S. Baird Papers, SHSW Archives.

11. Chute to G. W. Ewing, 27 March 1850, Ewing Collection, ISL.

12. Rosholt and Gehl, *Florimond J. Bonduel*, 85–86; Transcript of letter written by Father Bonduel, published in the *Boston Pilot*, 1 August 1857, republished in the *Green Bay Register*, 19 July 1957, Menominee Tribal Archives (hereafter 1857 letter from Bonduel).

13. Bonduel to George W. Ewing, 19 February 1850, Ewing Collection, ISL.

14. Agreement between P. Choteau Jr. and Co. on the one hand and David Olmstead and W. G. Ewing on the other hand, 11 September 1850, Ewing Collection, ISL.

15. The Ewings' intentions are made clear in Ewing to Wright, 21 November 1852, Ewing Collection, ISL.

16. Carron in council, 8 September 1855, from Council Proceedings attached to Francis Huebschmann to Acting Commissioner of Indian Affairs Charles E. Mix, 28 September 1855, Ex. Doc. No. 72, Senate, 225.

17. Powell recalls that statement as being made in an interview with President Fillmore, in "William Powell's Recollections," 175.

18. Carron in council, 8 September 1855, Ex. Doc. No. 72, Senate, 225.

19. See Manypenny to McClelland, 22 December 1855, Ex. Doc. No. 72, Senate, 154–203; Rosholt and Gehl, *Florimond J. Bonduel*, 103.

20. "Memorial from Thompson to the Senate," 9 January 1855, and Council Approval, 4 October 1854, Ex. Doc. No. 72, Senate, 5, 26.

21. "Report of the Senate Committee on Indian Affairs," Ex. Doc. No. 72, Senate, 40–41.

22. Thompson to McClelland, 19 January 1855, Ex. Doc. No. 72, Senate, 75; Rosholt and Gehl, *Florimond J. Bonduel*, 154–55; Ourada, *The Menominee Indians*, 118–21.

23. Rosholt and Gehl, *Florimond J. Bonduel*, 106–9; affidavit signed by Simon Bopre witnessed by Wm. Powell and W. H. Bruce, 31 December 1850 at Lake Pow-ha-gon-nu, in Henry S. Baird Papers, box 2, folder 2, SHSW Archives. A good discussion of the division of the non-Indian population regarding opposition to and support of Menominee removal is Shaler, "Negotiating the Treaty Polity," 278–91.

24. The mutually beneficial relationship between the Ewings and Murray is discussed in Trennert, *Indian Traders on the Middle Border*, 167, 171.

25. Ourada, *The Menominee Indians*, 119–20.

26. Wright's contractual obligations are outlined in "Memorandum of an agreement made and entered into this day between Richard W. Thompson and George W. Ewing, under the name of Thompson & Ewing, on the one part, and George F. Wright of the other part," 20 October 1852, Ewing Collection, ISL; the contract is discussed in Trennert, *Indian Traders on the Middle Border*, 187; Jacob's receipt for eight hundred dollars for his part in the removal is dated 13 November 1852; and notation of this agreement by G. W. Ewing is in Jacobs to G. W. Ewing, 16 October 1852, both in Ewing Collection, ISL.

27. Wright to G. W. Ewing, 15 May 1851, Ewing Collection, ISL.

28. Chute to G. W. Ewing, 27 March 1850, Ewing Collection, ISL.

29. W. G. Ewing Jr. to G. W. Ewing, 3 March 1851, Ewing collection, ISL.

30. Two messages from E. Murray, Superintendent, to the Menominee Tribe, 4 October 1852, Ewing Collection, ISL.

31. Jacobs to G. W. Ewing, including a penciled-in note signed by Thompson and the Ewings, 6 October 1852, Ewing Collection, ISL.

32. A document dated 8 November 1852 shows the Menominee paid $2.50 each for 588 blankets, 248 of them 3-point English Mackinaw blankets and 304 of them 2.5-point French blankets, for a total of $1470. The division among the ten bands went as follows: Oshkosh band, 71; A-yam-e-tah band, 97, Lamotte band, 65; Sho-ne-niew band, 29; Sagatoke band, 67; Menominee River band, 52; Pish-ti-go band, 40; Oconto band, 56; Wau-ke-chon band, 37; Ah-kaw-mote band, 15; chiefs and headmen, 43; and destitute persons, 16. Ewing Collection, ISL.

33. Murray to Lea, 2 November 1852, Green Bay and Prairie du Chien Papers, vol. 76, doc. 1, SHSW Archives.

34. Rosholt and Gehl, *Florimond J. Bonduel*, 144–47; interviews with Menominee people.

35. Wright to Thompson and Ewing, 1 December 1852; H. W. Jones to Geo. W. Ewing, 15 December 1852; Murray to My Dear Friend, 20 December 1852, all in Ewing Collection, ISL.

36. Rosholt and Gehl, *Florimond J. Bonduel*, 145–47; population figures at the time of removal are on p. 147. Figures for 1870 cited as based on 1870 annuity payroll are in Proceedings of a Menominee Council, 6 June 1870, *Letters Received* M234–327, frames 208–9.

37. Unsigned letter to Suydam, 23 August 1853, Green Bay and Prairie du Chien Papers, vol. 76, no. 30, SHSW Archives.

38. Rosholt and Gehl, *Florimond J. Bonduel*, 143.

39. Carron in Council, 8 September 1855, in Council Proceedings attached to Huebschmann to Mix, 28 September 1855, Ex. Doc. No. 72, Senate, 227.

40. Cope, "Visit to the Menominies," 23 (11): 82; 23 (12): 89–90.

41. Cope, "Visit to the Menominies," 23 (13): 97.

42. Cope, "Visit to the Menominies," 23 (15): 113.

43. Krog, "The Menominee," 27–30, Menominee Tribal Archives.

44. See, for example, "Hearing Before the Committee on Indian Affairs, United States Senate, On the Claims of Certain Menominee Indians to Enrollment as Members of the Tribe, April 15, 1910," in Central Classified Files (CCF) 1907–39 Keshena 053, in National Archives and Records Service, Washington DC. These claims all date to the 1849 buyout sanctioned by the 1848 treaty. The families who accepted the payment are referred to as "forty niners" by tribal members today.

45. Treaty with the Menominee, 1848, in Kappler, *Indian Treaties*, 573.

46. Shaw-ne-ke-ness-ish is possibly Asha'wani'pinas.

47. Manypenny to McClelland, 22 December 1855, Ex. Doc. No. 72, Senate, 183–85.

48. Rosholt and Gehl, *Florimond J. Bonduel*, 103–4.

49. Manypenny to McClelland, 22 December 1855, Ex. Doc. No. 72, Senate, 179–81.

50. Manypenny to McClelland, 22 December 1855, Ex. Doc. No. 72, Senate, 184.

51. Manypenny to McClelland, 22 December 1855, Ex. Doc. No. 72, Senate, 179–81.

52. All documents February–April, 1851, in Ewing Collection, ISL.

53. See Thompson to McClelland, 19 January 1855, Ex. Doc. No. 72, Senate, 66.

10. RECLAIMING THE HOMELAND

1. The successful passage of that bill led to the conversion of forty Menominee families to Catholicism, according to Bonduel. Rosholt and Gehl, *Florimond J. Bonduel,* 85–86, 149–52, 154–55; 1857 letter from Bonduel, Menominee Tribal Archives. See also Thompson to McClelland, 19 January 1855, Ex. Doc. No. 72, Senate, 75.

2. "Joint Resolution Concerning the Menominee Tribe of Indians, Resolved by the Senate and Assembly of the state of Wisconsin," 1 February 1853, Edward E. Ayer Collection, The Newberry Library.

3. Hill, "Northern Superintendency," *Historical Sketches,* National Archives and Records Service, Chicago (NARSC).

4. Ex. Doc. No. 72, Senate, 196.

5. Wright to Col. G. W. Ewing, 17 December 1852, in Ewing Collection, ISL; Hill, "Northern Superintendency," *Historical Sketches,* (NARSC).

6. *Annual Report of the Commissioner of Indian Affairs,* 1855, 40.

7. Huebschmann to Manypenny, 28 December 1853, *Letters Received,* M234–322, frame 344.

8. Huebschmann to Manypenny, 21 May 1854, *Documents Relating to the Negotiation of Ratified and Unratified Treaties,* reel 5, frame 73.

9. Report of Francis Huebschmann, 1 October 1855, *Annual Report of the Commissioner of Indian Affairs,* 1855.

10. Memorial of Richard W. Thompson to the Senate and House of Representatives, 9 January 1855, Ex. Doc. No. 72, Senate, 9–10. Francis Huebschmann, in a speech to the Menominee at the falls of Wolf River, 7 September 1855, told the tribe that the entire $242,686 was for the difference in value of the Minnesota land, in Ex. Doc. No. 72, Senate, 147–48. Manypenny to McClelland, 22 December 1855, confirmed this, in Ex. Doc. No. 72, Senate, 202–3. But Manypenny contradicted himself: in the 1854 *Annual Report of the Commissioner of Indian Affairs,* 20, he said

the money was to make up for the amount of land sold in 1848, in which the Menominees were underpaid. Huebschmann reiterated that he had said this money was to pay for both, as stated in Article 4 of the treaty, in Huebschmann to Manypenny, 23 November 1855, in Ex. Doc. No. 72, Senate, 214.

11. Huebschmann to Manypenny, 21 May 1854, *Documents Relating to the Negotiation of Ratified and Unratified Treaties*, reel 5, frame 73.

12. Huebschmann to Manypenny, 23 November 1855, Ex. Doc. No. 72, Senate, 217–18.

13. Huebschmann to Manypenny, 30 May 1854, *Letters Received*, M234–322, frame 410–11.

14. Huebschmann to Manypenny, 25 August 1854, *Letters Received*, M234–322, frame 426.

15. A hand-drawn map of the fifteen townships set aside for the tribe is in *Letters Received*, M234–322, frame 172. See also Huebschmann to Manypenny, 7 March 1854, *Letters Received*, M234–322, frames 372–73, and Huebschmann to Charles E. Mix, 13 April 1857, *Letters Received*, M234–323, frames 318–19.

16. Huebschmann to Manypenny, 7 March 1854, *Letters Received*, M234–322, frames 372–73; Huebschmann to Mix, 13 April 1857, *Letters Received*, M234–323, frames 318–19.

17. Huebschmann to Manypenny, 28 December 1853, *Letters Received*, M234–322, frame 344; Ex. Doc. No. 72, Senate, 41.

18. Huebschmann to Acting Commissioner of Indian Affairs Charles E. Mix, 27 October 1854, *Letters Received*, M234–322, frames 433–35.

19. Huebschmann to Manypenny, 30 December 1853, *Letters Received*, M234–322, frames 364–65.

20. *Annual Report of the Commissioner of Indian Affairs*, 1855, 40.

21. Huebschmann to Mix, 27 October 1854, *Letters Received*, M234–322, frames 433–35.

22. Report of Rosalie Dousman, Teacher; Report of Frederich Haas, Farmer; Report of A. D. Bonesteel, Agent, all in *Report of the Commissioner of Indian Affairs*, 1859, 38–47.

23. Petition from Menominee Chiefs and headmen to the United States

Senate, 3 July 1854, Green Bay and Prairie du Chien Papers, vol. 76, doc. 33, SHSW Archives.

24. Letter from 11 Menominee chiefs (Ah-ko-ne-may, La Motte, Ne-yah-tah-wah-po-ma, Wau-ke-che-on, Ke-ne-boy-wa, Wy-tah-sah, Kay-so, Wish-co-by, Ne-o-pet, Wah-pe-nah-nosh, O-ho-pa-sha) to Lt. Bourne, 30 July 1870, *Letters Received*, M234–327, frame 246.

25. Unsigned draft of letter to Senators Henry Dodge and J. P. Walker, 21 November 1854, in Green Bay and Prairie du Chien Papers, vol. 76, doc. 34, SHSW Archives. One of these was perhaps the American Fur Company claim pressed by Ramsay Crooks until 1894, when the Commissioner of Indian Affairs, Daniel M. Browning, finally decided against it, arguing that it was an attempt to swindle the Menominee. Claim case, Estate of Ramsay Crook, President of American Fur Company, against the Menominee, RG 75, CCF 1907–1939 Green Bay 253, National Archives and Record Service, Washington DC.

26. Unsigned document written in pencil on both sides, with ink note that says "1854 Ewings to Oshkosh," Green Bay and Prairie du Chien Papers, vol. 76, no. 35, SHSW Archives.

27. Brackets in original text. The Cown referred to is probably G. Cown, not J. Cown. Council proceedings attached to Letter from Huebschmann to Mix, 28 September 1855, Ex. Doc. No. 72, Senate, 221–29.

28. Council Meeting, 9 February 1856, *Documents Relating to the Negotiation of Ratified and Unratified Treaties*, reel 6.

29. Huebschmann to Manypenny, 23 February 1856, *Documents Relating to the Negotiation of Ratified and Unratified Treaties*, reel 6.

30. Treaty with the Menominee, 1856, in Kappler, *Indian Treaties*, 755–56.

31. Thompson "To my old friend *Oshkosh*," 19 May 1856, Green Bay and Prairie du Chien Papers, vol. 76, doc. 40, SHSW Archives.

32. Weshonaquet Mosehart, Deposition in Keshena, 25 August 1913, Menominee Historic Preservation Department.

33. Keesing, *The Menomini Indians*, 149–51. See Keesing's map, "Menomini Reservation Showing Progress in Settlement 1852–1882," 151.

34. Huebschmann to Manypenny, 28 December 1853, *Letters Received*, M234–322, frame 344; 1857 letter from Bonduel.

35. Brackets in text. Rosholt and Gehl, *Florimond J. Bonduel*, 24, 157–58.

36. 1857 letter from Bonduel, Menominee Tribal Archives.

37. For many years Corpus Christi remained a most colorful and joyous celebration on the reservation. See Nichols, "Corpus Christi on the Menominee Reservation."

38. If Bonduel's numbers were correct, there would have been a large growth of Catholic Menominees, since he served among six hundred Menominees at Lake Poygan. Likely not all of those six hundred were Catholic.

39. 1857 letter from Bonduel, Menominee Tribal Archives.

40. Statement by John Warrington is in Chronicle by Bishop Francis Xavier Krautbauer, *The Sacred Heart Province Franciscan Indian Mission Records*, reel 13, frames 470–72, Marquette University Archives.

41. Keesing, *The Menomini Indians*, 151–52.

42. Population figures at the time of removal are in Rosholt and Gehl, *Florimond J. Bonduel*, 147. Figures for 1870 are cited as based on 1870 annuity payroll in Proceedings of a Menominee Council, 6 June 1870, *Letters Received* M234–327, frames 208–9.

11. SIEGE AND SURVIVAL

1. Immanuel Wallerstein describes the development of this economic system this way: "In modern history, the dominant effective boundaries of the capitalist world-economy have expanded steadily from its origins in the sixteenth century, such that today it encompasses the earth." *The Politics of the World-Economy*, 2.

2. Adelman and Aron, "From Borderlands to Borders," 818.

3. Österhammel, *Colonialism*, 20.

4. *Letters Received*, M234–323, frame 60.

5. The ideas and some of the text for these conclusions regarding treaties were presented by the present author in "Commentary on Expert Witness Documents," 43–51.

6. Davis, *Sustaining the Forest*.

Bibliography

MANUSCRIPT AND ARCHIVAL SOURCES

Indiana State Library

George W. Ewing Collection. Indiana Division.

Interviews by the Author

Interviews with Menominee people, 1991–2001. The author interviewed
Menominees, elders and others knowledgeable of tribal history. The
author retains notes from all these interviews but offered anonymity
to the interviewees in this written study.

Marquette University Archives

Sacred Heart Province Franciscan Indian Mission Records. Microfilm.

Menominee Historic Preservation Department

Interview with Alex Askenette, 19 March 1993.

Interview with Earl Wescott Sr., 7 October 1993.

Interview with Marvin Steven Askenette, 25 April 1994.

"Monument to Chief Menominee in Indiana Is Linked to Mystery." *Antigo
Daily Journal*, n.d.

Weshonaquet Mosehart, Depostion in Keshena, 25 August 1913.

Menominee Tribal Archives, Keshena

Bonduel, Father. Transcript of letter published in the *Boston Pilot*, 1 August
1857. Republished in the *Green Bay Register*, 19 July 1957.

Krog, Carl. "The Menominee Indians on the Menominee River." *Wisconsin Academy Review*, 27–30.

National Archives and Record Service, Chicago

Hill, Edward E. *Historical Sketches for Jurisdictional and Subject Headings Used for the Letters Received by the Office of Indian Affairs, 1824–1880.* Washington DC: National Archives and Records Service, General Services Administration, 1967.

National Archives and Record Service, Washington DC

Record Group 75. Central Classified Files 1907–39, Keshena 053, Enrollment.

Record Group 75. Central Classified Files 1907–39, Green Bay 253, Accounts of Traders.

Record Group 75. No. 59. Green Bay [Factory] Accounts 1815–1823.

The Newberry Library

Edward E. Ayer Collection.

Smithsonian Institution, National Anthropological Archives

Jenks, A. E., 1899–1901. Letters Received 1888–1906. Entry no. 10, Bureau of American Ethnology Records.

Trowbridge, C. C. "Excerpts from C. C. Trowbridge's Account of the Menominee Taken at Green Bay, summer of 1823." Transcribed from Leonard Bloomfield Papers.

State Archives of Michigan

Records of Executive Office, 1810–1910.

State Historical Society of Wisconsin Archives

File: 1836.

File: 1846, 30 July. Medill, William. Box 142, Folder 8.

Green Bay and Prairie du Chien Papers. Wis/Mss/C.

Henry S. Baird Papers. Wis/Mss/V.

Keesing, Felix. "Leaders of the Menomini Tribe, A Sketch from the Contemporary Records and from the Memories of Old Indians of Today." Typewritten paper with hand-corrected notes, n.d., ca. 1930. US/MSS/ 7E, Folder 1.

Raney, William Francis. "The Grignon Family in Wisconsin to About 1760." April 1934. Unpublished paper. MSS/E902/GR, Box 69, Folder 18.

Tanner Papers. Correspondence, n.d. Wis/MSS/DJ, Box 17.

Boyd, James Madison, "Menominee Indian Payment in 1837." Typewritten transcript.

Tenney, Horace Kent. "A Case of *Lex Talionis*." Manuscript, n.d. Wis/Mss/BE.

State Historical Society of Wisconsin Library

Krautbauer, Rt. Rev. F. X. "Short Sketch of the History of the Menominee Indians of Wisconsin, and the Catholic Missions Among Them." *American Catholic Historical Researches* (October 1887). Bishop Krautbauer, "Missions Among the Menominees in Wisconsin," PAM 52–1474.

State Historical Society of Wisconsin, Green Bay Area Records Center

Satterlee, John V. "Menomini Legend very true On the Menomini River . . ." John Valentine Satterlee, ca. 1852–1935, "Writings, 1933, by John V. Satterlee . . . originally written for Earle S. Holman." Green Bay/SC/77.

BOOKS, ARTICLES, AND DISSERTATIONS

Adelman, Jeremy, and Stephen Aron. "From Borderlands to Borders: Empires, Nation-States, and the Peoples in Between in North American History." *American Historical Review* 104, no. 3 (1999): 814–41.

Anderson, Dean L. "The Flow of European Trade Goods into the Western Great Lakes Region, 1715–1760." In *The Fur Trade Revisited: Selected Papers of the Sixth North American Fur Trade Conference, Mackinac Island, Michigan, 1991*, ed. Jennifer S. H. Brown, W. J. Eccles, and Donald P. Heldman, 93–115. East Lansing: Michigan State University Press, 1994.

"Anis'e's Expedition." *Collections of the State Historical Society of Wisconsin* 12:84–91. Text also appears in *Michigan Pioneer and Historical Collections* 11:501–6 under the title "From Mr. Ainsse. Unaddressed."

Annual Reports of the Commissioner of Indian Affairs. 1854–62.

Barrett, S. A., and Alanson Skinner. "Certain Mound and Village Sites of Shawano and Oconto Counties, Wisconsin." *Bulletin of the Public Museum of the City of Milwaukee* 10, no. 5 (1932).

Beck, David R. M. "Commentary on Expert Witness Documents: *Menominee Indian Tribe of Wisconsin v. Tommy G. Thompson, et al.*, Case No. 95 C 0030 C (W.D. Wis. Jan. 13, 1995)." Prepared for Menominee Treaty Rights and Mining Impacts Office, 31 October 1996.

———. "The Historical Limits of Menominee Country." Prepared for the Menominee Historic Preservation Department, March 1995.

———. "'I Recommend You Will Not Drop My Bones': The Menominee Voice in the Treaty Making Process." In *Celebration of Indigenous Thought and Expression*, ed. Susan M. Branstner, 64–75. Sault Ste. Marie MI: Lake Superior State University Press, 1996.

———. "Proof of the Existence of Numerous Menominee Bands at the Time of Earliest European Contact." Unpublished paper, 1993.

———. "Return to *Namä'o Uskíwämît*: The Importance of Sturgeon in Menominee Indian History." *Wisconsin Magazine of History* 79, no. 1 (1995): 32–48.

Bemis, Samuel Flagg. *Jay's Treaty: A Study in Commerce and Diplomacy*. New York: Macmillan Company, 1923.

Biddle, James W. "Recollections of Green Bay in 1816–17." *Collections of the State Historical Society of Wisconsin* 1:49–63.

Bieder, Robert E. *Native American Communities in Wisconsin, 1600–1960: A Study of Tradition and Change*. Madison: University of Wisconsin Press, 1995.

Birmingham, Robert A., and Leslie E. Eisenberg. *Indian Mounds of Wisconsin*. Madison: University of Wisconsin Press, 2000.

Blair, Emma Helen. *The Indian Tribes of the Upper Mississippi Valley and Region of the Great Lakes*. Cleveland: Arthur H. Clarke Company, 1911. Includes Nicholas Perrot, *Memoir on the Manners, Customs, and Religion of the Savages of North America* and Claude Charles Le Roy, Sieur de Bacqueville de la Potherie, *History of the Savage Peoples Who Are Allies of New France*.

Bloom, John Porter, ed. *Territorial Papers of the United States*. Vol. 27,

Wisconsin. Washington DC: National Archives and Records Service, General Services Administration, 1975.

———. *Territorial Papers of the United States.* Vol. 28, Wisconsin. Washington DC: National Archives and Records Service, General Services Administration, 1969.

Bloomfield, Leonard. *The Menomini Language.* Ed. Charles F. Hockett. New Haven: Yale University Press, 1962.

———. *Menomini Lexicon.* Ed. Charles F. Hockett. Milwaukee: Milwaukee Public Museum Publications in Anthropology and History, no. 3, 1975.

———. *Menomini Texts.* Vol. 12 of Franz Boas, ed., *Publications of the American Ethnological Society.* New York: G. E. Strechert and Co., 1928.

Bradley, A. G. *Sir Guy Carleton (Lord Dorchester).* 1909. Reprint, Toronto: University of Toronto Press, 1966. Includes note by A. L. Burt from 1926 edition.

Brown, Charles E. "Battle of the Pierced Forehead." *Wisconsin Place Name Legends or Wisconsin Indian Place Legends.* Madison: Works Progress Administration, 1936.

Calloway, Colin G. *Crown and Calumet: British-Indian Relations, 1783–1815.* Norman: University of Oklahoma Press, 1987.

———. *New Worlds for All: Indians, Europeans, and the Remaking of Early America.* Baltimore: The Johns Hopkins University Press, 1997.

Carter, Edwin Clarence, ed. *Territorial Papers of the United States.* Vol. 10, Michigan. Washington DC: United States Government Printing Office, 1942.

———. *Territorial Papers of the United States.* Vol. 11, Michigan. Washington DC: United States Government Printing Office, 1943.

———. *Territorial Papers of the United States.* Vol. 12, Michigan. Washington DC: Government Printing Office, 1945.

———. *The Territorial Papers of the United States.* Vol. 17, Illinois. Washington DC: United States Government Printing Office, 1950.

Charlevoix, Pierre X. F. de. "Excerpt from Charlevoix's *Journal historique,* made after he traversed the west in search of the Western Sea." *Collections of the State Historical Society of Wisconsin* 16:408–18.

Charlevoix, Rev. P. X. F., S. J. *History and General Description of New*

France. Vol. 5. Trans. with notes by John Gilmary Shea. New York: John Gilmary Shea, 1871.

Child, Brenda J. "A New Seasonal Round: Ojibwe Families during the Great Depression." Paper presented at the American Society for Ethnohistory Conference, Tucson AZ, 18 October 2001.

Childs, Col. Ebenezer. "Recollections of Wisconsin Since 1820." *Collections of the State Historical Society of Wisconsin*. 4:153–95.

Clayton, James L. "The Impact of Traders' Claims on the American Fur Trade." In *The Frontier in American Development: Essays in Honor of Paul Wallace Gates*, ed. David M. Ellis, 301–9. Ithaca NY: Cornell University Press, 1969.

Cleland, Charles E. "Indians in a Changing Environment." In *The Great Lakes Forest: An Environmental and Social History*, ed. Susan L. Flader, 83–95. Minneapolis: University of Minnesota Press, 1983.

Clifton, James A. *The Prairie People: Continuity and Change in Potawatomi Indian Culture, 1665–1965*. Lawrence: The Regents Press of Kansas, 1977.

Codignola, Luca. "The Battle is Over: Campeau's *Monumenta* vs. Thwaites's *Jesuit Relations*, 1602–1650." *European Review of Native American Studies* 10, no. 2 (1996): 3–10.

Collections of the State Historical Society of Wisconsin. Vols. 1–20.

Cope, Alfred. "Visit to the Menomonies." *The Friend* 23, nos. 5–25 (1849–50).

Coues, Elliot, ed. *The Expeditions of Zebulon Montgomery Pike*. Vol. 1. New York: Francis P. Harper, 1895.

Cronon, William. *Nature's Metropolis: Chicago and the Great West*. New York: W. W. Norton and Co., 1991.

Current, Richard Nelson. *Pine Logs and Politics: A Life of Philetus Sawyer, 1816–1900*. Madison: State Historical Society of Wisconsin, 1950.

Davis, Thomas. *Sustaining the Forest, the People, and the Spirit*. Albany: State University of New York Press, 2000.

Day, Gordon M. "Western Abenaki." In *Northeast*, ed. Bruce G. Trigger, 148–59, vol. 15 of *Handbook of North American Indians*. Washington DC: Smithsonian Institution, 1978.

Day, Gordon M., and Bruce G. Trigger. "Algonquin." In *Northeast*, ed. Bruce G. Trigger, 792–97, vol. 15 of *Handbook of North American Indians*. Washington DC: Smithsonian Institution, 1978.

de Neveu, Gustave. "The Menominee Indian Payment in 1838." Trans. from the French. *Proceedings of the State Historical Society of Wisconsin at Its Fifty-Eighth Annual Meeting*, 153–64. Madison: Published by the Society, 1911.

Densmore, Frances. *Menominee Music*. Washington DC: Government Printing Office, 1932.

"Documents Relating to the Episcopal Church in Green Bay." *Collections of the State Historical Society of Wisconsin* 14:450–515.

Documents Relating to the Negotiation of Ratified and Unratified Treaties with Various Indian Tribes, 1801–1869. National Archives and Record Service Microcopy T-494.

Eccles, W. J. *The Canadian Frontier, 1534–1760*. Rev. ed. Albuquerque: University of New Mexico Press, 1983.

———. *Essays on New France*. Toronto: Oxford University Press, 1987.

———. *France in America*. Rev. ed. East Lansing: Michigan State University Press, 1990.

Edmunds, R. David. *The Potawatomis: Keepers of the Fire*. Norman: University of Oklahoma Press, 1978.

Edmunds, R. David, and Joseph L. Peyser. *The Fox Wars: The Mesquakie Challenge to New France*. Norman: University of Oklahoma Press, 1993.

Ellis, Gen. A. G. "The 'Upper Wisconsin' Country." *Collections of the State Historical Society of Wisconsin* 3:435–52.

Ellis, Gen. Albert G. "Some Account of the Advent of the New York Indians into Wisconsin." *Collections of the State Historical Society of Wisconsin*, 2:415–49.

Extract from letter by Du Lhut, 12 April 1684. Trans. *Collections of the State Historical Society of Wisconsin* 16:114–25.

"Extrait de la Lettre du sieur Du Lhut écrite à Michilimakinak, le 12 avril 1684." In *Memoires et documents*, ed. Pierre Margry, 6:38–50. Paris: Maisonneuve et Ch. Leclerc, 1888.

Forum on Sovereignty: Divergent Jurisdictions. Conference at University of Wisconsin-Stevens Point, 7–9 October 1990. Poster.

Fries, Robert F. *Empire in Pine: The Story of Lumbering in Wisconsin, 1830–1900.* Madison: State Historical Society of Wisconsin, 1951. Rev. ed., Evanston IL: Wm. Caxton Ltd., 1989.

Gibson, Charles. *The Aztecs under Spanish Rule.* Stanford: Stanford University Press, 1964.

Goddard, James Stanley. "Journal of a Voyage, 1766–67." Ed. Carolyn Gilman. In *The Journals of Jonathan Carver and Related Documents, 1766–1770, ed.* John Parker. St. Paul: Minnesota Historical Society Press, 1976.

Grant, Bruce Herman. "Spirituality and Sobriety: The Experience of Alcohol Use and Abuse among the Menominee Indians of Wisconsin." Ph.D. diss., Catholic University of America, 1995.

Grant, John Webster. *Moon of Wintertime: Missionaries and the Indians of Canada in Encounter since 1534.* Toronto: University of Toronto Press, 1984.

Grignon, Augustin. "Seventy-Two Years' Recollections of Wisconsin," *Collections of the State Historical Society of Wisconsin* 3:197–295.

Haeger, John D. "A Time of Change: Green Bay, 1815–1834." *Wisconsin Magazine of History* 54, no. 4 (1971): 285–98.

Harris, R. Cole, and John Warkentin. *Canada before Confederation: A Study in Historical Geography.* New York: Oxford University Press, 1974.

Hart, Paxton. "The Making of Menominee County." *Wisconsin Magazine of History* 43, no. 3 (1960): 181–89.

Heidenreich, Conrad E. "Huron." In *Northeast*, ed. Bruce G. Trigger, 368–88, vol. 15 of *Handbook of North American Indians.* Washington DC: Smithsonian Institution, 1978:

Hemphill, W. Edwin, ed. *The Papers of John C. Calhoun.* Vols. 5–9. Columbia: University of South Carolina Press, 1971–76.

Hill, Edward E. *Guide to Records in the National Archives of the United States Relating to American Indians.* Washington DC: National Archives and Records Service, General Services Administration, 1981.

Hoffman, Walter James, M.D. *The Menomini Indians.* New York: Johnson Reprint Organization, 1970. Originally published as one of several reports attached to the *Fourteenth Annual Report of the U.S. Bureau of Ethnology, 1892–93*, Washington DC: Government Printing Office, 1896.

Horsman, Reginald. "The Origins of Oneida Removal to Wisconsin, 1815–1822." In *An Anthology of Western Great Lakes Indian History*, ed. Donald L. Fixico, 203–32. Milwaukee: American Indian Studies, University of Wisconsin-Milwaukee, 1987.

Humins, John Harold. "George Boyd: Indian Agent of the Upper Great Lakes, 1819–1842." Ph.D. diss., Michigan State University, 1975.

Hunt, George T. *The Wars of the Iroquois: A Study in Intertribal Trade Relations*. Madison: University of Wisconsin Press, 1940.

Hurley, William M. *An Analysis of Effigy Mound Complexes in Wisconsin*. Anthropological Papers, no. 59, Museum of Anthropology, University of Michigan, Ann Arbor, 1975.

Hurst, James Willard. *Law and Economic Growth: The Legal History of the Lumber Industry in Wisconsin, 1836–1915*. Cambridge MA: The Belknap Press of Harvard University Press, 1964.

Innis, Harold A. *The Cod Fisheries: The History of an International Economy*. Rev. ed. Toronto: University of Toronto Press, 1954.

Jacobs, Wilbur R. *Wilderness Politics and Indian Gifts: The Northern Colonial Frontier, 1748–1763*. 1950. Reprint, Lincoln: University of Nebraska Press, 1967.

Jenks, Albert Ernst. *The Wild Rice Gatherers of the Upper Lakes: A Study in Primitive Economics. Nineteenth Annual Report of the Bureau of American Ethnology for the Years 1897–1898*, 1013–1137. Washington DC: Government Printing Office, 1901.

Jennings, Francis. "American Frontiers." In *America in 1492: The World of the Indian Peoples before the Arrival of Columbus*, ed. Alvin M. Josephy Jr., 339–67. New York: Alfred A. Knopf, 1992.

———, ed. *Iroquois Indians: A Documentary History of the Diplomacy of the Six Nations and Their League*. Woodbridge CT: Research Publications, 1984. Microfilm.

"Journal of a Council Held at Green Bay, Michigan Territory, by George B. Porter, Commissioner on the Part of the United States, with the Menomonee Nation of Indians." *Michigan Pioneer and Historical Collections* 37: 263–77.

Kane, Paul. *The Wanderings of an Artist Among the Indians of North America, from Canada to Vancouver's Island and Oregon, Through the Hudson's Bay Company's Territory and Back Again.* Toronto: The Radisson Society, 1925.

Kappler, Charles J. *Indian Treaties, 1778–1883.* 1904. Reprint, New York: Interland Publishing Co., 1972.

Kasprycki, Sylvia S. "'A Lover of All Knowledge': Edwin James and Menominee Ethnography." *European Review of Native American Studies* 4, no. 1 (1990): 1–9.

———. "Sirens, Tapirs, and Egyptian Totems: Toward an Interpretation of Menominee Religious Iconography." *Archiv für Völkerkunde* 48 (1994): 93–120.

Kay, Jeanne. "John Lawe, Green Bay Trader." *Wisconsin Magazine of History* 64, no. 1 (1980): 3–27.

———. "The Land of La Baye: The Ecological Impact of the Green Bay Fur Trade, 1634–1836." Ph.D. diss., University of Wisconsin-Madison, 1977.

Keesing, Felix M. *The Menomini Indians of Wisconsin: A Study of Three Centuries of Contact.* 1939. Reprint, Madison: University of Wisconsin Press, 1987.

Kellogg, Louise Phelps. *The British Régime in Wisconsin and the Northwest.* Madison: State Historical Society of Wisconsin, 1935.

———. *The French Régime in Wisconsin and the Northwest.* Madison: State Historical Society of Wisconsin, 1925.

———. "The Menominee Treaty at the Cedars, 1836." *The Transactions of the Wisconsin Academy of Sciences, Arts, and Letters* 26 (1931): 127–36.

———. "Old Fort Howard." *Wisconsin Magazine of History* 18, no. 2 (1934): 126–40.

Kemper, Jackson D. D. "Journal of an Episcopalian Missionary's Tour to Green Bay, 1834." *Collections of the State Historical Society of Wisconsin* 14:394–449.

Kingston, John T. "Early Exploration and Settlement of Juneau County." *Collections of the State Historical Society of Wisconsin* 8:397–407.

Krug, Merton E. *DuBay, Son-in-Law of Oshkosh.* Appleton WI: C. C. Nelson Publishing Company, 1946.

Lavender, David. *The Fist in the Wilderness*. Garden City NY: Doubleday and Company, Inc., 1964.

"Letters of Bishop John Martin Henni." *Wisconsin Magazine of History* 10, no. 1 (1926): 67–82.

Letters Received by the Office of Indian Affairs, 1824–81. Microcopy 234. Washington DC: National Archives and Records Service, General Services Administration, 1959.

"Lieut. James Gorrell's Journal." *Collections of the State Historical Society of Wisconsin* 1:24–48.

Lockwood, Hon. James, of Prairie du Chien. "Early Times and Events in Wisconsin." *Collections of the State Historical Society of Wisconsin* 2:98–196.

Lurie, Nancy Oestreich. *Wisconsin Indians*. Madison: State Historical Society of Wisconsin, 1987.

Margry, Pierre, ed. *Mémoires et Documents pour Servir a L'Histoire des Origines Françaises des Pays D'Outre-Mer*. Vol. 1. Paris: Maisonneuve et Cie., Libraires-Éditeurs, 1879.

———. *Mémoires et Documents pour Servir a L'Histoire des Origines Françaises des Pays D'Outre-Mer*. Vol. 6. Paris: Maisonneuve et Ch. Leclerc, 1888.

Martin, Lawrence. *The Physical Geography of Wisconsin*. 3d ed. Madison: University of Wisconsin Press, 1965.

Martin, Paul S., George I. Quimby, and Donald Collier. *Indians before Columbus: 20,000 Years of North American History Revealed by Archaeology*. Chicago: University of Chicago Press, 1947.

Mason, Carol I. "The Historic Period in Wisconsin Archaeology." In *Introduction to Wisconsin Archaeology: Background for Cultural Resource Planning*, ed. William Green, James B. Stoltman, and Alice B. Kehoe. Special issue of *The Wisconsin Archaeologist* 67, nos. 3–4 (1986): 370–92.

———. *Introduction to Wisconsin Indians: Prehistory to Statehood*. Salem WI: Sheffield Publishing Company, 1988.

Mason, Ronald J. "Archaeoethnicity and the Elusive Menominis." *Midcontinental Journal of Archaeology* 22, no. 1 (1997): 69–94.

[Mazzuchelli, Samuel]. *Indian Almanac: Kikinawa dembamoiwewin; or Almanac wa aiogin obiboniman debeniminang leso*. Green Bay[?] WI, 1834.

Mazzuchelli, Samuel. *The Memoirs of Father Samuel Mazzuchelli, O. P.* Trans. Sister Maria Michele Armato, O. P., and Sister Mary Jeremy Finnegan, O. P. Foreword by James P. Shannon. Chicago: The Priory Press, 1967.

"M'Call's Journal of a Visit to Wisconsin in 1830." *Collections of the State Historical Society of Wisconsin* 12:170–205.

McDonough, Kathy, with the assistance of David Grignon. "Menominee Indian Tribe of Wisconsin: The Importance of Menominee Culture and Tradition." Unpublished paper, ca. 1993.

McKenney, Thomas L. *Memoirs, Official and Personal: With Sketches of Travels among the Northern and Southern Indians, Embracing a War Excursion, and Descriptions of Scenes Along the Western Borders.* New York: Paine and Burgess, 1846.

McKern, W. C. "The First Settlers in Wisconsin." *Wisconsin Magazine of History* 26, no. 2 (1942): 161–69.

Menominee Indian Tribe of Wisconsin. *Menominee Tribal History Guide, Commemorating Wisconsin Sesquicentennial, 1848–1998.* Keshena WI: Menominee Indian Tribe of Wisconsin, 1998.

Michigan Pioneer and Historical Collections. Vols. 11, 37.

Miquelon, Dale. *Dugard of Rouen, French Trade to Canada and the West Indies, 1729–1770.* Montreal: McGill-Queen's University Press, 1978.

———. *New France, 1701–1744: "A Supplement to Europe."* Toronto: McClelland and Stewart, 1987.

Moranian, Suzanne Elizabeth. "Ethnocide in the Schoolhouse: Missionary Efforts to Educate Indian Youth in Pre-Reservation Wisconsin." *Wisconsin Magazine of History* 64, no. 4 (1981): 243–60.

Morse, Jedidiah. *A Report to the Secretary of War of the United States on Indian Affairs.* New Haven: S. Converse, 1822.

Nichols, Phebe Jewell (Mrs. Angus F. Lookaround). "Corpus Christi on the Menominee Reservation." *Wisconsin Magazine of History* 34, no. 1 (1950): 17–19.

O'Callaghan, E. B., M.D., ed. *Documents Relative to the Colonial History of the State of New-York* . . . Albany NY: Weed, Parsons, and Company, 1853–58.

Österhammel, Jürgen. *Colonialism: A Theoretical Overview*. Princeton: Markus Wiener Publishers, 1997.

Ourada, Patricia K. *The Menominee Indians: A History*. Norman: University of Oklahoma Press, 1979.

Overstreet, David. F. "Overview of Theoretical Frameworks Addressing Models and Probable Correlates of Menominee Protohistory and Prehistory." United States District Court for the Western District of Wisconsin, File No. 95-C-0030-C, *Menominee Indian Tribe of Wisconsin v. Tommy G. Thomson, et al*. Document 103.

The Papers of Sir William Johnson. Albany: The University of the State of New York, 1921–65.

Parker, John, ed. *The Journals of Jonathan Carver and Related Documents, 1766–1770*. St. Paul: Minnesota Historical Society Press, 1976.

Perrault, Jean Baptiste. "Narrative of the Travels and Adventures of a Merchant Voyageur in the Savage Territories of Northern America Leaving Montreal the 28th of May 1783 (to 1820)." Ed. with introduction and notes by John Sharpless Fox. *Michigan Pioneer and Historical Collections* 37: 508–619.

Peterson, Jacqueline. "Ethnogenesis: The Settlement and Growth of a 'New People,' in the Great Lakes Region, 1702–1815." *American Indian Culture and Research Journal* 6, no. 2 (1982): 23–64.

Porlier, Louis B. "Capture of Mackinac." *Collections of the State Historical Society of Wisconsin* 8: 227–31.

Powell, William. "William Powell's Recollections." *State Historical Society of Wisconsin Proceedings, 1912*, 146–79. Madison: Published by the Society, 1912.

Price, Jacob M. *France and the Chesapeake: A History of the French Tobacco Monopoly, 1674–1791, and Its Relationship to the British and American Tobacco Trades*. Ann Arbor: University of Michigan Press, 1973.

Prucha, Francis Paul. *American Indian Treaties: The History of a Political Anomaly*. Berkeley: University of California Press, 1994.

———, ed. *Documents of United States Indian Policy*. Lincoln: University of Nebraska Press, 1975.

Quimby, George Irving. *Indian Life in the Upper Great Lakes, 11,000 B.C. to A.D. 1800*. Chicago: University of Chicago Press, 1960.

Radisson, Pierre d'Esprit. "Excerpts from the Journal of Pierre d'Esprit, Sieur Radisson, the Fourth Voyage." *Collections of the State Historical Society of Wisconsin* 11:71–96.

Raney, William F. "Pine Lumbering in Wisconsin." *Wisconsin Magazine of History* 19, no. 1 (1935): 71–90.

Records of the Wisconsin Superintendency of Indian Affairs, 1836–1848, and the Green Bay Sub-Agency, 1850. National Archives and Records Service Microcopy M-951.

Reese, William L. *Dictionary of Philosophy and Religion: Eastern and Western Thought.* New Jersey: Humanities Press, 1980.

Ritzenthaler, Robert E. *Prehistoric Indians of Wisconsin.* 3d ed. Rev. Lynne G. Goldstein. Milwaukee: Milwaukee Public Museum, 1985.

Rosholt, Malcolm, and John Britten Gehl. *Florimond J. Bonduel: Missionary to Wisconsin Territory.* Rosholt WI: Rosholt House, 1976.

Royce, Charles C. *Indian Land Cessions in the United States.* Eighteenth Annual Report of the Bureau of American Ethnology, 1896–97. Part 2. Washington DC: Government Publications Office, 1899.

Sagard-Theodat, F. Gabriel. *Histoire du Canada et Voyages que les Frères Mineurs Recollects y Ont Faicts Pour la Conuersion des Infidelles.* 1636. Reprint, Paris: Librarie Tross, 1866.

Schmitz, Neil. "Wisconsin's Fox River Valley and the Mesquakie: A New Local History." *Wisconsin Magazine of History* 80, no. 2 (1996–97): 83–105.

Shaler, Bethel. "Negotiating the Treaty Polity: Gender, Race, and the Transformation of Wisconsin from Indian Country into an American State." Ph.D. diss., University of Wisconsin-Madison, 1999.

Sims, Catherine A. "Algonkian-British Relations in the Upper Great Lakes Region: Gathering to Give and to Receive Presents, 1815–1843." Ph.D. diss., University of Western Ontario, 1992.

Skinner, Alanson. *Material Culture of the Menomini.* Vol. 20 of *Indian Notes and Monographs,* ed. F. W. Hodge. New York: Museum of the American Indian, Heye Foundation, 1921.

———. *Medicine Ceremony of the Menomini, Iowa, and Wahpeton Dakota, With Notes on the Ceremony Among the Ponca, Bungi Ojibwa, and Pota-*

watomi. Vol. 4 of *Indian Notes and Monographs*. New York: Museum of the American Indian, Heye Foundation, 1920.

———. *Social Life and Ceremonial Bundles of the Menomini Indians*. Vol. 13, pt. 1 of *Anthropological Papers of the American Museum of Natural History*. New York: Published by Order of the Trustees, 1913.

Skinner, Alanson, and John V. Satterlee. *Folklore of the Menomini Indians*. Vol. 13, pt. 2 of *Anthropological Papers of the American Museum of Natural History*. New York: Published by Order of the Trustees, 1915.

Skinner, Claiborne. "The Sinews of Empire: The Voyageurs and the Carrying Trade of the 'Pays D'en Haut', 1681–1754." Ph.D. diss., University of Illinois-Chicago, 1991.

Slotkin, James S. *The Menomini Pow Wow: A Study in Cultural Decay*. Milwaukee Public Museum Publications in Anthropology, no. 4. Milwaukee: Milwaukee Public Museum, 1957.

Smith, Alice E. "Daniel Whitney, Pioneer Wisconsin Businessman." *Wisconsin Magazine of History* 24, no. 3 (1941): 283–304.

———. *The History of Wisconsin. Volume I: From Exploration to Statehood*. Ed. William Fletcher Thompson. Madison: State Historical Society of Wisconsin, 1973.

———. *James Duane Doty, Frontier Promoter*. Madison: State Historical Society of Wisconsin, 1954.

Snelling, Wm. J. "La Butte des Morts—The Hillock of the Dead." *Collections of the State Historical Society of Wisconsin* 5:95–103.

Snow, Dean R. "Eastern Abenaki." In *Northeast*, ed. Bruce G. Trigger, 137–47, vol. 15 of *Handbook of North American Indians*. Washington DC: Smithsonian Institution, 1978.

Spector, Janet D. *What This Awl Means: Feminist Archaeology at a Wahpeton Dakota Village*. St. Paul: Minnesota Historical Society Press, 1993.

Spicer, Edward H. "American Indians, Federal Policy Toward." In *Harvard Encyclopedia of American Ethnic Groups*, ed. Stephan Thernstrom, 114–22. Cambridge MA: Belknap Press, 1980.

Spindler, George, and Louise Spindler. *Dreamers with Power: The Menominee*. Prospect Heights IL: Waveland Press, Inc., 1984.

Spindler, Louise S. "Menominee." In *Northeast*, ed. Bruce G. Trigger,

708–24, vol. 15 of *Handbook of North American Indians*. Washington DC: Smithsonian Institution, 1978.

——. *Menomini Women and Culture Change*. Millwood NY: Kraus Reprint Co., 1974.

Tanner, Helen Hornbeck. *Atlas of Great Lakes Indian History*. Norman: University of Oklahoma Press, 1987.

——, ed. *The Settling of North America: The Atlas of the Great Migrations into North America from the Ice Age to the Present*. New York: MacMillan, 1995.

Tanner, Herbert B. "Sketch of George and James M. Boyd." *Collections of the State Historical Society of Wisconsin* 12:266–69.

Terrell, John Upton. *Furs by Astor*. New York: William Morrow and Co., 1963.

Thwaites, Reuben Gold. "Preface." *Collections of the State Historical Society of Wisconsin* 17:xi–xix.

——, ed. *The Jesuit Relations and Allied Documents*. Cleveland: The Burrows Brothers Company, 1896–1901.

"Treaty of Ghent, 1814."

Trennert, Robert A. *Indian Traders on the Middle Border: The House of Ewing, 1827–1854*. Lincoln: University of Nebraska Press, 1981.

Turner, Frederick Jackson. *The Character and Influence of the Indian Trade in Wisconsin: A Study of the Trading Post as an Institution*. Ed. and with an introduction by David Harry Miller and William W. Savage Jr. Norman: University of Oklahoma Press, 1977. Originally published in Herbert Baxter Adams, ed. *Johns Hopkins University Studies in Historical and Political Science*, 9th ser., vol. 11–12 (November and December 1891), 547–615.

Unrau, William E. *White Man's Wicked Water: The Alcohol Trade and Prohibition in Indian Country, 1802–1892*. Lawrence: University Press of Kansas, 1996.

U.S. Congress. House. Ex. Doc. No. 4. 36th Cong., 2nd sess. (1860).

U.S. Congress. Senate. Ex. Doc. No. 72. 34th Cong., 1st sess. (1856).

Viola, Herman J. *Thomas L. McKenney: Architect of America's Early Indian Policy, 1816–1830*. Chicago: Sage Books, 1974.

Wallerstein, Immanuel. *The Politics of the World-Economy: The States, the Movements, and the Civilizations.* Cambridge: Cambridge University Press, 1984.

White, Richard. *The Middle Ground: Indians, Empires, and Republics in the Great Lakes Region, 1650–1815.* New York: Cambridge University Press, 1991.

Wrone, David R. "The Menominee Perspective on the Oneida Treaties." Paper presented at the Oneida History Conference, Green Bay, 26 April 1990.

Index

Printed in the USA
CPSIA information can be obtained
at www.ICGtesting.com
CBHW020059201124
17694CB00009B/144/J

9 780803 213302